MUSiCMAN

EXTRAORDINARY JOURNEY

The Story is dedicated to GBITS, the Great Backpacker In The Sky.

Book Cover design by Wesley Holshouser, Westco Design
Draft editing by Betty Jane Gorin-Smith
Cover photo: Garlic
Back cover art: Priscilla Chandler

Connect with Music Man:
ATMusicMan12@gmail.com

FOREWORD

"If there is a story to tell, I'm sure you are going to tell it."

His sarcasm was so dry that I had to think about whether I should be insulted. The decision internally was "No, not today." Walls of red spruce and Eastern white pines lined the I-95 corridor under a clear blue sky in the Great North Woods as we crossed the state line from New Hampshire into Maine.

Two months prior, I didn't know a soul in the New England town to which I moved. This new friendship meant a lot to me. He could be counted on to tell me the truth when I needed to hear it, even if the truth ran the risk of hurting my pride. True friends are like that: honest and hard to come by. They simply want the best for you and only hope for the same treatment in return. Nothing more. A big part of me was sad to see him go. Like his mother, when she held her chest as we pulled out of his driveway earlier that day, I kept my own much milder emotions tucked away. I was excited as hell for him and his new plans for adventure. He had to stay committed.

"Rest up," I said. "You won't be seeing these trees pass by thru a car window for a while. You'll be back in them." The coniferous pine-top forest continued to zoom by outside at 75 miles per hour.

My clever new friend had been living a nomad's life for years—occupying Wall Street, hopping trains west, mastering the squat game in Oakland, eventually living in a tree igloo. After a rough winter he was looking for real change and had come back to his native New England town. He had spent the better part of the past three months working on himself without a bottle in his hand. But by early summer he had plateaued. The timing was perfect, and this type of journey was fitted for him perfectly. Mine too, given my role. I was thrilled to answer the call when he had questions about hiking the world's most storied footpath: the iconic American trekking adventure of thru-hiking the entire Appalachian Trail. History books about the colossal undertaking have fine patinas, and I knew a little something about it myself. I was on board as support and willing to do anything I could to help him see his newfound dream thru. Having had my own go at the pilgrimage two years prior, this was an opportunity to see if I could ultimately help someone else pull it off. Logistics and gear, I could assist. The stuff-sack and cooking stove I loaned him were more like good luck charms, and they were solid pieces of trekking gear. And I was more than willing to drive him up to the middle of Maine, to Baxter State Park, and climb the epic Mount Katahdin with him to start the endeavor. As a fresh sojourner of the wilderness though, he would have to walk the rest of the miles himself.

"I'm toast, I need to stop for water," he said after we had scrambled nearly four miles straight up the Hunt Trail balanced on the spine of Mount Katahdin the next day. We reached the Tableland with the summit in sight from a mile away, towering at thousands of feet above the forest floor. After a look-see, we pushed forward. When we finally reached the summit, he let out a huff of exhaustion and took a puff of his inhaler.

After the Albuterol filled his lungs, he sat down to take in the stunning view of the Maine wilderness below and his jaw dropped. It was a clear mountain afternoon and the sharp ridge of the Knife Edge loomed out in glory to divide the high winds. The endless mountain tarns below glistened with dark blue water and White Cap Mountain appeared over the distant ranges from seventy miles away. It was a perfect summit day; my good friend was in awe and enthralled.

"I have never been on such a mountain. It's incredible. Are they all like this?"

"None of them are like this one, Hard Way. Relish this day and know that you will never forget it. Nice climb and well done."

Suddenly, I longed for the adventure again. The majestic Maine scenery can cast a spell on hikers who look for sunbeams on the path while the wind whispers sweet nothings to eager ears. Furthermore, there was unfinished business. But I quickly accepted that the trail had already provided me with just what I needed. Hard Way would also find what he was looking for, when he realized where it is he would have to look.

"Music Man, do you want to take a picture with me?"

"Absolutely, Hard Way. But not on the summit sign. My brother's opinion is the sign is sacred and I tend to agree. It is for thru-hikers first and I won't go near it unless I have earned it. I had my chance. Today, you have earned that right by declaring your intent to follow the AT all the way to Springer Mountain, Georgia."

"Damn," he said, "that's regal sounding."

I took a picture of him standing on the famed KATAHDIN sawhorse sign, then we had a picture taken together a little below the summit. I shook his hand and wished him "Good Luck, Godspeed." I had to catch the shuttle out of the park from the foot of the mountain before the gate closed and I was passing my critical turnaround time. It would take Hard Way longer to descend the mountain, so I had to hustle on. Hard Way took his first steps as a thru-hiker with newfound friends he would make on Katahdin. They were attempting the same thing he was, also masking similar anxieties with a humble strength: the hopes and fears of walking 2,193 miles from Maine to Georgia, up and over the peaks and valleys of the oldest mountains on the continent. Deep in my soul, I believed that Hard Way would make it.

From the summit of Mount Katahdin, Hard Way voiced a final suggestion for me when I hit the white blazes of the AT, as I ultimately left him to it:

"Yo, Music Man! Remember to take care of her!"

I gave him a thumbs up in agreement then headed down the mountain by myself.

Later, he texted me that he had lost his bug spray. In addition to being allergic to peanuts and having asthma, he informed me that he hates bugs too. I shook my head and chuckled. With the brick wall emotion of misinterpreted texts, my response was:

[Don't Fucking Quit! Write your own story, Hard Way!]

The next morning, I watched the Millinocket town parade with new friends from the Appalachian Trail Lodge, then I drove home alone. It was the 4th of July.

THE STORY

.1

"TRIP-PUFF...TRIP-PUFF...TRIP-PUFF..." scratched the sound of my suitcase dragging on a downtown sidewalk with a broken wheel. The late afternoon sky was gloomy, and the bitter cold brought a swampy thickness to the air as it filled my tired lungs. I was out of money, ideas, and places to go. Just breathing in the bone-broth fumes of frozen downtown Louisville exhausted me. Like the handicapped wheel of my suitcase, I, too, was broken and moving like a footless apparition as the dope wore off and the crash came on. A glimmer of hope flashed as a familiar face approached. It was Black Face, and we met yet again in the wrong end of town.

"Black, what happened yesterday?" I asked, expecting a dubious response. I already knew what happened: he robbed me. The day before, commerce was typically bustling at the main library downtown. For me that day, business as usual had ended in the dreaded waiting game. And I had lost. He never came back with my money or any dope.

"Census Man! My dude, I'm sorry about yesterday. You know how it is. The monkey was on me, man." He babbled with a drunken attempt at sincerity as he waved around a brown-bagged Screwdriver, spilling some of the precious juice. I had known Black Face on the streets for a few months. He was volatile and quick tempered but reliable for decent dope and he knew that I almost always came with folded cash. His coming was a welcome beacon on that dreary January day.

"Let me go scoop my stash then come back, D. I'll get you together on that twenty from yesterday. Go up to Shorty's tent and tell him you waitin' on me. Give me twenty minutes," he said.

Twenty... the magical number in the hood.

"Bet on a dub or better, Black."

I continued toward the viaduct near the corner of 1st and College Street, next to the J.C.T.C. campus parking lot. College kids hurried to their cars after class trying to get out of the depraved neighborhood as quickly as possible. I often thought that if I could go back and talk to my college-aged self, sleeping thru Latin class, I'd smack his desk to wake him and pray that he "do anything else but that."   I hid my suitcase behind a guardrail before ducking under the bridge to make my way up the graded cement of the freeway viaduct. From the sidewalk under the bridge rose a smooth ramp of concrete leading to a row of tents on a platform. The "homes" of the homeless lined the upper enclave and it was ten degrees colder beneath the bridge compared to the exposure outside. One could easily catch their death by nodding off for too long on the ground allowing the concrete to suck any remaining heat out of the body, quietly sending them on. Nobody would notice for hours or even a day, and then it's too late for street style arrangements.

Shorty's tent was near the middle of the row. I approached in a pre-rehearsed fashion and announced my presence.

"Shorty, It's D! You home?"

"Yeah, come on up. What's smackin'?" His voice carried from inside the Sterno lit and heated tent.

Everyone had an alias on the streets and even the nick-names have nicknames after a while. Shorty unzipped the front door of his home and invited me in. The walls of the tent were lined with meticulously placed cardboard, used as insulation to keep the wind out and the heat in. The four-man Coleman tent floor was also covered with many layers of blankets, pillows, food wrappers and general tweaker paraphernalia. The Salvation Army usually donated tents and Sterno fuel cans to the homeless in late fall, knowing many would try to brave the elements and some would die. Shorty had been homeless for years and this was his comfort zone regardless of the weather. He knew all the tricks and cons. I made my way in and sat down on a pile of soiled looking fabric.

"So, what's up?" Shorty rubbed his chin and scratched his forearm. He was wearing two different shoes, both showing toes.

"Black is on his way up here to get me together from yesterday. He owes me."

"Coo cool, you got a buzz for me when it's done?"

"Am I free, white and over 21?" I joked.

"You're crazy as hell, D."

Black Face's call from down below bounced off the support beams of the underpass: "Yo! Census Man! You up there?"

Some of them called me "Census Man" because I would brandish a not-yet-expired but invalid United States Government identification card from my recent tenure at the Census Bureau, which by itself could have gotten me killed or arrested. People of the night generally don't like the authorities, perceived or real, and a government I.D. is a government I.D., whether it's from the D.E.A. or the National Park Service. By then, my job with the Census Bureau was long lost to the rubble that included my family and friends, my house, personal assets, or anything else you or I didn't have nailed down. I didn't *lose* anything; I gave it all away for my addiction.

I was completely powerless over dope and within a year, everything I could claim as my own would fit into that small and dirty suitcase with a broken wheel. And it was virtually empty. In fact, the empty suitcase itself might have been all I owned sans the clothes on my back. It's amazing how much can fit into the bottom corner of a baggie: everything.

Somehow, I still owned a truck, an old Ford Escape. But it was stashed at my brother's house and there was no way I was going to con anyone out of the keys. I had surrendered the oh-five Ford Escape on the way to a recent stint at the nuthouse. Captivity was the only way I could stop running: Four walls and a locked door, one way or the other. I was stuck on the streets of downtown Louisville, Kentucky, spending my days chasing the next high for $8 at a time. There I was again in a piss-stinking, cardboard-lined polyester walled maison de la mort...about to cop more than I bargained for. A lot more.

Miraculously on schedule, Black Face had shown up to Shorty's front door. He came into the tent and sat down with his Screwdriver in one hand and several tied baggies in the other, all containing different types of dope. After nearly two decades of dancing with the devil, the current drug of choice and I were locked in a cold embrace, and I had a firm grip on not letting go of it.

"Alright, alright, twenty bucks' worth. You want to add to it?" He slurred as he tried to find the right knot of dope in his hand without spilling his Screwdriver.

"Nah man, just clean up the cash I gave you yesterday."

"You got a baggie?"

In that moment, a flash of the blues and reds filled the tent followed by a "whoop-whoop" from the cruiser that had just pulled up below.

"Ah, damn, stash...stash...stash!"

The scramble to ditch all potential felonies was on! The sounds of cellophane and plastic baggies disappeared under the blankets and pillows covering the tent floor.

"Hey, anybody in there?" the first officer asked.

"Can you unzip the door, please?" the second officer asked before we had a chance to respond. (The good-cop-bad-cop game?)

"Yeah, we're here," Shorty announced, sounding dejected as he unzipped the tent just barely a foot from the top. Two officers stood above the tent. It appeared that all the other residents had retreated to their humble abodes. In the darkness, the flashing lights were flickering off the badges and faces of the cops, a man and a woman.

"We're not here to hassle you," they claimed, "we're looking for this girl. Have you seen her?" The woman officer held up a head shot of a young brunette that we all recognized. I had seen her in an apartment building a day or two earlier, but it seemed to me that she didn't want to be found. She barely resembled the class picture in our faces, but it was her. I didn't say anything to the cops about her whereabouts, nor did anyone else except for grumbles of "Maybe" and "I don't really know, officer". We just wanted them to leave us alone. There was rarely an honest thought or action from anyone on the streets. Instead, total apathy.

"It's gonna get cold out here tonight, y'all." The cops asked again, "Are you sure, you're going to be, okay?" Their tones had genuine concern. But we assured them we were fine, and we tried to vibe that we wanted to be left alone. With heads waving, they got in the cruiser and drove away.

"That was close," Shortly sighed with relief.

"Yeah, man they was…wait, where's my dope?" In an instant Black Face's voice turned from relief to anger. "Nah…nah, motherfucker!"

He scanned his body and pockets, eventually shuffling the blankets under his seat more and more frantically as he realized he couldn't find his hidden products. The last few inches of his cocktail spilled into the corner of the tent, further infuriating him.

"Man, where's my dope! One of you punks took it, I know it!" He was tossing linens thru the air with the desperation of an addict who has lost his drugs. Waves of his manic paranoia burst forth.

"Black, it's here somewhere, we gonna find it," eased Shorty, trying to offer some reassurance. "*We* ain't gonna find shit! Put your fucking hands up, BOTH OF YOU!"

Suddenly, he pulled a rusty machete out of his trench coat and turned the edge in our faces. Shorty and I slowly raised our hands and sat motionless in our corners of the shrinking tent. The four walls were closing in and I felt the proximity of his deadly weapon, but I was not totally gripped by fear…yet. I was no doubt acting stupidly to put myself in this position. However, a certain fearlessness is required to walk the streets of any urban city, or at least the perception of having no fear. Best get used to it fast.

"Man, Black, put that blade away. Ain't no need for this. Your stuff is on the floor somewhere so just chill out ⌐ Shorty was trying to talk him down.

"Don't tell me what to do, Shorty! Last I checked, I had the blade! So shut up and give me my dope! Somebody better give me my dope back, or somebody else is going to jail tonight," he said in a semi-veiled threat. It was the plea of a desperate man. An addict in fear of being dope sick; in fear of taking a financial loss he couldn't afford. Those drugs were both his lifeline and hangman's noose. I related to that.

"Black, I ain't got the hank. I don't do that other shit anymore," I pleaded.

"You shut the fuck up, white boy, unless you plan to tell me where my dope is," Black exclaimed.

We couldn't convince him that it was simply lost in the sea of blankets. The panic of the police visit had prompted reflexed reactions. In the commotion, the drugs surely had to be stashed somewhere underneath him. Amid the cop's presence, I was not thinking about what I could do to steal his bag of stashed dope. Then again, that's just me. None of it made sense to anyone. The rusted blade was flying around the inside of the tent as he continued to tear thru all the shit.

"Man, I'm going to jail tonight," he threatened, like he was about to do something final. If he didn't get his hands back on his medicine, there would be hell to pay. After searching Shorty's footprint, Black Face turned on me.

"Time to move, white boy."

He wanted to search under me. I moved to pull my pockets out like a pauper during the Great Depression.

"Get-cho hands out-cho pocket, goddammit! Move over...*Move!*"

I started to slide over to the side. At that point, others had gathered outside the tent. I heard them trying to talk to us, but I couldn't concentrate on what they were saying. With his permission (I thought), I started to shift again, and this set him off.

"Hey! I didn't say move again!" Black Face raised his arm then tucked and turned his shoulder down whipping the wielded weapon. I sensed the rusty blade bearing down on my head in a blur. Instinctively, I lowered my face away from the surging machete just in time for the dull edge to bounce off my skull at the crown. I barely felt it. Black Face bound toward me, grabbed my collar, and tossed me to the other side of the tent. My adrenaline was pumping, but mounting fear was overcoming any motivation to move away from imminent danger.

"Let that white boy go!" The woman cried out in tones.
Her voice was trying to conceal a different fear, from the outside looking in, of what might happen. Something within Black Face must have been affected by pleas from the outside. As he tossed fabric in the air like juggling scarves, he started chanting to himself:

"You can run if you want to. You can run if you want to."

I couldn't tell if he was talking to me or the monkey on his back. After the blade hit my scalp, I was completely frozen in fear and could do nothing. I felt buried alive in a pine box and each shovel full of tossed dirt made it darker. It finally dawned on me that I had lost all control over my fate. The dull blade had pulled a flap of skin back from my skull beneath and blood was dripping down the back of my neck and cheek.

"You can run if you want to..." his voice bounced off the walls with slaps of cave-like echoes.

"You can run if you want to...."

****

Bro's voice came from below me as we scrambled up the chain-linked slab of Half Dome's backbone, after the ascent from Yosemite Valley in golden Northern California.

"Ain't gonna outrun that bear down there. He likes what he smells in our packs," said my fraternal twin brother.

"Where is Goldfish hiding out?"

We spied our backpacks far below down at the trail junction. It was the first day of our attempt to hike the 211-mile John Muir Trail, a famed section of the Pacific Crest Trail. The track ran thru Yosemite, Sequoia and Kings Canyon National Parks, then past Guitar Lake to the epic southern terminus of the JMT atop Mt. Whitney. It was June 27th.

Our 27th birthday that day had been wonderfully spent climbing out of Yosemite Valley and then up the spine of the iconic Half Dome. He had talked me into the long-distance backpacking adventure for our golden birthday in the Golden State, along with Goldfish who was fresh off a successful Sobo hike of the Appalachian Trail the year before. Maybe Bro thought I needed something different in my life. Having had some struggles of his own in our late teens, someone led him into the woods for recalibration. Bro entered the wilderness as a glassy-eyed, defiant, and pissed-off kid. He emerged as a man poised with a new sense of service, leadership, and purpose. Bro eventually blossomed into a passionate and successful arborist and conservationist.

Day-One of the John Muir Trail ended with the two of us bouldering up the granite spine of Half Dome to the summit. The reward center in my brain burst open like a penny-slot jackpot. It felt great to have the heavy pack off my back while hoisting myself up and down the giant chain links of the "Oh, shit" handles on either side of the route. One misstep could spell mortal disaster. In good form, we raised ourselves up to reach the summit with the late afternoon sun.

"Look at this view!"

"Wicked, yeah man, yes!" Bro returned with a high five. "Look at El Cap over there! And the Falls... Wow, that's a long way down." In awe, he pointed across miles of the valley covered with dark green trees, silver cliff faces and waterfalls silently tumbling a thousand feet down. Gazing upon the majesty of Yosemite Valley, he put his arm around me.

"Just think of all there is to see in this world, Brah. No need to crawl or run. We can just walk."

"Hiking in the mountains is simple but not easy." Later in life I would chase a demon repeatedly. The wisdom of the phrase "simple but not easy" would become clearer and more haunting, especially right before the final bottom-out. While struggling with active addiction, I would periodically get the monkey off my back. But the circus was always in town. For years, I had circled the drain like it was a black hole, caught in a vicious cycle, with narrowly escaped freefalls to the singularity. But out in the wilderness my skin fell in love with the air; my eyes soaked in the colors; the rest of my senses sang whilst my heart kicked like a drum. The path ahead was already marked. It was suggested that I simply follow the trail blazes.

"We better head down," said Bro, "Goldfish is still watching our packs."

"Yeah, she's been hanging out with those bears for a while."

"She can handle that. What a first day of hiking."

"Amazing day. Happy Birthday, Bro. I love ya."

"Same to you, Brah. Happy Birthday. Love you, too."

"Race you down?"

****

"You can run if you want to!"

The sound of Black Face's voice was coming back to center. How could I run? I was trapped in this tent with no way out and little hope of surviving further harm. Even if I did run, I would look guilty therefore not safe on the street anymore.

That is the selfish delusion of an alcoholic in his cup. Our minds are forever zeroed in on getting the next hit by any means necessary.

"Black, this is fucked up! Quit this shit!" snapped Shorty.

"Let him go!" came the girl's voice from the other side of the tent. Black Face had enough. In the confines of the tent, he swung the machete at Shorty's neck. "Here it comes," I told myself. But Shorty, living up to his name, ducked just in time. The blade went over his head and slashed thru the sidewall of the tent.

Instantly, my window of opportunity had opened. The survival instinct jolted me out of a freeze and into flight mode. Diving headfirst, I leapt across the tent and out of the opened sidewall, bouncing off the concrete floor of the viaduct. "Stop, drop and roll" training from elementary school came from somewhere as I tucked and rolled twenty feet down to the sidewalk below as if I were on fire. I might as well have been... I had set fire to everything else in my life. But escaping the stale and deadly air in that tent brought forth a burst of energy. I landed on my feet and ran away as fast as I could.

A FEW MONTHS AGO, I met a cook at a deli who told me a story about a former hiker of mountains:

"Fairly recently, a man came into the deli and told us that he had just completed backpacking the entire Appalachian Trail. After pressing him for more about his adventure, he offered his initial thoughts about the journey's end. He said that when he stood atop Mount Katahdin, looking at the famed wooden sign that demarcates the northern terminus of the trail, there was no one else there to take his picture. The man was cold and soaked thru with rain and he was hungry and emaciated. He started to wonder what he had accomplished. 'Nothing', he was sad to say. He surmised that he had not accomplished anything of real value, and he felt totally alone. I felt sorrow for this man over his confession of confusion," said Delhi, "yet I couldn't help but agree with his analysis. Not surprisingly, he never left us. His story is common in our house, although we speak of it not."

Delhi reflected upon his own spiritual adventures in silence for a moment. Then he smiled and fried up a salmon patty good enough to bait an Alaskan grizzly from across the continent. His tale, however, was not a sparkling review of long-distance hiking. The hiker's accomplishment can surely be viewed as one of physical endurance if nothing else. But it raises the larger question of purpose: Why hike long distances to begin with? There are as many reasons to thru-hike a long trail as there are people who attempt it. Anyone who considers the challenge has probably come up with at least one plausible reason to try, and that's all it takes. Or, if you like, one decision followed up by the necessary action. Lo, the lucky ones make the trudge of a lifetime as variations on a theme, regardless of how far they make it.

The good cook also said this about music: "If you listen to the radio today, there's no hope in it. Popular music just flips the bird at any sense of morality or community or showing of love. There's a lot of pain in secular music. It screams from the hilltops 'I'm gonna do whatever the hell I want! I am not going to be obedient...and so what if I am scared?' Nope, no redeeming qualities of faith or hope. Music is powerful stuff, man. It can lift the guardrails up and let the enemy in."

Popular music has always had a rebellious quality to it, like the half-insane idea of walking from one tip of a country to the other. But I respectfully disagree on his last point: Interestingly for the hiker and human, lifting the guardrails empowers the ego to purge the enemy out thru a natural exorcism of sorts. The difference being that a wilderness-creature-spirit wields a power much greater than the wrinkled hands of false oracles.

****

On that dreary run thru the winter from hell, I had been awake for days. My menacing presence had quickly festered like a boil on the city's ass. After trying to get clean for a couple years, I had picked back up and was running wide open. Managing to put some brief periods of sobriety together, there still were no signs of real change. Only hints, here and there.

By February 29th, I was so leaping-high, I ditched going to a release-party where I was expected to attend and perform my song, on a bill with other artists from the record. The poet-laureate of Louisville, Dr. Ron Whitehead, had graciously produced a song of mine for his latest compilation album featuring local songwriters. He paid for my studio time and shared his priceless wisdom about healing thru the arts.

While attending one of Ron's creative writing workshops, he said something to the group that hit me like a water balloon and soaked me thereafter. It was a suggestion of how to go about writing something truly good. He instructed that "artistic creation is most expressive or emotive when you are willing to be completely vulnerable and speak your truth from the soul. It is with patience and practice that we get better and cleverer with how we do it. 'It' refers to connecting with another human being thru a chosen medium." At the time, the song that Ron financed for me was my very best songwriting attempt at three chords and the truth. But I torched his recording gift like a broken bulb on a Christmas tree. I had sobered thru the creative process but started using again just days before the album release party which featured artists on the record. There was no way I could show up in such a state. No one could guess that two weeks later, I would be in a North Georgia motel with an angry proprietor banging on the door while the President yelled "Fire!" on the blaring television (for good reason), and me grappling with the idea of walking off the hangover of life for about two-thousand miles.

My hindsight ran a reel-to-reel horror flick queued on repeat. Active addiction cost me my family, my job, my home, and any sense of social responsibility. All I had to do was surrender. Still, I couldn't do it. I hadn't truly hit rock bottom. My family was informed that they were enabling me, and I was in turn using them, so that I could keep using drugs. The information checked out. As I felt the quicksand starting to take me down, my survival instinct growled. Some say I had a moment of clarity. I made a call to the last person that I knew would answer. I called my twin brother.

"Bro?"

"Brah."

"I am thinking about trying a thru-hike of the Trail."

"You are...."

"What do you think?"

It gave him pause and our conversation fell silent on both ends of the "AT phone call".

****

The first trail I technically "thru-hiked" was the Knobstone Trail, which the State of Indiana boasts as its longest continuous backcountry footpath. At a rough and rugged 50 miles give or take, the "KT" was a training run for what would become the bid to hike the John Muir Trail later that summer. At the time when Bro and Goldfish first suggested that I tag along with them to the High Sierras of California, to attempt the crowning jewel of the Pacific Crest Trail, I had never even heard of the John Muir Trail, the Pacific Crest Trail, or the Continental Divide... let alone the KT, that ran right thru our front yard. Well, across the Ohio River from Louisville, Kentucky, to be geographically correct. But I was familiar with the Appalachian Trail because of the numerous friends and relatives that had attempted to walk the entire length from Springer Mountain to Mount Katahdin. Some had succeeded and some had failed. But all had returned with sparkles in their eyes and fiery secrets in their hearts. There was a humble new wisdom about the world that they possessed upon their return from the wild. And they spoke about places and things that seemed like distant fantasies: long views of tall mountains; waterfalls of the clearest blues and grays that seemed to fall from the heavens, and shaded ground covered in pine needles that was soft enough to comfortably lay bare asses on. And the people they spoke of...a lot of folks who usually would not mix in civilian life come together on the essentials of supporting each other's sustainability. What was this whole "hiking" thing about, really?

"Tell me more about this Knobstone Trail, Bro."

"Rugged and steep, Brah, it's going to be a long weekend of 50 longer miles. But it will give you an idea of what to expect on the John Muir Trail. Only the JMT is over 200 miles long, and in much different terrain," he explained.

"So, this long weekend-warrior expedition is just a dry run? Like, training ground or something?"

"*Proving* ground. It's a chance to see how your moxie matches up to the elements with thirty pounds strapped on your back."

The idea of "climbing mountains with thirty pounds on my back" didn't exactly shake my tambourine at first. There was no way for me to know that one day, I couldn't imagine a life without hoisting thirty pounds up and over mountains. Day-hikes with just a water bottle in my hand would feel like streaking naked.

Eight weeks before the trip to California, we donned our packs at the head of the Knobstone Trail to try for three fifteen-mile days, to get home by Sunday night. The trailhead, at Deam Lake State Park in Southern Indiana, was just ten miles from Louisville's city limits. But it felt like a world away from the tall buildings and busy streets of Downtown Anywhere, USA.

"Come over here, Brah. Let me help you with that pack harness. Cinch down the straps, so the weight is equally distributed across your back. You want most of the tonnage in that waist belt so it's carried on your hips."

"Bro has your pack in good shape," Goldfish said with encouragement, "You've got perfect gear for this. The Black Diamond single-wall tent, light and durable; the Mountain Hardwear sleeping bag, and you're gonna love that Therm-a-Rest pillow sack. I wouldn't have carried it across thirteen state lines myself if it wasn't a solid piece of equipment."

Bro pulled the straps of my brand-new Osprey backpack and I chuckled with embarrassment, feeling like a grown-ass adult getting strapped into a car seat.

"Really," I begged him, "does it have to be that tight?"

"Trust me. You don't want all that weight sliding around on your shoulders. It's a burden on your back. We've got you dialed in pretty good there. Okay Brah, how does it feel?"

"Like a straight-jacket."

"Perfect. Let's kick this thing off."

And off we kicked, starting over a soft and flat stroll around Deam Lake, which was busy with boats, beer and boys baiting fishing-rods on the shore. It was clear and sunny, low humidity, and generally a great day to walk.

"This isn't so bad!" I reported, pleased with my positive attitude. But I spoke too soon.

"That's great, Brah! Now get ready to climb."

As the trail turned away from the lake, we immediately began a steep ascent into the deep forest that was full of red and black oaks, dogwoods, pines, and an occasional American sweetgum. But it was hard to appreciate the beauty, as my legs and lungs burned from the never-ending staircase of steps. I reached a limit and stopped the train.

"Y'all, I need a break. We've been climbing forever. How far do you think we've gone?" (The classic "Are we there, yet?") I was expecting them to say we were halfway there.

"We've gone about a mile and a half," said Goldfish.

"What?! A mile and a half? How far are we trying to go today?" My backpack started to feel like a satchel of gravel. What the hell was I doing out here, anyway? This isn't much fun, I thought. This is crazy! Why carry a bag of dead weight up the side of a mountain? What's the use?

"Hang in there, Brah. We have a great stop planned for lunch in about five miles."

I took a long, deep breath and put my head down. A little bit further up the path, the sight of some easy wildflowers lightened the burden of the heavy load on my back and something in my spirit flickered like the flint of a lighter strike. But the kindling on my fire had not fully dried out; the flame wasn't holding yet. That is, until we hit Round Knob. As we carved up the side of the escarpment and landed on the treeless bald, my jaw dropped. To the south, a panoramic view of the Ohio River valley stretched out for dozens of miles. The river looked like a snake wrapping around the summits of the city buildings from a dozen miles away. In nearly twenty-seven years of living, I had never seen my hometown from this vantage point, and it looked like a painting; a piece like my Aunt Pris would do, when something in the world stops her daily motions and compels her to sit and paint. But it's hardly "forced" when divine inspiration fills our soul enough to allow self-expression thru artistic creation. The key is to be ready at any moment for that inspiration.

"Bro! Goldfish! What a view! I've never seen the city from a thousand feet up unless I was flying. I always saw these hills over here, but never even considered...."

"Climbing mountains every day is tough, Brah. But the payoff is usually worth every mile. I know we still have a way to go... but what do you think so far?"

I was wide-eyed and winded, mostly in awe. They let me sit in silence, gazing out over the open valley to the home I thought I knew so well. From that vista, though, it looked like some weird and distant destination. The shape of the skyline was beautiful, and its location appeared out of place in the green expanse of the river valley.

I was seeing it from a brand-new perspective. Upon reaching the northern terminus of the KT, I had the feeling that I had genuinely accomplished something. Maybe there was something to this hiking thing after all? My Uncle Ron, trail name: No Trail Name

(NTN for brevity), picked us up from the trailhead parking lot after a tiring but rewarding thru-hike of the Knobstone Trail.

"What'd you think of the hike?" NTN asked.

"Awesome," I said.

"I know it," he chuckled with reminiscence, "After thru-hiking the AT, I can't drive past a trailhead anywhere and not look for a white blaze beyond the tree line."

Back then I didn't understand what he meant, but now I know exactly what he was talking about. And so does Bro, in his own way. That wisdom is ultimately what moved Bro to break the silence of our "AT phone call", when times of desperation conjured up ideas of my attempting a thru-hike....

****

"Yes, that is exactly what you should do. You've gotta do something different, Brah. This real-time tragedy is slowly killing you, and the rest of us are forced to watch. Something's gotta give."

Watching a loved one diminish into addiction carries its own type of convicted sentence. Oh, how it must feel, when there's nothing left to do but close the door on your own flesh and blood. But in that moment of unique desperation that we both shared, Bro's wisdom took subtle charge. He agreed to lend me some extra trekking gear. I drove over to his house to pick up.

"So, you still have your old Osprey rig and the Black Diamond gear," Bro probed, referring to my weathered old backpack, single-wall tent, and trekking poles.

"Yep. And a friend gave me a cooking stove. A Jetboil."

"That was nice of him. Good piece of gear if it works. Here, take these. The Western Mountaineering 20° sleeping bag, and here is the Therm-a-Rest pillow sack that Goldfish carried on her AT thru-hike. The same one she let you use on the KT and JMT. This bag already has many successful thru hikes to boast. It'll go the distance again if you can. And Brah, treat people the way you want to be treated. I love you. I hope you make the drive safely. You don't look good." He shook his head after he hugged me.

"I love you, too. Thanks Bro, I'll see you sooner than later."

"Not too soon. Stay out there and finish the damn thing...

...Don't Fucking Quit."

I called upon Quest Outdoors, the local outfitter, just before they closed that night. Bro had worked there for a few years in our twenties and many of the employees knew who I was. I looked like I had just barely survived an explosion in a meth lab. Plopping a new headlamp and water filter on the counter, I informed the horrified staff of my plans:

"I'm going to hike the Appalachian Trail, end to end!"

"Whatever you say, pal," the chiseled cashier mumbled. My hands were trembling so badly when he handed me the change that I dropped a quarter onto the glass counter. It landed with a clank that made me jump. Instead of handing me the receipt, he wadded it up and tossed it over his shoulder into the trash can, then crossed his arms in a symbolic gesture of "all sales final, no returns."

"Good luck and Godspeed," he prayed over me with a sigh. When it comes to the adventures of the outdoors, these cats were professional. They knew of that with which I spoke—more so than I. The AT was not for the faint of heart or the weak in spirit. Surely, they observed a scant chance of my success. But they had class and never said "no, you can't" (or "I told you so"). Quest Outdoors would support an adventure for any soul who needed a vacation, a change or a challenge. On that night no one seemed to recognize me or let on that they did. Hell, I didn't recognize me anymore.

I proceeded on to the highway riding dirty. There was dope in my head and more in my pocket. I was in no shape to travel, especially alone thru the middle of the night into the Deep South. The drive to North Georgia was an overnight hell ride down I-65 South. Mania drove the truck and paranoia checked the rear view mirrors every few seconds. Sometime late in the night, I was southbound on a two-lane state road that ran parallel to the interstate, flying at blistering speeds with my headlights off. I saw the faintly lit speedometer hit 100 mph; the needle was a wobbly blur. I used the distant interstate lights for navigation and could have killed anything on the dark pavement, including myself. Something was out there chasing me. One grass-munching deer crossing the road could have ended in both of us being smacked, spun out and splattered, with my body hanging from a rack of antlers pinned to a tree trunk. My savage state of mind turned a six-hour ride into nine hours, even after burying the needle of the old Ford a few times.

Passing the city limit sign into Dahlonega, Georgia, I somehow arrived in one piece and not in handcuffs. I checked into a motel and fell onto the bed in total fatigue as sunrise appeared on the horizon. I do not know how long I slept. The phone rang and I managed to scratch out a "Hello?"

"Sir, would you like to extend your stay another night?"

"Ugh...what time is it? Yeah, just run the charge on the same card again."

"Wait, Sir, you need to—" *click.*

I hung up the phone and stood up in the dark. After a few minutes, I pulled the curtains back to blinding sunlight. Jesus, what's today? What time is it? Where is my cell phone? Oh yeah, I sold my phone to a grocery store kiosk back in Louisville during a drug-induced blackout. They were on me, man. Whoever "they" were. Sitting on the edge of the bed, I turned the television on. My head was pounding, and the contents of my old Osprey Ether pack were strewn out all over the other bed. I didn't recall unpacking my hiking gear like a tag sale. The TV blipped on to a live feed of the President briefing the White House press corps to introduce an esteemed new panel of "experts."

"It's called COVID-19, and it's a deadly coronavirus from a lab in China," squawked the talking heads on cable news. The roundtable of reporters rambled on about the potential of the crisis to reach epidemic levels in very little time. Click. I splashed some cold water on my face.

"Ahhhhh, hissssss," I sucked air thru my teeth in pain.
The stinging water forced me to look at the mirror, something I hadn't dared to do in days. Squinty-blinking then wide-eyed, I strained at the sight of the ghastly chemical burns beneath my unkempt beard and mat of hair. Goddammit, I had done it again. I stumbled back to bed and fell fast asleep.

****

"Daddy!" My daughter's voice reverberated in my shifty consciousness, triggering memories of a whiteout scene in our backyard. It was two weeks before the Kentucky Derby and a series of late-season storms had piled up nearly two feet of snow on the ground. The fresh powder was fluffy and cold.

"Daddy, there's snow!"
The full-grown ash trees covering the backyard sprinkled tiny crystals of ice and snow thru the air as a gentle breeze tossed around the tops of the swaying giants with crackling frozen delight.

"Play in the snow with me, Daddy! Let's build a snowman! Yea!" She dropped to her knees and made a powdery snowball that broke apart in her mittens. Licking the snow from her thumb, she looked up and giggled: "Yummy!"

"Come get this butterball!" My wife cradled our infant son who was wrapped up in winter textiles and puffy coat like a burrito in over-protective mommy-style. He must have been miserable in all seven layers and one and a half years. But it was his first real awareness of snow and I'll never forget the look on that sweet little boy's face. In fact, it's all I saw in my mind's eye throughout one particularly hellish night that following winter. Homeless in January, I stumbled down to the waterfront in a desperate condition of failing health. It was twelve degrees outside, and my protective layers consisted of a thin autumn jacket, blue jeans, and imitation Chuck Taylors on my feet. It was close to midnight and my body temperature was plummeting. Even in my delusional state, I knew if I stopped moving I would likely pass out of exhaustion and die of hypothermia. The Ohio River had begun to freeze, and I could see the moonlight shining on the frosted ice covering the surface of the water. There was a row of permanent brick bathrooms, built at the waterfront, placed there for seasons-gone festivals of waving trees, warm waters, and the rootsy sounds of electrified Bluegrass music on the green. The men enjoyed draught beers in Dixie cups and wore ball caps and tank tops touting truck companies and jam bands. The women wore spaghetti-strap sundresses and Derby hats over rose-tinted sunglasses, with umbrellas in their melting neon cocktails. All were laughing in noodle-dances to summer vibes of the good ole' times.

Back in the arctic-like January night, no party was popping. It was a full-on crisis as my desperate scramble to stay alive ushered me down the row of bathroom doors, frantically jiggling each handle, hoping to find shelter behind a steel door. I surmised it would take pallbearers to bring me back out in a window of thaw. Each locked door handle brought me closer to the frozen river and nearer to my demise. I began to resign myself to the trauma-tundra of frozen shore that awaited; I almost welcomed it as I tried the last handle...*Pop*. The handle dropped, I pulled, the door swung open, and the motion-sensor light clicked on. Oh my, the relief to step in, slam the door shut behind me and latch out the cold—only to find that it seemed ten degrees colder inside the frozen brick enclosure. Something under the sink caught my eye....it was a knob, a timer— It was a heater. I scrambled to turn it on, twist... Nothing. Dammit. And then, I heard a crank, and the engine turned over as a coil started to glow orange. (Forever my favorite color.) Within seconds, the fan was blowing warm air onto my feet. I dropped to the ground, shivering, and rocking back and forth, trying to absorb every vibrating molecule of warmth. The feeling in my arms and legs started to come back. The will to live was no longer outmatched by exposure to the outside elements, and the temperature rose as I drifted into sleep while leaning against the door. I was startled awake in the morning to the sound of a groundskeeper banging on the door from the outside.

****

BAM, BAM, BAM!

Feverish knocking at the door startled me from rest, as the North Georgia motel door flew open via the proprietor's key. Before the light of dawn, the motel owner decided he'd had enough of me, and his swift action caught me off guard. He had wanted me out yesterday. Especially now, seeing the condition of the room after multiple days of shutting the world out, the boil came to a head. With an Indian accent, the motel owner teed off into a rage.

"Sir, you must check out! No more reservation extensions."

"Ok, what time is it?"

"Check-out is NOW!"

"Bullshit! It's dark out. I paid for this night. I will check out at...check-out. When is breakfast?" I rubbed my eyes and remembered my facial wounds.

"Now, OUT, please!" The Indian motel proprietor was furious. I back peddled him thru the open door as he raved on:

"No! Sir! you must go..."

"Thank you!" I slammed the door and fastened the chain.

"You will be trespassing, Sir...." His voice muffled behind the closed door.

Inexplicably, he didn't call the police. By 7:30 next morn, I had packed up the hatch of my Ford Escape and was headed for Amicalola Falls State Park less than a dozen miles away. It was a foggy and rainy morning on March 16th, in North Georgia, and my "friend-count" was zero.

A northbound thru-hike attempt of the Appalachian Trail typically begins with an idyllic experience at Amicalola Falls State Park. It's an opportunity for making last minute purchases and preparations, meeting other hikers, and officially registering the hike with the Appalachian Trail Conservancy. After a picture under the famed stone arch behind the visitor center, the Springer Mountain "approach trail" is the final kick-off to the southern terminus of the AT, which is the summit of the mountain itself. My experience was a far cry from the typical northbound start.

I registered my hike with the Appalachian Trail Conservancy (A.T.C.) at the Amicalola Visitor Center, receiving the "AT thru-hiker" tag number 1317. Then I left without saying another word to anyone. I did none of the other things either. I skipped the blue-blazed approach trail, thus avoiding the four hundred stairs that switch back and forth ascending the grand waterfalls. Climbing the amazing water cascade after which the park is named would have to wait. I would eventually make amends to the sole proprietor of the motel. But that would have to wait too. At that moment, what seemed like the end of days had authority over my every move. The feeling of imminent doom loomed large, but somehow I kept going.

The approach trail to the summit of Springer Mountain doesn't technically count as AT miles, so I concluded that I didn't need to hike it. My lack of schooling on the traditions of the trail was evident from the start. But as they say, "Hike your own hike." I decided I would drive my truck up the windy and rainy mountain road to the summit's trailhead parking lot and start my journey on the white blazes. Halfway up the rutted service road, something in my spirit moved me to stop the truck. The windshield wipers swathed the rain from the glass. Out of the driver window stood a lone tree. An Eastern white pine. As I rolled the window down the maroons and greens vibrantly burst into life. The muddy rain looked clearer. The wind on the hill was clean. Branches of the lone pine danced in the rain and pointed at the clouds above. Everything had seemingly been in black and white until I saw that tree emerge from the waking winter forest. I took a deep breath, then exhaled, emptying my lungs. Closing the window, I continued up the muddy service road to slowly wrap around the shoulders of the mountain. It was the first whiff.

Springer's trailhead parking was empty when I limped my exhausted truck into the parking lot. It was still a mile's hike south to reach the summit, two miles out and back on virtually flat terrain. I opened the hatch to an explosion of hiking equipment falling out onto the gravel. I found my rain jacket and put it on, feeling totally overwhelmed and exhausted already. What was I doing? What was I thinking? My head had begun to clear after coming down from a horrible spree of drug use and I could hardly make simple decisions. Moreover, what was I going to do with my truck? I really didn't care what happened to it but leaving it in the parking lot seemed like bad form. I considered leaving the keys with it and signing the back of the title, as a recompense for the chap that would have to deal with schlepping the damn thing off the mountain. Seemed fair. Then I got distracted and forgot about the fate of the truck. So many thoughts raced around my head. I dropped worldly possessions by the wayside, I was inadvertently lightening the burdens of weight; I was approaching the gate.

The thought crossed my mind that maybe the hardest part was over. What was there left to do but put foot to dirt and leave it all behind? Still, I hesitated. Instead of stuffing my backpack with wrinkled gear, I laced up my boots and looked for the sign marked "Springer Mountain Summit →" ...I found the trail heading south toward the top of Springer Mountain. I had no phone, no camera, and no way to commemorate the moment. It was for the best. The thought of what the picture would look like made me bristle with insecurity. I passed the blue-blazed trail leading down to Springer

Mountain Shelter and continued to the unassuming summit of the most storied hiking mountain in the South. Hovering over the bronze plaque and first white blaze that demarcates the southern terminus of the Appalachian Trail, I took another deep breath. A last-century fashioned historical marker showcasing a beautifully molded hiker preserves a bygone era that still had resonance.

The bronze plaque reads:

"A footpath for those who seek fellowship with the wilderness."

Being a World War combat veteran, Earl Shaffer, the first person to thru-hike the Appalachian Trail in 1948, later claimed that he hiked the trail to "walk off the war." Under the plaque, I saw a compartment with a metal door on the side of a rock slab. Opening the box, I found the first trail register and thumbed thru the pages containing clever passages from other hikers who had come this way before.

"Hawk was here". Who? I turned the page: The ink from Darwin's autograph was barely dry. Who the hell were these people? Travelers from all reaches of the earth had signed this book with sacks stuffed for a quest to remember. I sat down and wanted to cry but I figured that it was already raining, so what was the use anyhow. The ink-penned hopes and dreams were beginning to bleed on the page, so I closed the rainy notebook and put it back in the compartment under the rock. Flexing my core muscles and stretching my back, I prepared for the mile back to the truck.

For a moment, the clouds let a single ray of sunshine down to warm my face and fill me with a sliver of hope. It was not a hope for anything. Just the feeling. It was needed after the longest mile. Turning north with heels firmly on the earth, I took my first steps as a Nobo of the Appalachian Trail. From that moment on, I owned the fact that I was a thru-hiker. I would trudge as far as my feet would take me and try to get something out of this experience. Arriving back at trailhead parking by evenfall, I climbed into the way-back of the Escape and closed the hatch.

Early morning brought rumbles of large vehicles pulling into the parking lot. The windows of my truck were totally fogged up and I took an opportunity to slip out of the driver side door when I thought no one was looking. My appearance was hellish, but I was gaining nerve. I had done this before, trekking long distances in the past with my brother. The John Muir Trail, Knobstone Trail, the Red River Gorge and the Smokies. Trail and park patches from previous adventures covered my ancient backpack. The presence of the moderate credentials was comforting. I knew I had the fortitude to hike, at least for a little while and the patches proved it. They didn't prove a thing. Anyone can take a drive to Maine just to get a lobstah stickah for the cah. The winter-bare oak and poplars hid behind the evergreens that towered above the perimeter of the parking lot, which was now bustling with activity. Fresh-skinned detergent-fuming hikers donned overstuffed packs as they laughed and gave each other high fives. A huge black bus with pop-outs and chrome wheels was supporting a large group of hikers that looked like they were gearing up for the long haul. I was quiet, shy, and unsure as I approached a couple of them, who seemed a little less testosterone-driven than a certain faction that quickly headed for the trail.

"Hey guys. What is this? I mean, who are you guys?" My voice cracked.

"Damn, son, where are you from?" He was an upper middle-aged guy with a large brim fishing hat on and a wad of Copenhagen in his lip.

"Kentucky."

"Well alright, Ken-turkey! I thought I heard some Mason-Dixie in there... What's that, they say? *Undecided?*"

"Undecided? That was a century and a half ago."

"Oh, don't mind me, I'm just joshin' with ya." He laughed and dropped his fist like pile-driver on my shoulder. "As for us, we're from the Wounded Warrior Expeditions." He pointed at the motely crew of comrades in the parking lot. "WWE sponsored thru-hikes for our crew. There's about thirty of us...clowns, tag-teamed out here in duos and trios. But we're one unit."

He motioned to the trainwreck of egos already butting heads near the trail-map kiosk. The call and response between a pair of very Honorably-Discharged corporals called many to amusement. Recollecting with all due respect, they started in with the trash-talk:

"I'll make the falls in thirty minutes!" declared one to the other.

"That's miles away, peg-leg! Do some theater logistics!"

"You're an asshole, Debronske! Take your meds!"

I turned away from the lively scene and back into our conversation chuckling. These guys were wounded heroes but didn't take themselves or each other too seriously. These men were still a unified front, poised for glory.

"That's amazing. You guys are all military veterans?" I was awkwardly trying to be friendly for the first time in ages and the Lone-Star soldier responded in kind.

"Yep. And we are all twisted up in some way! I see the battlefield in my mind's eye— but thank God I have two working legs. There are vets out here hoping to hike that are missing much more than the innocence of youth." A light-hearted laugh bellowed from all. "My name is Don...from Texas." he reached out his hand. "Good to meet you, Don. So, this bus..." I pointed over my shoulder to their mobile command center that seemed to have anything that a hiker might need to kick off and keep going. The first bit of generosity from the heroes that came my way was camaraderie.

"Yeah, that's us," said Don, "Our hikes are sponsored by Wounded Warriors, all the way from here in Georgia to middle Maine. We're veterans with service-connected...ratings. We each have a list of different sponsors along the trail that have agreed to help us out when we pass thru. That resource bus is supporting us thru Neel Gap." He pointed to the brand-new Transit van in the middle of the parking lot behind me. "Trail-Com. Care to join us?"

"That's nice, Don, but I'm not packed yet. See you on trail." I walked away trying to mask anxiety at my unpreparedness.

"Hey!" Don called to me, "Do you have a name?"

"Not yet."

Don turned sideways and furrowed his brow. I headed for for my truck to start packing up the gear.

My equipment consisted of the worn and storied Osprey pack; the Western Mountaineering 20 degree sleeping bag my brother had given me; one Black Diamond single wall two-person tent; a pair of Black Diamond ski poles (with giant baskets that gathered jokes from other hikers); Ridge Rest sleeping pad; a Mountain Hardwear puffy coat; a Sea to Summit food sack; one very special Therm-a-Rest pillow sack that doubled as a clothes bag; and an original JetBoil stove that my friend Jimmy Banks had given me on the day I departed. Jimmy passed it along with a message:

"This was my wife's JetBoil. Take it with you and may it bring you good luck...and may you bring it back. Permanent loan."

I met Jimmy Banks in a treatment center the summer before the "long-walk" idea. He was a great nylon-string guitar player and had a saucy Tracy Chapman-like baritone thing going with his voice; he was all-dude but equally as lamenting. The year before our paths crossed, Jimmy Banks' wife died of a heroin overdose in Guatemala, where they had escaped the West Coast in a fiendish frenzy. He woke up to find her dead in their bed above a bodega, on an otherwise picturesque tropical day with the breeze gently blowing the curtains behind open sliding doors to a view above the water. Her death really tore him up and he had spent the worst parts of the previous year turning his arm into a pincushion, with only brief periods of sobriety. I usually knew if he was using dope or not, because his weight could fluctuate a hundred pounds in a matter of weeks. I told him I would give the bequeathed Jetboil back the next time I saw him. He waved me on, saying "A longer-than-usual hike, huh... Sounds crazy...I like it. Good luck, man."

So, there I was, a Nobo on the Appalachian Trail. What it meant; I didn't know yet. But I would come to learn that "Northbound AT" was a special circumstance for a human being, and not to be taken for granted. I was beginning to feel a sense of purpose I had lacked for a long time. That purpose was still cloudy and not fully defined, so I considered the basic principles that seemed appropriate for a thru-hiker. I reminded myself of what Bro had told me. Goal #1: Go the distance. Rule #1: Don't be an asshole. Set my sights on Katahdin, then take it one day at a time. The old way of living was not working anymore. I had been fighting a war that was long ago lost, re-entering the bloody battlegrounds, and stepping over the bodies of lost comrades in search of a dominant enemy. I had given up everything that mattered to me in life for my addiction. Even after realizing that I was a very sick person, I kept on wrestling with the demons, believing that I could subdue the enemy within me. I wanted control of all the external forces that kept me from living the life that I wanted to live. I would look him square in the face and tell him that today was the day we would walk past the barber shop without stopping. GBITS had other plans.

"What do you do?" Don asked, as we began carving the rugged miles of North Georgia.

"I have played guitar for a living, mostly. I pick a banjo on occasion. Short stint in government, too...civil duty stuff."

"No kidding? My father played banjo for a living back in Texas, God rest his soul! When I was a kid, I used to sit at his feet and watch him pick and grin. Musicians have a hard life though; you know I'm sure. Not a lot of money in it. But he loved it...wait, that's it!"

"What?"

From a distance, the "Call to The Post" trumpeted like it was Kentucky Derby Day. But this wouldn't be a time trial. (And who was that long-haired old man in the white suit hiding behind the rocks over there?)

"Don, did you see that...."

"Your trail name. You need a trail name," he insisted. "What about *Music Man*?"

.3

PLAYING SIMPLE MUSIC came naturally to me, but I have never thought of myself as an inherently gifted or talented "musician." My insecurity constantly reminded me that I was the least proficient "musician" of my colleagues and band members, but for some reason they kept me around. Maybe because when I put my hands on it, my fingers did what I wanted them to do even if my mind wasn't that creative. In my humble opinion, "Clapton is God" was a direct result of his ability to eliminate any filter between his head, his heart, and his hands. "Slow hand" they called him. I didn't understand his nickname until I went thru my first heartbreak. Then I understood. If Eric Clapton felt it in his heart, we did too when he played it. He told stories with melodic lines, like so many greats that came before him and have come around since. Overrated? I think not. I wanted to be just like that. Another great one comes to mind, Buddy Guy once claimed "I ain't the best, but I'm the best till the best comes around." These guys could really play, and I was captivated by the raw emotion that poured out of them and into me. Certainly, there are brilliant minded and big-hearted heroes who can arrange and produce great harmony. But when it comes to playing the music themselves, they couldn't hit a baseball with a banjo. Then there are those who possess the coordination to play strange feeling instruments but sneak into a deeper musical understanding over time. Even though I had no idea what I was doing (and still don't), "emoting" came early on for me, after I learned "the hundred songs" that would eventually leave behind scant traces of formal musical theory.

Acid-rock kings and guitar gods were my early idols. I was easily swept into the lava lamps and liquids day-dreams of psychedelia. Just like Allmans biographer Alan Paul, I'll never forget the moment I first opened the *Eat A Peach* album cover. Duane Allman and Dicky Betts, Trey Anastasio, Michael Houser, Warren Haynes, and Jerry Garcia spoke to me in the fluid style of long-jam storytelling. At college I traced a backward number line of roots that led from Stevie Ray Vaughn to Albert King to Robert Johnson.

I studied Grant Green's trumpet-like guitar playing and I was wowed by Led Zeppelin and Pink Floyd and Queen and the Moody Blues. Dad turned me on to all kinds of other stuff, the Beach Boys and the Journeymen, Smokey Robinson, and Stevie. One evening he blew my mind open with the Who's Quadrophenia album when he cued up Rain O'er Me. Daltrey's scream at the end of the song has haunted my soul forever after. I developed a love of songwriters like the Beatles and the powerhouse songwriting craftsmen Elton John and Bernie Taupin. And there was Tim Buckley and Cat Stevens. Edgy stuff too, like Deep Purple and Iron Butterfly. I found Tommy Bolin on my own. GENESIS. There were other greats. There were old standards from Cole Porter and the opera romantics of Pavarotti. Classic records by ABBA, Fleetwood Mac, Steely Dan, and Chicago filled the record shelves, which have expanded over the years with my own tastes and fancies. Dad's favorite song: "A Whiter Shade of Pale" by Procol Harum. The index is seemingly endless, but that initial collection of my father's vinyl was my education in the art of music. 100% squeezed juiced.

Moving art in any medium turns me on. Time is a dimension, after all. I would rather watch the Native American mother make turquoise jewelry by the light of a ceremonial fire than pick out a piece from the overwhelming collection of doubtless treasures laid out in front of me. Observing the creative process gives me a giddy feeling inside. The experience of eyeing a good glassblower rolling a Christmas bulb in front of a piping hot oven, for me, is like sitting at a tiny round table next to a brick wall in a 1930's basement lounge on 4th Street listening to sizzling jazz.

The dark side of my love affair with music was the accompanying pleasures of the flesh. Performing was my first drug. There was something about the lights, the sound, and my newly long hair. I had found an identity. No longer shy and unsure when I had a guitar in my hands, all was right with the world. I was good at something, and when I played people watched and listened. Talking to girls became easy. An inexperienced mind and confused spirit can get easily intoxicated with pretty girls around and money getting stuffed into pockets. People would say things like "You're really good at that," and "You are going places". The child I was, lacking in life experience, happily bought into the fairy tale. It seemed that my mind never had a choice because I just didn't know better. My ego wanted to believe the things that people predicted for my future and I lusted for it.

I hid behind a talent for playing guitar. When I felt like someone was getting close enough to figure out who I really was, the "real me" (which was a fraud surrounded by fog machines and stage lights), I would pick up my guitar and play as if to say "Hey, look at what I can do, not at who I am! Don't look at the real me but listen to this instead!"

When Lone-Star Don suggested the trail name "Music Man" my gut fluttered like the butterflies of stage fright that I had not felt for many years. I could relate to a "music man" as being one of the many masks I wore over the years. It had been quite a while since I had anything of real substance that I could identify with. For a host of reasons, I didn't veto the new trail name. Did I love the name at first? No. But the traditions are what they are, and I wanted to commit to them. Who was I to break ranks, or worse: Name myself? I know what'd I'd be if I did: self-named. Alas, Lone-Star Don cared enough to peg me with a trail name that meant something to me, and to him too. It reminded him of his old man. He named me, and I accepted it. (It's that easy, hikers.)

This time, I wanted to do right by the "Music Man". The first few suns and moons on the trail brought immense challenges, but the vibrations of my embroiled cities and homesteads slowly faded into the distance. I ventured deeper into the sleepy jungle. Blood Mountain, Tray Mountain, and Unicoi Gap are rigorous expeditions for day-hikers and thru-hikers of any fitness level. But I was hanging in there. In late March the trees still had no leaves on their branches, except for the conifer's needles. Mountain slopes seemed to be moist and mossy, given the exceptionally dry weather conditions on the trail. The bright greens of the mosses and lichens invoked a mystical quality to the trail, as the path often encircled mountaintops like stripping a candy cane. Giant poplars, oaks and Georgia pines covered the trail with a spring shadow that brought the mossy bark glowing to life.

Usually beautiful and peaceful and forever weird in a good way, my hometown of Louisville had become ground-zero for social unrest in the spring of 2020. Adding to the uncertainty that the pandemic ushered in, frustrated citizens wreaked havoc on the streets in Louisville in the wake of the Breonna Taylor tragedy. A change in policing tactics was long overdue. And not just for Louisville, but for many cities around the country facing systemic socio-economic issues that strangle access to opportunity. The bottleneck at the exit of the hood in Louisville is not unique. But the situation in town was extraordinarily desperate at that time. While part of me wanted to be there, to show some form of solidarity with the constantly dividing and reunifying communities back home, I had my own demons to face.

Selfishly, perhaps, I stayed on the Appalachian Trail and prayed for my home instead. Even if the powers-that-be did not want thru-hikers to continue, I had different plans along with a few other mercenaries. When I registered my hike with the Appalachian Trail Conservancy at Amicalola Falls, I provided them with my email address. While at a motel in early April, I received an email rescinding my privilege to be recognized as a thru-hiker if I continued to hike. The email further instructed me to vacate the AT as it was, due to pandemic-related park and trailhead closures. At the time, I didn't know what to think about being abandoned by the folks in the trail-offices. There was confusion, then resentment began to well up. The abandonment would take some time (and perspective) fully process and understand; perhaps longer than a thru-hike. Humans living within the social constructs and limits of civilized Earth were just doing the best they could with what they had in front of them.

The natural scenery and solitude of the trail inspired much self-reflection. Finally, I had the space and time to think with a clearing head. I was there to hike and to try and save my own skin from the horrible path of self-destructiveness that I couldn't shake back home. My children deserved a healthy father, and I desperately wanted to be happy again. Is it selfish to wish for one's own happiness?

****

In those last days of active addiction, I roamed the streets of Louisville in a desperate condition. Music was absent from my hollowed-out existence. Once the hardest drugs took hold of me, my poker face couldn't hide the tells of real lethargy. Sort of like an old sedan with a decent paint job but a bong for a muffler. Once I started showing up in detox wards and rehabs, all the cards were finally down.

Everyone saw that I had been bluffing for years and some rightly suspected I had been stacking the deck. My sedan had only been making left turns, vainly and foolishly attempting to hide the two missing hubcaps on the driver side. But dirt always comes out in the wash. At two years divorced, I was a homeless unemployable deadbeat. Just as the cycle of street-institution-street-institution had me at spin-dry, I would crank the dial and hit the "fuck it" button again. Close family and a few loyal friends never turned their backs on me, but they knew when to close the door and turn the porch lights off. I sank further into addiction. Then there were the auto accidents...

For nearly twenty years, I had a perfect driving record without so much as a fender bender to report. Only a handful of moving violations. That sparkling history came crashing down in a matter of months when I found a substance that kept me awake for days at a time. My body would finally start to crash when I stopped moving, and that included waiting for red lights. One time, I awoke to a knock at the window as I waited for a green light to change. I wrecked four cars in less than a year while blacking out behind the wheel. I nearly bit my tongue off when I flipped my mother's Lexus while overdosing in a dealer's driveway. I turned the car around and pulled away but that's the last thing I remember. I "came to" hanging upside down seeing red, as blood ran from my mouth into my eyes. My body jolted as I unclipped the seatbelt and fell onto my head. I climbed out of the smashed driver's window and into the arms of first responders who tried to get answers out of me. I ended up confessing my life story to the medic in the ambulance, then got scared and ran from the hospital. My car must have reached a speed near fifty miles per hour on that narrow trailer park drive. I clipped the bumper of a parked pickup truck and rolled over in the bristling white Lexus. That trailer park has a yellow road sign on the sidewalk that reads "Children at Play". Still, no charges or threats to my driving privileges though I was running out of vehicles to total out. How I survived that year without killing myself or anyone else is nothing short of a miracle. Real change, however, was still many miles away and I was adrift with no beacon of hope in sight. Life appeared black and white with sounds muffled and jostling, like I was living deep underwater and caught near a black hole. I could not stop using, and most of the time I didn't want to. When far from the respite of the wilderness, relief from the cyclic agony was found in the fleeting moments after a fresh hit of dope. Eventually, that stopped working too. That's when I truly hit bottom. No more rescue canes flew from the wings. The house lights came on and the curtain lifted to reveal the pock-faced Wicked Wizard to himself. I had no idea yet of why I thrust myself face first into addiction.

One sullen night, I walked out from under a bridge and looked around at the paleness of the city. I vaguely sensed the mobile travelers zooming by on the highway above. Where were they going? The sounds of cars careening by became clearer and the silhouette of a tree came into focus under the full moon. As I searched for a newborn sky, my daughter's voice entered my consciousness. She was singing and laughing under a familiar Norway maple tree, sitting on my shoulders with her tender hands holding the purple leaves in mid-September.

****

The Wounded Warrior Expedition project managers reluctantly pulled funding for the sponsored hike, leaving the boots-on-the-ground trekkers to make their way into Neel Gap self-supported. The giant black transport was gone, and with it went almost all the Veteran hikers. I heard that one of them, called Turtle Wolf, stayed on the AT and completed a Northbound thru-hike, though I never saw him again, after a chance meeting in North Georgia.

The same day that the Vets announced that they would be leaving the trail, I met another hiker near Cooper Gap on Sassafras Mountain. His name was Donatello. Small in stature, but strong as an ox and big on heart, he had a great sense of humor. Walking with him for a few miles really brightened my often snow-balling self-deprecation. With long and matted dirty-blond hair and a scraggly beard, he laughed with rasp and looked older that he was. Donatello carried a walking staff taller than he was and wore a giant coolie on his head, giving the impression he could be easily located on a trail or as difficult to spot as finding "Waldo" in a Cambodian rice field at harvest. His pack was something off the cover of an ancient "Hike the Appalachian Trail" brochure; an overstuffed old frame-pack that towered two feet above the coolie he wore, and constantly interfered with his ability to wear the hat with any stability. It all seemed so difficult and secretly funny, but he managed it.

There was something about his nature that I liked, but he seemed shy and clever. Pinning trust on anyone was something that I had not done for a long time. The streets back home had washed away my ability to have faith in a stranger but hanging with Donatello helped me recover a bit of that willingness. If we both had skeletons in our closet, it didn't matter. Trust is gifted; it's not built. It may be *rebuilt*, if its broken. And maybe not. But initially, trust is a gift from the willing, for a chance at the potential reward of authentic human connection. It's generally worth the risk.

Donatello loved to stop for any good photo opportunity. After hiking together for a few days, I sensed that he was laying the groundwork for a photo-journal of the Appalachian Trail, although he never outright claimed that was the intention. Stopping every mile, and sometimes more often, for a click of his GoPro, wasn't terribly vexing at first but it began to wear on me eventually. It did, however, rekindle a creative spirit within me. Exciting were the moments we would simultaneously howl in agreement under a tunnel of rhododendrons or at a surprising stunner of a view:

"Now there is a great shot!" Eventually, after a few pack shake-downs, he had trimmed his base weight down to a more manageable number and we could pick up the pace between stops. He didn't need the six pairs or socks, four pairs of underwear, and the emergency fishing kit that only sounded like a good idea at home, when considering luxury items. His classic one-liners and fits of stubbornness to relieve his back of extra gear reminded me more of Captain Jack Sparrow than a Ninja Turtle. He garnered laughs from me sometimes, even when he was trying to be a serious as he could, which frustrated him. If he stopped too often, then I gave him shit. It had been quite a while since I had a genuine companion, so our evolving partnership was a port in the storm. Even if the new vessel turned out to be a pirate ship.

NEARING FONTANA DAM, we started to get trail news about other park closures due to the pandemic. In addition to Great Smoky Mountain National Park, Shenandoah National Park was closed along with White Mountain National Forest. How to safely cross the dam at Fontana became a deepening mystery as we approached the village and park. There were grumblings of a tent city forming at Fontana Village because local authorities, in conjunction with federal marshals, were not allowing anyone into the park. Even with the required permits to go thru, hikers were effectively being shut out. It was a different kind of tent city than the one on the banks of the Ohio River, underneath Interstate 64 in downtown Louisville. There, group quarters were a classified homeless camp where hundreds of the down-and-out live. You would never know that it was there, for all the beautiful art, culture, and community of the Derby City. Louisville is a liberal oasis in a vastly conservative state and all the flags and colors of self-expression wave and pulse. Summer of 2020 was different. The exercise of "freedom" was motivated by a social narrative that the city must never forget or repeat. Circumstantially, I was better off in the forests.

Back on the Appalachian Trail, rumors floated of hikers who were ready to get moving after being stalled at the entrance to the Smokies. Ostensibly, the authorities had run everybody off with threats of legal consequences if we dared to try anything rogue around the park entrances. Donatello and I pitched our camp four miles south of Fontana Village and planned to go into town the next day to pick up mail drops. The rations we would collect were critical to our safe passage thru the park in one pitch. Late in the afternoon, we were relaxing at a campsite just off the trail when another young hiker stopped to introduce himself. He had a thick west European accent, and he was very curious about what we had heard regarding access to the Smokies.

"We are going to try and go thru the park. What about you?" I asked the young man with the European accent.

"I'm gonna try to push thru it in three days if I can get in. I don't have a choice, I am almost out of food," he said, as he began to dump items from random food groups into a Tupperware bowl for a meal. He opened a can of tuna and scooped it onto a melted looking foam.

"What is that?" I asked.

"Oh, it's tuna and bacon bits and ice cream."

"Well, split open and melt!" Donatello blurted.

The friendly foreign hiker seemed baffled and embarrassed by the criticism. Donatello sensed the good man's self-conscious reaction and tried to clean it up with a subject change.

"Where are you from, brother?"

"Amsterdam."

"Good for you!"

"Thanks brother! Isn't this great out here? I just love hiking in these old mountains. Hey, has Garlic come thru?"

"What? Who?"

"Garlic. She's a Nobo too. You know her?"

"No, no one else has been thru. I don't think I know Garlic."

"Right on, okay, okay." His Dutch accent was thick with good natured warmth. "So, getting thru the park is going to be crazy, no? I heard there's mounted rangers up there with German shepherds, too. And they're wrestling hikers to the ground, man! Then hauling them off da mountains to town and making them appear to pay big fines, man! I don't know about you guys, but I don't have a thousand bucks to hand to your government, ya know what I mean, guys?!"

I just loved listening to the Dutchman talk. He was so positive and spirited and deeply adventurous. His name was Grand Master, and he made us feel like we were all in it together. It strengthened my resolve. Our new friend said his goodbyes and headed north on the Appalachian Trail with Fontana Dam in his crosshairs. We never saw him again but later heard that he made it thru the park in less than four days.

Two years on, that same hiker would fall to his death at McAfee Knob while his father and Tramily (trail family) watched in horror. The wilderness is a dangerous place, even for the most seasoned woodsman. There will always be risks associated with spending consecutive days outdoors, far from the tiled ridges of city skylines.

The next morning, Donatello and I made the road walk into Fontana Village near the entrance to the park. The post office was our primary goal. We needed to get in and get our mail drops, then get out of town without drawing too much attention. Donatello found a muddy bottle of vodka with a couple shots left that someone had tossed onto the side of the road. The liquor rolled like lava in the bottom. After a quick sniff and a shorter hesitation, he threw it down the hatch. He could tell by the look on my face, I didn't want any. Not that I wasn't drinking... I'd had some real brown water and weed every now and again, but not often. Drinking before actually hiking was not practiced. Besides, what was waiting for us in Fontana? The suspense was killing me, and I figured I ought to have a sober mind for the engagement. After hearing rumors on the trail about what a nightmare the town had been for other hikers, I wondered if we could possibly make it into the park. Even if we could cross Fontana Dam, could we then traverse the national park's 71 challenging miles safely and undetected? Donatello and I descended into a ghost town. Fontana Village would normally be a bustling vacation destination that time of year. The hamlet should have been full of tourists and hikers and families playing mini golf on sunny days with ice cream carts darting around like Roman chariots. Instead, gray-skied tumbleweeds blew across the mini golf course as the last hole's windmill pitifully lost a blade in the breeze. The post office opened at 0900. We were ten minutes early and not a soul was around.

The civilian-robed postman was chewing on a piece of hay straw when he motored up in his pickup truck at three minutes till nine. We knew he'd be there. My mom (a proud retiree from the United States Postal Service) assured me it would open.

"That package is there, Son. It's been tracked. And they'll staff that depot with the National Guard before they shut it down. The post office *will* open on schedule, I guarantee it." she said.

"Jesus, it's not wartime, Mom."

"Yes it is, Music Man. It's a pandemic."

"You boys must be fixin' to get a box," the postman easily judged our status as hungry hiker trash.

"Just passing thru," Donatello casually stammered like Captain Jack Sparrow, but the postman had a quick draw too.

"Boys, there's a pane-*demick* going on, in case yuns don't knowed it. Whatchu boys plannin' t'do?" the Fontana Postman asked with a Tennessee drawl thick as Jack Daniels, himself.

"Well, seein' as we got parcels to *re*-ceive, I think we're fixin' to get a snack as soon as you pass them-there pony-packages over the bar. The corner store on the way into town was closed. Any open place a-pourin' draughts around here?"

Donatello was in fine form; generally bullshitting like the best I've seen. Also from Tennessee, D knew how to 'tawk American' with this Appalachian postman, and he said the least that he could get away with, whilst *h*wearing him out with *h*words.

"Marina's still open," said the Fontana Postman, "You'll pass that on the way to the dam. But I can tell you this, boys. This town ain't gonna survive this here *pane*-demick. Seein' as we *re*-lie on the tourist dollar. This Covid is a bad deal, yuns heard me? We's *all* could be zombies soon. Like the Walkin' Dead. And you should knowed it, boys, it's *eel*-legal to go up in that park. *It's closed.* Come on in, let's git them boxes. Any-ya need to use the phone?"

"Um, yes, I would love to use the phone," I responded, sounding too bougie. I took the opportunity to call my parents and confirm the pickup. The postman gave us our boxes, then he stood outside with us as we packed our food sacks. He then said something that hit me like a ton of bricks, summoning my first on-trail feelings of doubt about what I was even doing on the Appalachian Trail in the first place.

"Ya need to be home with ya families..."

It struck me like a thunderbolt. He was right. I should have been home taking care of my family the whole time. It got into my head. I was lost in the echo of the postman's words as we donned our packs and received his last message:

"Well, now that yaws got your boxes packed, I got's to call the law."

"What?!"

"Yep, I got to call 'em. Gotta let the sheriff know yuns fixin' to cross that dam. Be awares that lawmen's up at the Forest Service office. They ain't gonna let you thru. And that's if the Sheriff don't catch you first. I seen't 'em send them other hickers away. *Beware*. There ain't gon' be no rescue if y'all get stranded up on that ridge, hurt or starving, or anything. Besides boys, you need to be home with your families. But I'll give yuns a head start."

Donatello and I put our best Mississippi half-step underfoot and began hustling (our packs now very heavy with a six-day resupply) back up toward the trail. We checked over our shoulders every few steps, further adding the strain on our necks and backs. It was nearing high noon as we approached the Marina.

"Man, I'm thirsty."

"Me too. Dry as a bone. There ain't no Sheriff on our tail, least none that I can see." "Let's grab a beer at the Marina."

"Bet."

We skipped down the long parking lot and across the dock toward the placid water, surrounded by a cirque of smoky mountains. Fontana Lake was a calm blue and the sun had appeared thru the clouds overhead. We were exhausted from running our heavy packs up the trail and cold beer seemed the next logical choice.

"We're just out for a hike! Hell no, we don't have permits "occifers," but it's because of Corona...virus. Coronavirus! Yeah, that's it!!" It should have been all joking aside.

We sat on the deck for an hour putting down a six-pack of tallboy cans and having a good ole' time. No one else was around except for the owner, who introduced himself as Chester.

"Why are you even open?" I inquired.

"The bulk of our business comes from boat rentals. We do a lot of funerals, Music Man," answered Chester, with a razor face.

"Funerals?"

"Yep. Lots of locals want to be buried at the lake. We do funeral services on the water, especially in the spring thaw. You know, helping people scatter remains. It's a big margin and pays a lot of bills," explained Chester.

I looked at all the empty vessels moored to the slips of the dock. They lined up like a shopping mall parking lot on Black Friday. Nobody was going anywhere around here. Fontana Lake commerce had run aground.

Such a beautiful thought: My mortal remains scattered into these gentle bobbing waters under the protective shadows of the Smoky Mountain cirque that surrounds the tarn...that didn't sound too bad to me. Nice place to spend eternity. And their boats were spectacular. Everything from canoes, fishing boats and Jon Boats to large pontoons and even a yacht.

"We were gonna do a service today for some folks, but they canceled. All cause of COVID," Chester complained.

Bloody Covid-19. People couldn't even lay their loved ones to rest in peace out of fear they'll catch the shit at the funeral and be the next layer on the bottom of the lake. That beautiful thought of a golden-blue urn fell out of my brain like a cast anchor.

"It ain't right."

"No, sir. You got that right. Say, we haven't seen that many hikers lately. You boys trying to go into the park?"

Donatello and I looked at each other like made rats.

"Oh, guys, you ain't gotta worry about us," said Chester. "Go for it. All the other hikers that were camped out here packed up and left. Feds ran them off. Some of them said they were going around the park, then gettin' back on trail at Davenport Gap. And some said they's quittin' altogether. But none of them got past the marshals that were blocking the dam. The last I heard, the authorities packed up and left too. But there may still be a game warden up there keepin' an eye on the dam. Locals can give 'em hell just like you *hickers*. You want my advice? Wait until dusk, then go up and see what it looks like. It ain't even a half mile to get across that dam. Then the trail cuts straight up the ridge of them mountains, and into the park. You can get a head start over the dam and be on that ridge before they knowed yuns even there, if you stay invisible and quiet."

By dusk, Donatello and I were doing reconnaissance from some bushes on a grassy knoll above the south end of the dam near the U.S. Forest Service offices. There were two barricades still blocking access to the road over the dam. One black SUV filled a parking space marked "OFFICIAL," but the area was quiet, except for the frogs and crickets. *"Area secured, Sir."* Flood lights filled the parking lot with a wash of bright white. Old Glory gently wobbled at full staff, like us after a few beers. The bushes gave us cover as we looked over the dam. The external scene was tranquil, but we were on edge and listening intently for any signs of trouble on the horizon. The onyx-like shine of the lake water around the area teased like a temptress. The dam whispered to us, "Come on, men, who's got a number?" For the moment, the bushes felt safe.

****

Found her! Krystal was her name, and drugs were her game. She was settling down under the Breckenridge Street viaduct on a cold January night. We were both homeless and I had no truck to huddle in anymore but that didn't deter me. Her dope was cheap and decent so I copped from her whenever I could. As a bonus, she was attractive for a street girl. Krystal had athletic thighs, clear skin and all of her teeth. Her old man was known for good drugs and loaded guns. Reliable. There she was, all alone up there and casting her bait. She had sent seductive glances my way before, but she was very good at throwing shade. Depending on the season or the run I was on, good physical condition was intermittent. I wanted both dope and a date. On that night, I thought I had the right stuff. I was penniless with just a bus ticket left, but otherwise.... pretty, pretty...pretty good. The drugs were still working. Worst case scenario: I would talk her into fronting me a shard for double nickels on the dime. Best case scenario: she was holding our dope and she's coming with me, man.

Nearing the end of that run, I didn't spend any more time downtown than I had too. I had been spending a lot of money, marking me as an easy target to rob. The safety I found was at a squat in the East end of town. The abandoned ranch house that I called home for the night quite a few times, used to be owned by a lady that collected candles. She and the mister had passed away years ago. But the house was still full of all kinds of stuff. Most importantly for me in that wasteland of a winter: candles. So, I would slip in an open window after dark, go down to the ballroom in the basement and light a hundred candles for light and warmth. It didn't do much in the way of warming the giant ballroom, but I am convinced that it saved my life a couple times during that hard winter. I was acclimated to cold weather for long periods of time, and generally adjusted to stressful conditions. I could have been preparing for the Karakoram Range and been adjusted. But the glacier in my mind on that night was Krystal.

"Hey, I've got an offer for you," I approached.

"What's up Census Man?"

"I need a front. I don't have cash, but I can get you off the street tonight if you want. I know a warm place to squat if you've got a little dope and bus ticket."

The appropriate conversation was made, and she was game. Speed put my sex drive into overdrive depending on how long I'd been awake. Here was a window of opportunity.

"Well, sounds okay to me," said Krystal, "but I ain't got any dope."

Strike one.

"Damn."

"Here." She pulled a fifty-dollar bill from her sports bra and handed it to me. "Go get us something from the King."

She knew what was up. The King wouldn't deal with straight street folk. You had to have a little class and decent cash to pay the King a visit. I was one of the few street wanderers that he would deal with. Most of the time I was driving the Escape, and that was all the clout needed for the King. That and cash. I would never go to the King without at least fifty dollars in crisp new bills that folded nicely. Most folks doing hand-shake drug deals on the street couldn't afford the drugs or the risk when dealing with the King. Even though I thought it was too late in the evening to find him, I stayed in character for Krystal.

"It's probably too late for the King. Why not Kalik?" I asked.

"DO NOT go to College Street. I ain't fucking with him tonight." She said with a disgust and finality over her sugar daddy.

"Fine." I lied like Nazi.

She might not be dealing with him, but I sure as hell would. Past dark was too late to bother the King. Besides, whatever was going on between Kalik and Krystal wasn't my business. If they had some beef, it wasn't in my front yard. I had my own business to pursue in his backyard with his girl, if I could get away with it.

"You hear me, dude?" She warned, "Don't go over there."

"Take it easy. I'll be back soon." With that I departed.

I walked straight over to College Street where I knew I would find her old man, Kalik. And there he was. I approached the barrel fire and got his attention. He seemed lucid and unaffected.

"What's up, K, I need an eight-ball."

"Cool, cool, D. You know I got you."

I could taste it already. It had been a couple hours and all I wanted was my next hit. He cut out the dope then knotted the baggie and handed it to me. I gave him the $50 bill.

"Alright, D, always a pleasure…. hold up."

He looked me square in the eyes then down at the bill I had just placed in his hand.

"Where did you get this fifty?" He asked gravely, snatching the dope back from my hand.

"Wait, what?" I looked at him under furrowed brow.

"I ain't gonna ask you a third time, now WHERE DID YOU GET THIS FUCKING FIFTY DOLLAR BILL?"

"Kalik, I got it from Walgreens," I blurted on a whim. Walgreens was the closest store to us, on the corner of Brook and Broadway. It just came out. "Don't give me that shit. I know where you got this bill. I know because I made this fifty, mothafucker! Pressed it myself."

Krystal had warned me.

"Kalik, I swear, I got that bill at Walgreens."

"Where is she?" he snapped, "What y'all think you can run one over on me with my own merchandise? My dope *and* my cash? Fuck y'all. Where is Krystal?"

He pulled a .22 from his jacket and put it across his chest. I raised my hands at my elbows casually and managed to stay calm.

"Kalik, I..."

"D, I ain't trying to do this right now. Where is she? I know you didn't get this fifty at no Walgreens. Facts."

I stuck to the story.

"What are you talking about, K?"

"Goddammit, don't argue with me, D!"

He really didn't want to hurt me, and I could sense it. Plus, he knew she was trying to throw me like dice too. The addict in me exploited what I saw as a weakness in him. Insanely, I still thought that I could get the dope and the girl. What the addict is willing to risk in the madness—it's baffling. I was getting a new lesson in the morbid game that the disease of addiction plays with its host. He was holding a gun and I still couldn't come off the truth that would literally free me. Everything is a gamble until snake-eyes end the game.

"Fine. We're going to Walgreens then. Find out for sure. Start walking." Irritated, he waved me toward the direction of Broadway with the gun. He got on his bike and started to pedal slowly behind me as a safety measure. If I were to take off running, he could catch me. He kept pleading with me to tell him where she was, but I wouldn't budge. I kept thinking to myself, 'She's one block over, you lazy motherfucker, go look for her yourself.' But I had enough sense to just stick to the script. After all, I was still without bullet holes. Ride the storm out, I told myself. Krystal had warned me. How could I be so stupid? Trust no one, trust nothing. That was the rule on the streets. And always factor in Murphy's Law.

"Man, just tell me where I can find her, and I'll let you go. We ain't got to do this shit no more. She probably put you up to it."

Kalik was trying to get into my head, and it was working on my weakened mental state. That's when I officially got scared. I was about to crack, and I felt a confession about to come out of my mouth. Could I trust him to trust me? Nope. I took off running.

"Son of a bitch! Stop!" I heard him scramble to get his feet firmly on the pedals. Lucky for me the bike was stuck in a low gear, and he couldn't get it moving quickly. I had a head start. I pounded out a block running as fast as I could run then turned the corner at a brownstone apartment project. Taking one moment to look back over my shoulder, I observed him flying up the street and gunning for me. I took off again, running along another block to the next corner where I turned again. Across the street I noticed a hedgerow and bolted for it. I dove headfirst into the thick bushes and grabbed the lower branches to lift myself up off the ground. It was a dense thicket and I had dug in deep, given what little time I had. Sticks and thorns poked me everywhere from my earlobes to my elbows and kneecaps. Just as I stopped moving, I heard the chain of his bike come around the corner as he depressed the brakes into a slow coast. He patrolled from corner to corner before I saw the tires pull up and stop right in front of the bush I clutched to, for dear life (or just life). One of his tattered Converse Allstars lowered to the pavement mere feet from my head. Neither one of us moved or made a sound. A game of cat and mouse. My lungs wanted to explode from all the sprinting, but I held my breath firm and watched his feet, one held a bike pedal and one on the street. After what seemed like an eternity of ten seconds, he said something.

"Mothafucker," he mumbled one last time.

Kalik raised his feet to the pedals and slowly kicked the bicycle away with the gun still on the handlebar as he rounded the corner and out of sight. When I was sure I was alone, my lungs heaved out fear and gasped for life. I crawled out from the bush and ducked away thru the shadows.

I was convinced that the police were now chasing me. Threading my way thru alleys, between houses and parked cars, and generally moving like a cartoon character hidden in a bush, I tip-toed all the way across the east side of town and into Shelby Park. I sat down and leaned up against a pavilion pilar, where I had a view of whatever might come my way next, but I slept instead.

****

"It's time to get across the dam," I declared, "We've got this, D. Let's go." I donned my pack and emerged from the bushes with confidence and focus, and quickly moved toward the dam. The sudden wide-open felt vulnerable. I picked up the pace and Donatello struggled to catch up. He had been caught off guard by my impulse to push forward and it irritated him. But once we were moving, we skipped past Old Glory bathed in light, and crossed the dam under the cover of night. If, at last, the blackness of the water below was still guarded, Fontana Lake's own Nessie let us pass above and undisturbed. Never stopping, we reached the other side and quietly vanished into the Great Smoky Mountain darkness.

Sometimes I ponder poor decisions that I have made and wonder what I could have possibly been thinking. The rooms of recovery are filled with stories of addicts who will, in error, confess to a slip and say, "Well, I made a mistake." Careful reflection and personal experience have taught me that there is a fine line between a mistake and a poor choice. I cannot, in good conscience, claim to have "made a mistake" when the choice to do wrong was evident as just that: a conscious decision made while knowing the consequences would be harmful to someone or something. For example, if I fail a test that denies me a driver's permit, then I have made a mistake. I wanted that driver's license, but I didn't want to smack the curb. It was unintentional in nature. I didn't choose to fail the test; I made a mistake. If I pick up a bottle or a pipe, however, that is my choice. I cannot turn around and say that I "mistakenly picked up". I knew it was the wrong choice but chose to do it anyway. Sooner or later, I had to start taking responsibility for the choices that I made and find the humility to admit the error of my ways. I can learn from both experiences. There will always be new mistakes to make. But I don't have to make the same ones repeatedly, expecting a different result. That is insanity. If I want to succeed in anything, I'll do better when I know better. Just as with most mistakes, I have made certain choices and will have to deal with any consequences that arise because of those choices. Summarily, with all choices, there is calculated risk and potential culpability to weigh.

Finally, I had entered the national park. Albeit highly illegally. Already fatigued, the first steps of the trail took us straight up a brutal climb. After less than a mile we reached a bend in the trail where our bodies fell to the ground in victorious exhaustion. Fontana Lake reflected lights from many hundreds of feet below, revealing sparse traces of the civilization that surrounds it. There was a blue light moving on the water and we convinced ourselves it was the police patrolling the shores and scanning the ridgelines for anything that resembled rogue hikers. We kept our joy quiet, but we felt great. Crossing the dam was exhilarating and we would survive to hike at least another day. After a deep drink of water, I pitched my tent under a tree near the edge of the mountain while Donatello cowboy camped under the stars. We both soaked in solitude and could sense the enormity of the mountains around us.

Around 5 am, I awakened to the sound of Donatello's voice. "Ah.... Ah.... Shit, shit!"

Rain started pouring down. I heard him shuffling his gear around as rain pelted the fly over my tent. He tried to fashion a shelter out of the tarp he used as a ground quilt. But it was too late and everything Donatello possessed was getting soaked. His shelter was normally a hammock strung up under an A-frame tarpaulin pitch, but late-night laziness had bit him in the ass. Drenched in the cold air temperature outside, I knew he was in trouble.

"Dude, throw the tarp over your stuff and come over to my

tent. You need to get out of that cold rain," I warned him.

"Okay, thanks Music. I'm coming in."

But just as he rounded everything up under his tarp the rain stopped. The forest was still dark and dribbling as he trembled under a tree with his body temperature dropping.

"Music, I am freezing. I need to get moving," he chattered.

He was right. Hypothermia was a real threat in those conditions. He had gained enough trail experience to listen to his survival instinct. The impetus to hike was correct: it was time to go. We struck our camp quickly in the dark then rolled and smoked a cigarette. After donning our packs, we were on the trail with our headlamps on in a matter of minutes. Another small victory that brought about a new problem: our headlamps. Now moving, Donatello was mitigating the hypothermic threat. But we were now visible to anyone down on the lake or any rangers that might be making early patrols of the park's trail systems. We continued to climb up toward Mollie's Ridge, now hypersensitive to anything that moved or any light that flickered. Not thirty minutes into the climb I noticed a red glow a couple hundred feet below us and coming up the trail fast.

"D, look back there. Do you see that? Someone is coming up behind us in stealth mode with that red beam," I whispered.

"Yep, you're right. I see it."

"Is that a ridge runner? A park ranger?"

"There ain't supposed to be anyone up here. No ridge runners anywhere on the AT this year after the Harpers Ferry office called the season a bust."

"We gotta outrun them, whoever they are. We can't take the chance they'll out us. Let's put an extra step on it."

Only three miles into the park and they were already coming after us! It appeared that Operation Smoky Rogue was the precarious choice after all. There seemed to be some validity to the horror stories about tight security around the park. It was looking like we had a stressful stint of hiking ahead if we could even survive.

"Do you still see the red light?" I asked him after three dimes of heads-down hauling. "Son of a bitch, there it is!"

Still there, the red was rising fast and gaining on us, and I was exhausted already. Mentally pressed and stressed from the previous twelve hours, totally soaked from the early rain, and a bit hung over from the day before, we decided to stop and hide for logistics, reconnaissance, and our own security meeting.

"Over there, behind that felled oak tree," I huffed in exhaustion, "I'm toast."

"Yeah man, me too." Donatello agreed.

We plopped down behind the tree and caught our breath.

Donatello rolled a joint while I feverishly watched the trail corridor for the red headlamp, but it never came. We had a smoke while the sun rose over the mountains, then we pushed on after a half-hour of quietude. We were convinced that we had outrun the threat. Thanks in part to GBITS, it appeared that we had escaped.

For the next two and half days the Appalachian Trail freely gave us precious gifts. We never saw a soul and it felt like we owned the park. The southern Smokies are rugged and remote. I felt as though I had escaped into a mountain paradise. The valley vistas on both sides were breathtaking at every turn and the weather was spectacular. Days were sunny and hot while the nights were clear and cold. The section from Russell Field up and over Thunderhead and Rocky Top were a dream come true. We hiked slowly and stopped at long views for longer breaks.

There is something mystical about the Smokies in any season. Hiking thru the deserted Smoky Mountain National Park was a once in a lifetime opportunity and I enjoyed every step. The problems of society wrangled far below the majestic and menacing ridges of the mountains. We stashed our packs at the base of Clingmans Dome's paved day-use path, then skirted up the spiral ramp of the observation tower to an uninhibited experience at the highest point of the Appalachian Trail. The 360° view from the observation deck is one of the finest vistas on the entire trail, at over 6,600 feet in elevation. Tall peaks sketched onto the horizon for dozens of miles in every direction, reminding me of how small I really am. Just a grain of sand on an earth sized grain of sand, in a cosmos unfathomably large. We snapped photos of Mt. Guyot and savored the experience we were having.

I thought about my daughter. She would want to draw these mountains with a pencil and show her little brother which colors of paint to mix. She would brush the canvas of the sky with her smile. I wished she was there with me. In a way, she was. My heart was aching for her and my son. As I shuffled down the ramp from the Dome, I made a commitment to myself and my children. I would reach them. I would walk all the way to Massachusetts and tell them: oh, how I love and long. I would ask them about their art and toys. It was a solemn oath that I intended to keep. They didn't ask for their daddy to go away. They didn't deserve to grow up without a father. I would finish the trail on my knees if my feet were shredded; on my hips if my knees were blown out. "I will reach the end," I told myself. I needed to do this. I prayed that the path would lead me home. For some reason, more than it ever had before, thru-hiking seemed like the right thing to do. If I were to ever be a father again, I would first find peace for myself. My children patiently waited near the trail's terminus, and I had to get there before they forgot about me. A bigger purpose was forming, and I began to feel like I was not in control anymore. Joy held sadness in embrace.

.5

DONATELLO AND I DESCENDED from Clingmans Dome in a spiritual state. We eased back into the sport of hiking at no rush. After doing some trail data, we decided to head another two miles to Mt. Collins shelter for the night. It was getting late in the afternoon and another couple miles up and over Mt. Love seemed a reasonable way to close out a spectacular day. There was no way we could have known what was coming in the next mile. The excitement was far from over.

As we were getting back into a stride, I felt a faint vibration. A thumping in the air. At first, I thought it was a Ruffed Grouse drumming somewhere near, as can be felt deep in the Southern Appalachians. The mating call is an inaudible vibration that bubbles up like an accelerando drum roll on the eardrums. This is quite an experience of its own, to hear what feels like something lightly tapping on your eardrum with soft mallets. But this was no mating call from a hidden grouse. From the ridge, I looked west over the valley. Nothing. I looked back to the right to see Donatello looking east.

"You heard that too?" I asked.

"Yeah. Maybe some grouse?" He guessed while looking out over the other side of the ridge. "I don't hear it anymore."

He turned to face me as the rumble quickly rose again. As we stared at each other, a chopping black helicopter rose over his head out of the valley, and it was hovering right on top of us in seconds!

"Shit! Shit! Run!"

No sooner did we turn north; a silver helicopter rose out of the west valley triangulating with the black chopper. They were no more than a hundred feet above us, and a couple hundred feet apart from each other.   *"AHHH!"*

"Oh, my gawd! Who the hell is that? The Federales?"

"Rambo and Airwolf have entered Operation Smoky Rouge!" announced Captain Jack Sparrow, "Run, goddammit!"

Down the north slope of Mt. Love, we ran for our life! We ended up under a small canopy of limbs that covered the trail, and one of the birds buzzed us so low we could feel the blades chopping the wind above our head. The helicopters then exchanged places and dipped back down into the opposing valleys below, leaving the cores of our bodies vibrating.

"What the hell are we gonna do?"

"Not get caught," Donatello said like a bandito, looking up over his shoulder as we hid in the canopy. Rumbles continued rising from unseen hollers below. Like us, the choppers were regrouping in their own airspace.

"We gotta get beyond the treeline, D! This is crazy!"

"Nuts, Music! Totally NUTS! Pinkertons found us, but they ain't gonna nail us!" Donatello laughed with a black-throated bellow, as the sleek chopper rose out of the valley again and faced us dead ahead. I could almost see the pilot, with his helmet and visor driving at the heart of the rumble. The pilot pointed two gloved fingers in our direction as the silver-bird again gained elevation in a tactical flank. The roar of the rotor wash was deafening, and I was ready for the Men in Black to repel down from the helicopters at any moment. It was terrifying...and thrilling.

"We gotta run!"

And that is just what we did. We ran our asses off...again...for the second time at Great Smoky Mountains National Park, which was closed due to a government decree that we didn't want to obey.

The rest of the world saw us as traitors for even thinking we could pass thru this park undetected; seemingly committing acts of treason for trying to go thru with the clandestine operation. It was the wild west, and we were the last gangsters on the lamb. We ran for a mile straight before pumping the brakes just below the tree line. The thunder started to fade into the valleys. I prepared for the cavalry to come marching up the trail to catch us and put us in cages to haul us off for the barbecue pits outside the Gatlinburg Police Department. Once there, they would baste us with their best Tennessee barbeque sauce recipes trying to impress the stoic Federal Marshals visiting from Washington to oversee the mission. But no cavalry came. No marshals or deputies or park rangers or game wardens. We took the blue blaze over to Mt. Collins Shelter in the dark with our headlamps off and were finally off the beaten track. We ducked behind the tarp that hung in front of the shelter and into safety, praying it was all over. They had us on the mountain, but we hoped we had slipped off and into the shelter undetected.

"Holy smokes, Music Man! That was epic!" Donatello celebrated as we dropped the tarpaulin closing us into the lean-to.

"I can't believe that just happened!" I exclaimed.

"Yeah, man, but we got away! We got away!" Donatello declared with pride, while pointing his walking staff toward the sky.

"Donatello, they could be activating the Guard right now!"

"Chill out, Music Man, they ain't coming back for us. Those Airmen were having a field day with that game of cat and mouse. They had their fun." He leaned his coolie and staff into the corner next to the hearth.

"Damn cold in this brick house," I shivered.

"I'll get a fire started," Donatello said.

"I don't think that's wise, D."

"Dang and blast, Music Man, it's an indoor fireplace. They ain't gonna see the smoke rising from the chimney in the dark. Plus, the tarp hanging over the front of the shelter will keep the light from escaping. We're fine, my good man!"

"They could have some heat-seeking goggles or something." I could hear my own paranoia resurfacing from the trauma of drug-fueled running on the streets.

"I'll roll a spliff here in a few minutes after I get this fire started."

After a hot meal and a cup of cocoa, I relaxed a little. Still, I swore that the planet Venus was really a drone surveilling us while I was outside taking a leak. Again, Donatello told me to chill out.

"It's not moving," he said as walked away, clearly vexed.

The fireplace was stubborn to get blazing, but Donatello was determined to not go to bed cold. He didn't have the low-rated weather gear that I sported so he kept trying to get the fire going.
I laid down in my bed roll on the platform. It had been a hell of a day and sleep seemed near and fine.

Donatello blew another lungful of air onto the faint embers, but the damp wood just wouldn't carry a flame. I was too tired to help. I had almost drifted off to sleep when suddenly, the tarp to the shelter flew open. The bright glare of a headlamp hit my eyes like a laser beam....

****

The doctor waved his flashlight in front of my pupils to check for signs of mania. It wasn't just a formality. Everyone else knew I was acting crazy, but I thought I was just having a panic attack. The human resources office at the federal agency where I worked ordered me away for "health concerns" that day, but I never made it home. Instead, I got mixed up in a psych-eval while trying a routine check-in for a treatment center where I had been a repeat offender. That day had started like any other: me getting tight before work. But the morning took a thousand turns thru dawn, as the spirit that always wore dark didn't go back under the bed.

During the drive to work, the music on the radio started doing impossible things. The notes of the pop song were bending and turning like rubber bands in my ears. It sounded like the record was spinning backwards. When the music became completely senseless, I knew something was wrong with my brain. Perceptions of reality had warped into a paranoid frenzy and the fact that I even attempted to go to work that day was a mark of the illusory state my mind had entered.

"You're having a panic attack, Sir. Try to calm yourself," the doctor informed me.

"Thank you, Captain Obvious! And do I look like a "sir" to you? If one more prig calls me sir" ...

"You are having a panic attack, *Sir*. Try to calm yourself."

I had figured as much by that point. My chest felt like Mayzie's egg with the weight of Horton crashing down on me. I had been up on dope for too many consecutive days in a row and any sanity I had left was long gone. But I was still showing up to my HR job at the federal office. Wisely, they sent me home. There was no other option really. They couldn't outright fire me without processing, like a boss in the private sector could. The perceived security of a tenured government job enabled me to continue the destructive path I was on. I would continue to manipulate the system for as long as possible. A couple folks in the office knew exactly what was going on. They just hoped I would pull myself out of it after the divorce decree was issued. At some point prior, a coworker intimated that his favorite Chicago song was "Hard Habit to Break". Then he slipped off hoping no one had seen us talking.

The only other panic attack I can recall having was the day my newlywed wife and I went to the courthouse to certify the marriage license and officially change her last name to mine. I was a little sick that day, but she didn't know it. It was an ominous warning, apparently missed by both of us. She didn't know that she had married a full-blown opiate addict. I was good at hiding my addiction and better at presenting the stage character that I wanted the world to see. But that façade would crumble. I started to frequent the detoxes and nut houses in town and the surrounding counties. There I was again, in a dual-diagnosis hospital for psychotic drug addicts, getting shot in the ass with enough tranquilizer to level a moose and flash-freeze my brain for two days. Memories of that trip to the psych ward only begin when the meds wore off. My wife told me that she and my parents had come to a family session that we all attended, while they had me heavily sedated on psychotropics. I have no recollection of that event, but I believe every bit of their account. She told me that I spent the entirety of the hour on the therapist's floor snooping under everyone's chair for a $20 that didn't exist. When I started to come around, I became horrified as I learned of my behavior. Something had to be done. I was powerless over drugs and becoming very desperate. Putting my family thru these horrible episodes was wearing them down, too. Selfishly, I used my own guilt and shame as excuses to dive deeper into the abyss. After a brief period of dry time, I decided that drinking alcohol wasn't my problem. It was the dope that drove me to madness. If I could manage to keep the straw out of my nose and in my mouth, I believed I could go back to drinking like a gentleman. Another tailspin soon followed. After just a cap full of beer, I was soon in a hospital with a doctor shining a flashlight in my eyes again, too high to remember how I got there. The doctor instructed me to "Blink again, stranger."

****

"I said...are you a ranger?"

A girl's voice tickled my ears with a sassy Yankee twang. She sounded younger than me. I could tell she was a New Englander but that was about it. My eyes were not adjusting to her lamp beam pointed squarely in my eyes, but I started to make out a blond braid on each of her shoulders underneath a winter hat.

"Are *you* a ranger?" I fired back.

"Do you always answer a question with a question?"

"Can you take that beam out of my face, please?" I insisted.

"Oh, yeah. Sorry." She moved the beam out of my eyes and shifted it toward Donatello at the fireplace. Then she walked in letting the tarp drop behind her. The blonde-haired hiker had a pro looking backpack and trekking poles and was clearly out for a long haul. After taking her pack off, she turned her headlamp beam to low, then...red...then off. She brushed past while looking at me thru oversized blue coral-rimmed glasses. Wow. Gorgeous! Eh-hem, I mean...She looked like...a very nice young lady. Perfectly tied pony braids of beach blonde hair decorated both of her shoulders. How could she look this good after a day like today?

"Did you guys see those helicopters?! Fucking mercenaries, I tell ya!" She proclaimed her lonely experience with the choppers and was clearly rattled by it.

"Yes! Did they get to you too? That was crazy, wasn't it?" I responded.

Donatello knelt close to the floor smoking a damp hand-rolled cigarette and quietly studied the new inhabitant of our dilapidated shack with pseudo-friendly skepticism. We had not seen another human being for three days and he was noticeably less comfortable with another hiker around. I too felt a fresh wave of self-conscious fear, silently acknowledging the ethical flaws in Operation Smoky Rouge.

"Who are you guys, anyway? You Nobo?"

"Um, well seeing as though you don't look like a park ranger to me...."

"My name is Garlic. Not a park ranger."

"Nice to meet you," I blinked. "I'm Music Man, and that's...."

"Donatello. A pleasure, my lady!"

"It speaks!" She quickly turned in the direction of the hearth. What do you say we get this fire started? I'm freezing!" Garlic purred with sass as she floated over to the fireplace like a Maine Coon cat.

At the snap of her fingers, she had the hearth blazing, as if by mixing witchy potions and powders. I sat up in my sleeping bag...for a spell had been cast. I got up and joined the fireplace chat to investigate the new hiker. Kneeling beside a newly crackling fire, she had displaced Donatello who walked away shamefully amused. Guarding the stone hearth, Garlic knelt by the heat as confident as a Clinton. She told the all-time greatest version of her helicopter story that rivaled our experience. Her telling was harrowing and exciting. She used her hands for helicopter blades and finger-whistles; she fake-fainted to silence, then bounced up into a performance of how she cursed the pilot while flipping him the bird. Garlic's charisma was mesmerizing. She owned my attention, as Donatello knelt in the corner and smoked cigarettes, rarely making eye-contact.

Our conversation burned on endlessly as Garlic's fire blazed higher and higher without any effort. We talked about the trail conditions and hiking in the cold. She told me that she had entered the park on her own three days before, in the middle of that stormy night. I wanted to know her age, and losing my manners, I asked.

"How old do you think I am?"

"Twenty-five," I guessed.

"I hope you are guessing that based on looks." She glared. Whoops. But she still gave it up:

"I'm thirty-three."

Perfect, I thought, pleasantly surprised.

"What about you, old timer?"

I liked her already, so I gave it up too:

"Thirty-nine."

"Ooh, just sneaking in there." Garlic teased.

"And where's that?" I regretted saying it immediately.

She changed the subject quickly as I had lost my manners again and embarrassed us both. Garlic conceded that the past two days had been stressful. The day's events had worn us all out and I couldn't imagine going thru the helicopter chase alone. It must have been terrifying from top to bottom.

"I'm really glad to see you guys," she concluded, "It's been tough wandering around these mountains alone. I was hiking with Grand Master and Boomerang, but they blitzed ahead and maybe off the trail, respectively. It's just nice to have some company."

Her tough exterior melted with the warmth of the fire. She took a breath of relief, as we all prepared to rest. Garlic came over to the bottom platform and rolled her bedding out between my bed roll and the fire. When she unfurled her Tyvek ground quilt, it sounded like popping popcorn. There was plenty of real estate open on the top and bottom platforms, but she set up her bedding surprisingly close for a first meeting with strangers. It was only survival.

"You don't mind, do you Music Man? I need a heat economy. My sleeping bag isn't rated low enough for this arctic cold."

"Be my guest," I said with one eye open.

I liked her. She was smart and beautiful, and she wasn't afraid to speak her mind. Garlic cared little about what others thought of her. She didn't even mind me asking her age, really. And she was curious about our thoughts. She wanted to talk about everything you can't talk about at your government job. Politics, spirituality, food (this is required workplace conversation; chocolate and sourdough bread in particular), she loved to quote Jordan Peterson and roast Alan Watts. Underneath her tough Yankee exterior (with judicious refinement) was a vulnerable human being...searching like the rest of us.

Uncharacteristic silence had fallen on Donatello. He seemed pressed out and stoned. Maybe I neglected communication with him while starting my friendship with Garlic. Either way, he seemed to smell a rat immediately. In the end, we all lay still and silent, letting the fireplace calm to a faint glow of soft crackles, before it made a final flicker leaving only orange embers. The logs puffed smoke at both ends as the last sensation in the darkness was the smell of smoky-sweet cedar....and the cold. Thus concluded one of the most memorable days of my life. I knew I would never forget it.

The next day, the three of us climbed the mountains of the national park together. Donatello took the point most of the day with Garlic in the middle and me bringing up the back. I couldn't take my eyes off her. Her gear showed off her sports body with sultry class. Black leggings with the vents on the side left just enough to imagination, and her blonde braids and oversized blue coral-rimmed glasses.... will somebody please bring a fire extinguisher to this beach? I had the hots for this strong young woman. We stopped at a shelter for lunch and Donatello snuck off to try the locks on the ranger box. He had swiped the combination at Mollie's Ridge and made a bad habit of rummaging thru the ranger boxes at all the shelter sites.

"You guys are slow," she jabbed as she snacked.

It was the first direct criticism of my hiking that I had received, and it instantly made me insecure.

"When did you start hiking?" She probed.

"March 16th. You?

"March 24th." Garlic proudly reported.

Damn. Were we slow? I hadn't really thought about it until my pace was being critiqued. "What's he doing over there?" She asked me, hairy-eyeing D's whereabouts.

"How'd you get the name Garlic? Are you trying to keep the vampires away?" I tried to get her attention back.

"I didn't name myself, dude. I put garlic powder on everything." She pulled out a baggie containing at least a street ounce of garlic powder from her food sack.

"Everything?"

"Damn near it. Everything except my breakfast...and even that meal isn't safe sometimes. Seriously, what the hell is he doing over there, at the supply shack?"

"He's looking at stuff in the ranger box, I guess."

"Aren't they locked?"

"He figured out the padlock code at Mollie's Ridge. Apparently, they all use the same combination. He's been checking the supply boxes at all the shelters."

"Well, *that's* super shady. I'm not sure I want to hike around that kind of nefarious shit," Garlic declared as she sealed her Ziplock bag of seasoning powder, putting clove-aroma in the air. As she packed up her gear, I caught resentment for Donatello.

"Hang on," I tried to dissuade her.

"Nope. See you cornpumps on the track.... maybe."

Off she kicked and that was that. Cold as ice yet cooking. With a quick turn at the junction, she was back up on the trail and out of sight. I wanted to chase after her but loyalty to Donatello kept me at the picnic table. He strolled back over and asked me where she had gone.

"She blitzed out."

"Darn it. Well, it's probably for the best," he said with subtle satisfaction. "She was a buzzkill." Failing to agree with him, I was finally beginning to question some things about my hike. Around that point, I began to identify and solidify a personal trail philosophy that was surfacing. It later came to be called "the philoSophy", emphasizing the letter "S". I could place everything that I did on the AT into one of these categories. And I mean everything.

✳✳✳✳✳✳✳✳✳✳✳✳

Spiritual: Wilderness, nature, solitude, prayer and meditation, reflection. Stay present in the moment. Enjoy my own company. Maybe, I need to hike alone for a few miles, or for the whole day. Am I learning lessons that the trail has to offer? I *am* a creature of nature, and this is my original habitat. I am connected to the trees and the rivers and the mountains and the sky. Groups of hikers can and will scare away wildlife by making noise. I should walk alone sometimes to increase my chances of seeing more and wilder animals. Always be ready to meet an animal friend, but especially when alone. Creation is everywhere, in all spacetime. The Big Bang happened in my heart. Remain alert and aware of my surroundings and not let my mind wander way down into rabbit holes; but allow thoughts to flow naturally and without constraint. Respect others on the trail and respect the trail itself. Practice self-respect by leaving no trace of presence here. Try to avoid judging other hikers, especially for trivial things like picking up a feather from the trail, which the "purist" claims are not practicing "leave no trace." Is she allowed to pick up a dirty Sour Patch Kid and eat off the trail? Good. Very good. Especially if it's a rare blue. Pack foods that I am excited about eating and stay grateful for Mom's scrumptious dehydrated meals. Lots of family experience, effort and love went into that magic in a pot. Appreciate the little things.

Mental health starts in the head and moves down. Stop at spiritual checkpoints often and say "Hello, me, it's time for a personal inventory." A beautiful valley vista or waterfall is a great setting. Don't just wait for spiritual experiences to happen, create them. Practice spiritual checks and balances for good mental health on the trail.

Social: Like it or not, hiking the AT is undoubtedly a social experience. Hikers will often take this category to extremes in both directions. Find a social balance that is natural and comfortable. By necessity, hikers interact with other human beings. There is no way to carry 5-6 months of food on my back. I must resupply. This requires an interaction with a cashier at the local Dollar General, or a postmaster for pickup of a mailed food drop. Limiting my social interaction to minimal opportunities for resupply implies one extreme on the spectrum and is bordering on anti-social. The other extreme is hiking only to catch the next "bar-bender" at a nearby hostel or town; or pink-blazing my way down the trail chasing a hiker(s). Not everyone hikes every mile, but that's fine. Who am I to judge what anyone else defines as acceptable travel? If you are going to call me a "purist" give me a sponge bath instead. Be patient tolerant and kind with self and others. Never pass up a chance to help someone in need. Everyone is hiking their own hike and deserves a warm smile until they prove to the contrary. It is impossible to know someone's story without taking the time to ask. Remember what it means to assume: It makes an *ass* out of *you* and *me*. (I'm probably not as good a judge of character as I vainly claim to be.) Stay neutral in social extremes but remember that absenteeism is not a good look either. Do organizational self-scanning regularly. "Who am I hiking with/around today? Are we getting along? Is there anything I should consider doing differently to foster a healthier social dynamic for myself, my partner, my Tramily, others from the bubble, or any other human being? Is there anything off-trail that requires my attention or anywhere I plan to be, specifically? (Doctor's offices, courthouses, family reunions, etc.) Am I calling home too much or not enough? Avoid conjecture and trail gossip. <u>The trail is long, but it is narrow</u>.

Emotional health starts in the heart and moves throughout the body. Pay attention to the needs of others and do "check in's" with other hikers when appropriate. Don't wait for social opportunities: create them. Practice social checks and balances for good emotional health on the trail.

Sport (Safety): Long-distance backpacking is undoubtedly an extreme endurance sport. There are many factors to consider when crunching data. The condition of gear; pack weight, distances, and trail conditions; don't fall under spells of expecting "trail magic" and always rely on self for the basics. Resupply often and treat hiker hunger accordingly. Camel up with purified water. Repeat, where is the water? If you hear a tree falling in the woods, yes, it is falling. So, look up! Not around, but UP, because sound waves can play all kinds of tricks in the forest. Try to avoid pitching tents under rotten old oak trees, especially if bad weather is moving in. These "widow-maker" events under the trees are rare, but they happen. Stay aware of one's surroundings, especially when it comes to wildlife. A serene stroll down the path can turn into a nightmare with a bite from the most feared and dangerous animals on the trail: Domestic dogs. Yes, unleashed dogs of irresponsible pet owners pose a greater risk to hikers than bears do. Encourage responsible pet practices and honest representation when it comes to service animals. Again, keep trekking poles ready for self-defense. A dog bite, like any other injury, can be a season-ender. Take advantage of easy trail conditions and opportunities for heads-up hiking to create enjoyment. Look around; get out of your head sometimes and come back to Earth! But be reminded that people die every year in the wilderness. There are many unpredictable factors as even the most experienced hikers can enjoy themselves into a serious jam. Carry a small first aid kit and extra power banks for electronic devices.

Physical health starts at the feet and moves up thru the body. Listen to your body and make wise tactical decisions based on experience and trusted input of others. Don't wait for opportunities to put safety first; before the "would-a, could'a, should-a's" come to call. Plan and practice personal wellbeing check-ins for maintaining good physical health on a long trek. Be ready to take a personal inventory in any of these categories when you least expect it.

In summary, the philoSophy helped me to organize the activities of the hike into manageable criteria that ebbed and flowed in an ever-shifting pie chart. If I kept the S's in decent balance, the result was simplicity for the hike with clear and reasonable goals. But plans are apt to change with just one thunderstorm, so I stay ready to accept those changes. Years on, it won't matter if my "end date" was on schedule or not. Odds are, I won't even remember the pre-planned schedule. But actual start and completion dates are keepers! The trail corridor is full of countless treasures, so take the time off from hiking to experience some of them. There is nothing quite like sitting under a waterfall during the heat of the day and letting the falls massage your aching shoulders. If the S's went too far out of balance, then stress could be the result (I know, two bonus S's). The sooner I could identify an imbalance in the trail philosophy causing me mental, emotional, or physical strain and/or stress, the sooner a recalibration could bring things back into focus. In times of uncertainty, try to pause and respond to internal and external forces, as opposed to having emotionally fueled reactions to things outside of one's own control. (Everything.)

An illustration of the philoSophy in practice would be something like this: While hiking in tough conditions alone, I meet other hikers and say something positive about the day or laugh at myself instead of complaining about the rain. Different hikers will have their own experiences, rituals and philosophies and they will invariably evolve with every step. Find what works; Hike Your Own Hike. Sometimes a good scream into a canyon can be cathartic.

Bernard of Clairvaux, a twelfth century Catholic abbot better known thru history as Saint Bernard, once said "You will find something more in woods than in books. Trees and stones will teach you that which you can never learn in books." Wise words from a man who spent his life immersed in the Word as a Cistercian monk. I enjoy the works of the great spiritual masters, stoics, and poets from long ago, thanks to my dad. Father earned a degree in English from the University of Virginia and mastered various nomenclatures as well. He read the classics and did his best to turn me on to them. Also possessing positive genius for numbers, he spent his career as a conservative financial advisor building consistent long-term growth for his clients' portfolios, bear market or bull. "Slow and steady wins the race," was his unspoken market philosophy. And he can play the ponies like nobody's business.

His lifelong buddies call him from near and far away places on Kentucky Derby Day to get his often-lucrative picks for the most exciting two minutes in sports. Everyone wants a chance to taste the victory that often results from Dad's number crunching on fractions, track conditions and jockeys that are hot in the saddle. Most importantly, Dad is deeply passionate about others and keenly attuned to anything that resembles suffering. He wants to help if he can. My father represents the best in human nature when it comes to generosity. Whether it's his children, the church, family, friends, or strangers, he gives. The cashier at McDonald's gets to keep the change, regardless of how much it is. However, his generosity is no better defined than by his willingness to give that of which is the greatest value, the currency of self.

My father's example illustrates a unique combination of spiritual, social and sports elements that, when applied well, helped me to fall into a natural rhythm on the Appalachian Trail. I took the best of what my dad had to offer in the way of practical guidance and crafted a new philoSophy for the hike. Whenever the footpath would come to an end, my aim was to pack it back out to everyday life. I often fall short, but thru failure I find success by learning what not to do. And this success is gauged by what my personal standards are; not standards set by any individual or institution. Am I productive and of service to others/nature? If so, I have a pretty good shot at another twenty-four hours with a sober mind and serene living. Still, when it comes to spiritual principles, I treat it like long-term parking with quarters. Without regular check-in's, my automated system of moral account corrections simply fails. The same brain trying to fix things is the very same brain in need of repair. The perspective I gain from transposing an honest written inventory of my behavior is vitally important to my serenity, as much as meditation and prayer.

I need help from other human beings. Don't miss that piece. If I am left alone to my own selfish desires, troublesome sapient instincts will eventually win out and I start treating people poorly to get what I want. All hell is bound to break loose as my track record shows. Distress codes from system scan at checkpoint: Just trying to save my own life over here, by doing what they told me to do. It's always time to act spiritually and not just think about it. Otherwise, I'm merely crafting a cathedral out of aluminum foil.

"Looks like rain," Donatello observed.

Thank you, Captain Obvious, my thought bubbles gurgled up. I was lost at the bottom of a mental shit-pond when his voice brought me back around. I didn't like Garlic's disappearing act and caught a resentment for Donatello because of his so-called "nefarious" behavior that had driven her away. Behavior that I had condoned long after I recognized it myself. Garlic carried herself with principles that I only claimed to stand for. Honesty was squarely in her nature while my loyalty to Donatello was becoming pacifistic and people pleasing. At last, with someone else's permission, it was right to feel flustered by his plundering of park resources.... Because it was wrong! (And it was ruining my chances at hanging out with Garlic. I would later discover other reasons that naturally separated us ALL on that gloomy day in the Smokies. Reasons that had less to do with Donatello.)

"Yeah. Rain. We better get moving," I said over my shoulder as I started to don my pack. He stopped chowing down on string cheese and cheap meat sticks to look up at me.

"Uh, maybe we should hang here at the shelter and ride the storm out. It's freezing, Music Man." He snapped back into his frozen Slim Jim, and I started to get a backbone.

"I'm gonna hike. We've been stopped for half an hour already and I would love to make it to Standing Bear by tonight."

Standing Bear Farms was many miles from where we stood, and we had already walked double digit miles since breakfast. The thought of the long haul sent a shudder thru him, but I didn't care.

"Dang and blast, Music Man. I guess you're right. We need to get out of this park anyway." His reluctance was poorly hidden.

Still, loyalty kept me waiting as he wrapped up his lunch and slowly put his pack together. We could sense the tension and neither one of us liked it. Donatello did his best to try and diffuse it by appeasing me, even if it meant the threat of catching up to her. In a way, we both stayed faithful to our hiking partnership at the shelter. But it was now on shaky ground.

We arrived back on trail and walked only a dime before the sky opened to a washout of a downpour. The path became a glacial river, with water beginning to cascade over the roots and rocks further limiting step placements if one wishes to keep their toesies dry. We stopped at a vista and covered up with jackets, doing our best to stay out of the sheets of freezing rain so our cigarettes would stay lit. Hand-rolled Buglers don't fare well in foul weather. But they're cheaper and not as harmful to the environment compared to butts with cotton filters. Suddenly, I wanted a drink. Time to do some trail data.

"Screw this. Let's kick, D. We can make it to Standing Bear by sundown if we hustle. The trail is mostly downhill into Davenport, and the hostel is just past that. We just gotta cross I-40 and it's right there on the other side."

Again, Donatello reluctantly agreed, and we were off. I led a ferocious pace, fully ready to out-pace the weather and safely exit the park. Though the Smokies had given us an amazing run for the price of admission, it appeared the cheap thrills were over. I wanted to get away from the stress of hiking thru the closed park and find a nip of bourbon, but Blue Ribbon would suffice. We hiked and climbed non-stop for hours and by early evening we entered Davenport Gap. Light rain still flecked at our faces. He stopped us again at the trail junction down to the shelter.

"I'm gonna stop in at the shelter for a minute," he stated. I knew what he wanted to do. Donatello just couldn't resist the potential for a five-finger discount at the ranger's supply box.

"I'm going to push on. I don't want to add the four dimes down to the shelter and back," I declared. "I want to get there."

"Alright man, I'll catch up to you there at the highway."

"D, I'll see you down there."

I hiked with a burst of fresh fervor. Down, down, down thru the gap and on my way. I reflected upon all that happened at Great Smoky Mountains National Park. The last day had some stains, but otherwise it was an adventure. There was excitement, nature, solitude, long views, helicopter chases, and personal challenges that were at least identified, if not overcome. The highest elevation in the trail had been tackled at Clingmans Dome. Was it all downhill from here? Discoveries and impressions made. I looked forward to seeing Garlic again. I immediately knew that the Smokies had been a singular experience. The remoteness and isolation of the park gave me a taste of what it might have been like for Earl Shaffer when he came thru these parts. Shaffer was the first hiker to complete a northbound thru-hike of the Appalachian Trail in 1948. He would return to the trail and thru-hike two more times, again setting a record for his southbound hike in 1965 as the first trekker to complete end-to-end hikes in both directions. And notably again in 1998, he would hike the trail a third and final time, in his late seventies, to commemorate the 50th anniversary of the first thru-hike. At age 67, Grandma Gatewood simply told her "growed-up kids" that she was "going for a walk". She became the first woman to thru-hike the AT in 1955 with essentially nothing but a bedroll on her back, thus pioneering the concept of ultra-light trekking. With our modern technologies, feats like theirs stand unrivaled in the minds of many. In my youth, I would carom around the famous Valhalla Golf Club for early rounds of the PGA Championship. One special year, I witnessed Tiger Woods join Jack Nicklaus and Arnold Palmer in a threesome monikered to "the Holy Trinity of golf," all pursuing the Wanamaker Trophy. My father leaned in to remind me that "We're not likely to see this again." Just as then, I prayed to walk the Appalachian Trail humbly in the shadows of giants.

Skirting the pandemic by attempting an end-to-end hike of the AT turned out to be a fine idea, and it happened by sheer accident. The country was locked down for a laundry list of reasons. Somehow, I was fortunate enough to enjoy the wilderness experience with little competition for limited resources. As it was, there were few people on the AT. Literally no one else was in the national park except for my hiking partner and the vixen I had met at Mount Collins Shelter, after Mt. Love. Where had all the people gone? The President first tells everyone to "Go out into nature, if you want to congregate!" And then weeks later, the Secretary of the Interior is ordered to shut down the entire National Park system? Talk about mixed messages.... Oh, fiddlesticks: I'm a registered Independent. I've got no room to talk or vote in the primaries, but if it would please the court, I'd like to enter this into the record:

People have so much more in common than we differ on. If we can first relate in the humanness that we all share, we can then begin to better understand and appreciate the subtle differences that make us unique and fascinating to each other. It saddens my heart: The powerful fear of each other's differences is so common; commanding a profound authority over the compassion that is instead found in celebrating our similarities. We should celebrate *both*. As a straight-white-male, the only real oppression I have ever experienced is that of being a homeless drug addict. But knowing that feeling, I strive to never again pop my collar to anyone ever again. I don't have to accept the unpolished lens with which different groups or societies view each other, and even themselves. For it is not my truth. Instead, I can change how I treat others on this Earth that we share. (Easy for me to say; I grew up playing golf at country club) I am not the poster child for perfect living. Of my own making, there will be plenty of poor choices and more mistakes to learn from. Clearly, though, these are two different concepts.

After crossing the bridge over I-40, I followed a service road with signage for the hostel, then made a turn at the bunkhouse that crossed a footbridge over a small creek. I stopped at the john: the glass tile work in the bathroom was exquisite for a see-thru shower. A "work-for-stay" hiker welcomed me and introduced himself as Feather.

"Are you planning on staying for the night?"

"Sure am, and *whew*, am *I* glad to be *here*!" I huffed and dropped my pack on the ground.

"Cool, cool. Wait, did you go thru the park?" Feather asked.
"Yep."

"Holy cow, bruh. Wow! You made it, congratulations! Not too many folks took that risk and came out clean on the other side. You're a lucky hiker."

Outwardly I kept my ego in check. Internally, my pride rolled like a Florida gator: "Yep, that's right. You can track me on the trail by my tread. It's the one that says, "bad mother fucker."

I met lots of other Nobo hikers for the first time at Standing Bear. John The Baptist was a young Amish man on a spiritual, social and sports trip like I had never seen. The man was devout, but also sowing wild oats (without the sex and booze) on his farthest trip from home, before setting into a spiritual life back at the farm. His daily distance averages were insane—

"Somewhere around 35 miles a day," he was cool as a cucumber.

"With that old frame pack? Wow, you're a monster!" I snorted. He looked at me like I had talked out the side of my neck, then he laughed with a childish oink.

Karma was there. Period. Dredds and his patchy pals were noodling trolling for trail chicks ("pink-blazing" they call it, nowadays). But then there was Potholder...a myth in the making. The legend who never fell; the original prognosticator, and humble guit-fiddler with the voice of God, who was missing a string for his mini-Washburn guitar, named "Red". It just so happened that I was carrying *the one* needed guitar string in my pack.

"I have an extra string," I informed him. "What?"

"Yep, the only string I have. Didn't know why I was even carrying it...until now."

"Dude, that is amazing!" Boomed Potholder.

"Next time, don't break the G string, just slide it over to the side!" We shared a laugh at my old-man guitar-slinger's lame-o dirty joke and exhaled over the good fortune of the guitar's repair. The string had broken after snagging on his pack somewhere, but it was fixed up in a flash as I procured one simple new string from my first-aid kit.

Potholder had a sadness about him that felt all too familiar. He was undoubtedly in some stage of Chautauqua, and I related to his quest for new modes of transcendental understanding. I instantly cherished his friendship like he was a long-lost cousin found after years of searching out souls that share a common seal. He was the nearest of distant spirit relatives and became my advisor when it came to trail etiquette. Potholder pulled me to the side and intimated that his key to successful thru-hiking was simple: "Humility, Music Man. Humility."

I needed to hear that. He added "Always step to the side of the trail and let the people climbing up pass you." After changing his guitar string for him, he let me play Red. But there was no sign of Garlic.

"Hey, have y'all seen Garlic? I thought she might be here already. We left camp together this morning, but I never caught her."

"Nope, Music Man. Ain't seen or smelt no Garlic," replied Feather, "but you walked a lot of miles today given the conditions on the trail. In this weather, she probably settled down back at Davenport Gap Shelter." I slumped. I had not considered that she might be down where I left Donatello. That night I had a dream, and she was in it. We had known each other for a lifetime, it seemed in the dream. We agreed to walk north in search of each other on the night of the nearly new moon.

With each northbound step I took, I knew that as she too walked north, and we would meet again at the top of the sphere. Or so it seemed; one of us would first have to figure out when and where to stop.

.6

MUSIC MAN WAS EXHAUSTED when I woke up the next morning. A quick decision was made that a zero-day was back on the menu. The breakfast and beer (and beer at breakfast) were calling my name. I happily reassured myself that I had earned a rest day. Plus, Garlic might possibly show up if she hadn't decided to walk past the hostel altogether. After the harrowing pass thru the park, I suspected she would be ready to exit early.

After breakfast, Feather called out my name:

"Music Man! There's a package for you!"

"A package? For me?"

"Looks like something swank. Open it!"

I opened the box to find a brand-new Osprey Exos 58l backpack. My jaw dropped. It was black and orange, fresh and bold, and all the straps of the harness were comfy and puffy. The note inside said   *"Happy Birthday, Brah. From Uncle Bill and me."*

It was an early birthday present from my support team back home. They knew that my fifteen-year-old pack was losing its lift, so they joined resources and treated me to a brand-new backpack with all the right bells and whistles: ultra-light and etc. Ryan, the owner of Quest Outdoors, had unlocked the store's front door and let my family in to set me up with a new pack. Ryan almost lost the store due to the pandemic, but he kept the faith. By that time, he was barely opening the doors to anything other than e-business. Even if the store was temporarily closed to avoid the worst of the crisis, Quest Outdoors still showed up to help. Heading the hero panel: Bro. Funding it: my loyal family. I didn't feel worthy, so I vowed to carry extra pounds of gratitude. It's amazing what some people will carry with them; and how it can transform thru spacetime. Just when rain was about to get in my eyes, Garlic walked onto the farm, followed (not too closely) by Donatello.

"Music Man, when do you get here?" Garlic bristled.

"I got here last night. You must have stopped at the shelter, huh?"

"Yeah. Donatello and I held up there in the weather," she replied wide-eyed and glaring. It was official— she hated the dude.

"Damn, you put a lot of miles away to get here. Is that a new pack?" Garlic asked, as she took off her oversized blue glasses to polish the lenses with her neck bandana. It felt like a compliment, so I thanked her. Wrong again. All things considered, she appeared happy to see me. My heart thumped like a hummingbird.

After I stuffed my gear into the new backpack, I called Donatello over to the bunkhouse and upgraded him with my old backpack. Even the old rag of a pack was an improvement from the even older external-framed boy scout behemoth of a sack he tossed over his shoulders every day. (My ego, called "Hero," took credit away from my family.)

"I don't know what to say, Music. This is just...amazing," Donatello intimated.

By the end of the day, more hikers had arrived at Standing Bear Farms hostel. Most of them decided to stay for another night. Some got vortexed in for the season, never finding the escape velocity to leave. The vibes were good and so was the weather. We sat around the fire ring that night, merrily drinking beer and moonshine and telling park tales that got more and more dramatic with each round of drinks. But the stories needed no stretching. The truth was riveting and unbelievable. Garlic and Donatello told of dam crossings and helicopter chases to the oohs and ah's of the captive audience. Operation Smoky Rouge had been a smashing success. Garlic was a stowaway added to the squadron mid-mission and gave her own captivating account of the events, as did Donatello in his typical pirate character. I perceived twinges of envy from other Nobos who had arrived there by way of hitch-hiking around the park. Many now wished they had tried their luck with the park rangers. The telling and listening of our story brought home how fortunate we were to have slipped thru.

"You guys are lucky as hell," said Feather. "Only one other hiker in the past few days claimed to have made it thru. Everyone else got here yellow-blazing via hitch or shuttle ride around the park. Oh, I also heard that a pair of hikers got picked up by a park ranger at Clingmans Dome. He drove them down to Gatlinburg and dropped them off with a warning: 'Don't let me catch you in the park again. Next time, it won't just be a free ride to town.'"

"We got away with murder.... well maybe just trespassing. But it seemed more serious. I could feel the heat, man."

"I don't think the ghetto-birds were necessarily flying around just to harass hikers," he suggested. "There was a lot of fishing and poaching in the park when they first closed the gates. It was a once-in-a-lifetime opportunity for the locals to catch a park bear for a trophy. But lawmen got that under control quickly, I heard. Either way, to hell with 'em. You won."

That made sense to me. It would explain why the pilots had fun messing with hikers who were already on pins and needles. What were pilots really going to do from the air? They were not going to rescue us if we ran into trouble, so why would they arrest us just for hiking? Who really cared if a few of us clung to the highest ridges with no skin in the same game that the locals were playing? Even if Dilbert Hayseed, future GREATNESS OF AMERICA, wanted to haul Smokey the Bear himself back to the hollers for a stew and a fireplace rug under the rocking chair, wilderness travelers were running from anything that so much as flapped its wings. Hikers just wanted to hike their own hikes and forget about the troublesome world for a few wake-ups. Simple as that.

Pickers and song sparrows traded tunes around the campfire while Garlic and I locked eyes in sultry glances all night. Nearing the bedtime hour, I played the song I had written about my children. Garlic stood alone and listening from across the bonfire. Transfixed, she clung to every word with her arms crossed. The look on her face was filled with dark yet romantic questions when she turned and headed for the bunkhouse. It got me into my own feelings. We were fighting an idea that might change the dynamic of our hikes...if we acted on it. "Don't think," my heart whispered, "just hike." I woke up early the next morning and struck out for the trail without saying goodbye to anyone. All that waiting around; and then I just left without a whisper.

Comfortably back on trail, I took it easy transitioning between the "social" and "spiritual". "Sports" would also wait for a full-stop at the crossroads of the heart. After seven miles of distracted hiking, I gave up for the day and unpacked at a quiet and empty Groundhog Creek Shelter. With the excitement of the park and hostel experience mellowing, I started to recenter somewhat. Still, Garlic remained in my mind. What was the real story with her? What had driven her to the skyline of the Blue Ridge, chasing the next horizon like the rest of us? Distracted, I needed to get focused on trail data. It was bitterly cold outside as the sun went down and I figured I had better get water before dark. I found the creek and begun filling my sticker-covered Nalgene when I heard a rustling down the trail. As I turned to look, a shapely creature came into focus thru the shades of evenfall.

Garlic came around the bend, alone, with her long blonde hair flowing over one shoulder and the day's last rays of warming sunlight curving around her hip-belt. I had never seen her braids untied and she was glowing with the sunset behind her. The woman had a pure talent for placing herself in the scenery. As she neared, Garlic became the scenery, like she had stars and comets crashing around her.

"Hey," she said.

"Hey, you. I'm surprised to see you." I genuinely was.

"Yeah, I had to get out of there. Too many hikers." She played it cool, but I suspected she had run me down on purpose.

"You're a hard hiker to keep up with, Music Man."

"I'm not hiking as slow as you thought, huh?"

"Yeah, you're still slow. Only seven miles since sunrise?"

"GBITS had other plans, I guess."

"You're right about that. The trail really does dictate, doesn't it? But I guess I walked myself here."

I should have kissed her right there, but I was still holding back. She sat down at the picnic table to have dinner and I joined her with our shoulders lightly touching. The temperature was dropping into the 20's.

"It's going to be freezing tonight," she said between bites of quickly cooling noodles and a tremble of nervous chill in her voice:

"My soup is getting cold...."

Enough of this.

"You should stay in my tent tonight. You know... we can keep each warm," I blurted out.

"My, my, Music. That's a little fresh, isn't it?" Garlic spied me from her oversized glasses filled with laughing blue eyes. She couldn't help biting her lip.

"Well, somebody had to put a voice to it."

She dropped her wooden spoon into her cooking pot and stayed with me in my tent that night. It was freezing cold, but we kept each other warm as promised. At one point we laughed at the condensation freezing to the ceiling of the tent as a fresh dusting of snow coated the campsite.

In the morning, things were different...or, shall we say, back to normal. Coming out of the hostel fresh and clean the day before meant I could still smell passion on both of us. But as soon as we pulled each other close, Garlic pushed herself away, apart, and back where we had started. All hints of our embrace evaporated. She fell silent at breakfast. The ice chipped off my tent in shards as I struck camp to the ground and stuffed it all away.

"I can't do this." Garlic announced as we donned our packs, "It wasn't a good idea. This was not supposed to happen." She had come to the wilderness to hike, and find herself, and get away from cornpumps like me, right? Fearing the possibilities, Garlic made a jumpstart for the trail. At the click of her heels, she skipped off without so much as a "goodbye." Little that I knew about her, I knew enough to recognize that fear had washed over her. I let her go to break the newly snow-covered trail.

The horror of late April 2018 is scarred into my memory like a grainy old black and white film. It was two weeks before the Kentucky Derby and nearly twenty inches of snow lay on the ground in Oldham County, twenty miles from the Twin Spires. The blizzard had lasted all night, but the cold morning sky was clear and blue. My condition that morning, however, was Dante's hell. I was dope sick and the roads were too bad to go anywhere and get my fix. Plus, I was broke. My daughter came into our bedroom at 9 am to wake me up. I had moved from the couch to the bedroom much earlier, after my wife got up to take care of the kids. They were excited about the fresh powder outside. I was useless and flopping around like a fish out of water with the sickness. When I heard the door to our bedroom open, I tried to stop squirming and pretended to be asleep. A shadowy little head covered with a winter hat tiptoed to the side of the bed.

"Daddy, will you take me out to play in the snow?"

I rolled over and pulled the sweat-soaked sheet over my head.

"Daddy?"

"I can't right now." My voiced was muffled under a pillow. "I didn't get much sleep last night. I need to rest a little longer, okay sweetie?"

"No-waah." She whimpered, "the snow is perfect. Pleeeease?"

Bundled up, mittens on, and scarf tied around her neck, her eyes sparkled. Still....

"Sweetie, I can't." I rolled over again shaking and nearly broke to pieces. But I didn't have one bit of energy or motivation to even cry. Anger and self-hatred fueled another shiver. My heart wanted to go play with her. Couldn't they see that I didn't do this to myself on purpose? It was complete madness, and it wasn't fair to anyone.

"Okay," she said with a dejected sigh. "Maybe later?"

"Maybe later, sweetie."

I could see the silhouette of my wife leaning against the door with her arms crossed. I saw her kneel and whisper to our neglected daughter as she left the room. Then my wife came in and closed the door behind her.

"What's wrong with you? What's going on?" She spoke calmly as she sat on the edge of the bed and put her hand on my side.

"Nothing, babe," I mustered. "Just need a little more sleep." I wasn't fooling anyone.

"Babe, tell me what's wrong. Let me help. I love you. Tell me what is going on? Please. Your children are waiting for their father to show up, and I'm waiting for my husband to come back."

I turned over and sat up, shark-eyed and jaundiced.

"I'm in deep again. I'm sick. I think I need some help." Truth be told, I didn't want help yet. I was lying about that part. Not fully at bottom, I was just trying to mitigate the current damage by telling half-truths when I was caught red handed. Back to my old tricks: Manipulation by way of letting just enough truth leak out to take the heat off. Typical behavior of an addict's honed craft. She stood up from the bed and pointed.

"GET OUT, NOW!"

"Whoa, whoa..." I tossed the covers off and found my feet, trying like hell to level up.

"No more "woe is me" bullshit, you bastard! Poor you, poor you, pour you another drink! Your family is falling apart, and you end up like this, again?!" The wife was fuming.

We had been going to marriage counseling for over a year. Neither one of us told the therapist how we really felt, and he must have known that at least I was full of shit (if not all three of us, to some degree). I'll give him credit for trying to help though. "The drugging is how I cope," I self-justified in silence. I knew better than to put a voice to such frustrations when I was in a vulnerable state.

"I'm packing the kids up and leaving this house. You had better be gone before we get home. And don't come back!"

Storming down the stairs, I marched behind her into the kitchen still pleading, but the gig was up. To make matters worse, the kids were now in the theater watching the horror show while frozen with shock.

"Get OUT!" she screamed as tears began to roll down everyone's face. Everyone except me. I was bone white as a blank canvas inside, outside and upside down.

"Okay."

She packed up the kids and ditched the area. Within an hour, I had fishtailed my truck out of the ice-covered driveway to our home in Oldham County with my backpack and a guitar in the hatch. I never stepped foot into my own home ever again. Ending up in a treatment center days later, I lost my government job (along with our family's insurance benefits) and was fully excommunicated from my world for the first time. It was like someone pulled the power chord of a spinning phonograph out of the wall. The cracked and wobbly Hank Williams record slowed to a stop.

Years earlier, going to college was the dawn of a new social age for me. I made it to class and tested well enough to make passing marks, so that meant I could party. The bands I played in gigged often. We traveled in all directions on brief tours whenever we could and played the local haunts regularly. Certain groups even managed to make a few records. Watch out College Town, USA, when the music men are in town! If I ever again tell anyone that I have arrived, then show me the door.

I lived on Transylvania Parkway for the better part of those years at the University of Kentucky. The "Transy House," as we called it, was pure debauchery in Lexington. There was no need for a formal fraternity membership. The group of rascals that lived in and out of our animal house put most of the fraternity row to shame. The house had a 24-hour open and revolving door policy for 365 days a year. The only consistent factor in that house for three years was a glassy-eyed me. After barely passing Latin class my senior year, the Sociology Department finally threw a degree like a paper airplane from a second story window of the Arts and Sciences building and bid me good riddance. Cheers behind the closing window drowned out with a slam: "He's gone!"

My college girlfriend, Cybil, still had another year of school so I didn't venture too far from our relationship. I moved back down to Louisville and got a teaching job at a mom & pop music shop. I ramped up the gigging life as well. My drinking and drug usage continued to progress, though I managed to save around ten thousand dollars that year. In my mind, I was fan-fucking-tastic. No one could tell me anything. It was an environment where the seeds of narcissism could sprout into poisonous orchids. Everybody around me was getting strange, but I still felt like a square peg in a round hole until I got a buzz on. I was an egomaniac with an inferiority complex. Strange sociopathic behaviors would emerge from time to time, but no one ever called me out for it. I was a lone ranger and completely self-absorbed. Sleeping the day away, teaching guitar lessons in the afternoon, and jamming all night became the new normal. On particularly bad runs, I started taking days off between just to feel the rush of dopamine after the first drink again. Real alcoholic shit. My control over quantities and frequency of use slowly worsened over time. I would dry out when I absolutely had to take care of whatever business was at hand. Then I would be right back to grimy living.

After Cybil finished school the following year, we took the summer off and drove out West. Cybil and I had the time of our lives! Spread out in my 1995 Buick LaSabre, we perused hard American countryside— the Dakotas and Jackson Hole, and way out on the Olympic peninsula, down to Coos Bay and the Redwoods, to Marin and Point Reyes, San Francisco, Death Valley and into southern Utah. Perusing the famous Wall Drug store gave us the feeling that we'd finally done something with our lives. We got a stickah for the cah. We paid visits to bygone friends and gave our woes to the rolling hills and desert plains. The picture of us on our patio date above Crater Lake at sunset...even Ansel Adams would nod in approval. Passing thru Idaho, at Craters of the Moon National Monument, we marveled at the jagged basaltic lava fields that spread out like a black-surfaced planet Mars. I recall leaning far over the edge of the Kings Bowl as sustained high winds cycled up to hold our bodies at nearly a 45° angle to the ground. We struggled to hear each other's voices over the roar, laughing all the while looking over the mighty carve in the Earth's crust. It is one of the deepest land rifts in the world.

However, our relationship started to get rocky somewhere around the Rockies and we finally broke up passing thru Memphis on the way back to Kentucky. Maybe we should have stopped for a drink on Beale Street instead of continuing to bicker down the road for miles upon miles. I-40 is a damn long highway, and we just couldn't break out of the argument, so we broke up instead. I have still never been to Memphis. As Cybil once lamented, "We did a lot of horrible things to each other, but I would not be who I am today without the time of my life I spent with you. It was the best of times, it was the worst of times, at the end." I still didn't recognize what was vaguely sensed in my mental periphery: I had a problem. A vital change would be in order if I even survived the shit. More wasted time and lost relationships might do the trick.

The very next summer, my brother and I traveled with our lifelong friend Andy O, going to Guatemala for a visit to "the Reserve." My great-grandfather purchased the roughly four-thousand-acre coffee farm in 1935 and it is still owned and operated by the extended family at the time of this writing. We decided to take a trip and see the Reserve for ourselves, as others in the family have historically done in their youth. It was a sort of rite of passage. The "finca" is a special place, serving as a home for the workers and their families that farm the mountain. Coffee bushes grow strong and healthy on the mountain slopes that are rich with volcanic soil and ideal for producing high yields. The red pulp-filled berry that grows on the trees and encases the bean gets harvested and dried by hard working farmers that live on the land they work. Built right there on the farm, in the shadow of active volcanoes, is a church and schools and other resources that provide for the many social needs of the villagers, as they dedicate their lives to the farm. Rumor has it that Señor, my father's first cousin who now owns and operates the farm, is one of the fairest and most desired employers in the country. From my humble observation, they looked damn happy to be there on that finca. It is a tropical paradise with tall palm trees that sway in the warm ocean gales that encircle the finca the Pacific Ocean and the Gulf of Mexico. Seeing the sights, we explored the finca's tropical jungle and went birding; we climbed sulfuric gravel to the active crater of Volcan de Pacaya, we toured historic Antigua, and drank beer at the bodegas in Panajachel. We ferried across Lake Atitlan to San Pedro Laguna under the sleeping eye of Volcan de Atitlan. It was a tropical paradise and we bummed around like the naive young gringos that we were, never worried about the banditos.

"Banditos?!" We ain't gotta worry about banditos! I am the boogie man!" Andy howled with youthful hubris as we sipped on Gallo in the Guatemalan sun. Sunburnt and hungover, we arrived back to the States just weeks before 9/11 while customs were still lax. We smuggling back textiles, raw coffee beans and other organic products not legal to carry across any border.

The social climate in the States was much different post 9/11, when I took my wife to Guatemala following her mother's death from cancer in 2011. We decided that a getaway was in order after the maelstrom of hospitals, doctor's appointments and hospice care that marked the tragic end to her mother's life. My wife had managed much of her mother's palliative care for years. I decided that she deserved to have someone take care of her for a change. Again, I took a guest to the finca, and back to Lake Atitlan and Antigua. Along the journey, we ventured deep into the north and toured the Mayan ruins of Tikal. In awe of the sacred geometry, we climbed the pyramids and sat above the canopy of rainforest that keeps all but the tallest capstones a secret from the sky. We toured the palace's interior and studied the masonry and artwork of the Mayan people, in a city lost to the mysteries of time. Sitting at the foot of The Great Jaguar temple was a spiritual experience unlike any other I have had. The grand staircase of the pyramid ascended into the heavens.

Arriving on time for our departure from the ruins that afternoon, we discovered that our tour bus had left us stranded in the pouring rain. We had to stow away on another tour group's bus, sharing a humped seat on the wheel well for the drive back to civilization. I'll never forget the harrowing ride out.

We thought we were going to die on that stormy road, filled with deep potholes that groaned the axles of the old bus with every dip. She sat on my lap and put her head on my shoulder as the van sliced thru mud holes, ruts and the crevasse left in her heart by her mother's gruesome death. I wanted her to know that someone loved her. But I didn't act like it when my back was turned. Once we were back to town, I went searching for the banditos.

"La...painkillers? Oh-pee-oids?" I queried at the Pharmacia back in Antigua.

"Codone?" The Pharmacist squinted and replied with a Tzotzil accent.

"Yes, goddammit, that's it. Codone. Got any?"

"Un momento, Señor."

I might as well have been the subject of a VICE documentary about a gringo who is bound to wind up trembling naked, in the public square after some Guatemalan gangster drugs him with scopolamine and takes me for everything I've got. But I managed to keep out of the gueto, copping at the local Pharmacia.   Whatever in the hell their version of Codeine was, I wanted it. The Mayan white-coat sold it to me cheap and without a prescription. Due to relentless doctor shopping back home, my name had been flagged on a controlled-substance watch list for years which prevented me from getting any form of narcotics via the old-fashioned way. Thus, a legal Rx for a pill bottle with my name on it was a pipe dream except for the occasional addiction-maintenance meds I could score to get the heat off me. But far from the restrictions of the States, I acquired fistfuls of the real fuckers for just a few quetzales. I had done so well for the first few weeks in Guatemala. I didn't use any dope until Antigua...but only because I didn't have any. Thanks to lax laws and regs of a foreign country, however, this tourist-with-cash was once again legitimately holding. I was buttered for the rest of the trip, and fully dope-sick from the pills by the time we landed at LaGuardia a week later. We went to the Cape straight from the airport, per the plan. But the first thing I did was drag her along with me, in her car, while I went doctor shopping in Provincetown. After striking out at the first clinic, one merciful physician's assistant finally gave me a script for some puny nerve pills just to get my whiny ass to leave. It tapped the kill switch just enough to temporarily get my twitching quelled.

After the drive back to her father's farm in Vermont, I raided the medicine cabinet for expired pills. Her father is a three-time AT thru-hiker with one Pacific Crest Trail thru-hike underfoot. He ultimately gave up hiking midway thru his Continental Divide Trail bid as he went for the career triple crown during his retirement.

"No navigation, no hiking," he said to me at some point while discussing his trekking experience, years before my own. Now his daughter was stuck married to the father of his grandkids.... a full-blown drug addict in a marriage headed Sobo. He came to Kentucky to help rescue his daughter from me in a move that was out of character for him, but necessary under the circumstances. They left Logan Airport bound for the Bluegrass during that depraved and snowy spring of 2018, just before the most exciting two minutes in sports, to whisk my family far away to safety.

After my wife had kicked me out of the house, she came to visit me in a treatment center a few days before she and the kids caught their own flights away. I was terribly sick when she came to the rehab for a visit. All I remember is this:

"I'm leaving you. I want a divorce. I am moving the kids back to New England." The news bounced off me.

"The kids will be waiting for you," she told me as we parted ways for the last time as a married couple, before the lawyers got involved.

"You want to hurt me?" I cursed, "I'll show you; *I'll* hurt me." I jumped the rehab fence that night in a crazed escape, falling ten feet farther than the drop appeared from the top, rolling my ankle.

I hobbled to my dope man's house in the middle of the night and hounded him until I got what I wanted, which was very high. Acting utterly selfish and delusional, I was in denial over everything that was happening "to me". I limped back to the same rehab the next morning. They found me humiliated and broken by the front door and wouldn't let me back in after the stunt I had pulled. I was now officially homeless. I had nowhere else to go. Being of no use to myself or anyone around me, I was spiritually dead. What was the use in staying clean anyway? I went back to the dope man, but even he wouldn't let me in. That's when I made my way downtown to join the ranks of the hound dogs and hellions of the street. The vicious cycle had entered a deathly turn and now I was the bandito.

Facts proved I had no love to give. It was impossible for me to be anything for anyone else while I was unable to take basic care of myself in the most basic ways. Would I ever let someone hold my son down and pour liquor and drugs into his system? No way! If that happened to him on my watch, I'd probably be in the penitentiary. So why do I do it to myself? How can I truly love anything or anyone if I don't treat myself with the same compassion? I had taken from everyone, and I had given it all away. I took from my family. I took from my friends and colleagues. I took their money, their things, their trust, their peace, and their serenity. I took their friend away; their son and their brother; their co-parent and husband; I took their father. I had reached a point where there was nothing left to take—but responsibility.

AFTER GARLIC WALKED AWAY FROM ME IN SILENCE, I sat down at the picnic table staring at the empty trail shelter. It was for the best. I felt I didn't deserve to meet someone special or be happy. Besides, no one wanted cause harm or hurt or jeopardize our chances at putting our best feet forward on the big hike. It was okay. For the first time in decades, true acceptance washed over me.

The weather was warmer and clear, while a gentle breeze turned the leaves around me. Passing thru Cherokee National Forest en route to Hot Springs, North Carolina, the miles pleasantly began to feel immeasurable. The previous night's snow had melted to reveal the diversity of the trail and its root-covered surface which made it difficult to hike with style. The focus that was needed to make progress often felt frustrating. "Heads-down hiking," we called it. However, it can be the conduit to powerful meditation when all available brain power is channeled into step placement. Managing challenges and mitigating stresses ebbed and flowed, but I stayed present and focused on the next footfall.

My brain and body were all over the place.

If the surface of the trail is rocky or braided by tree roots, each step can get increasingly more maddening as pain and frustration mounts. I came to look for the natural steps in the trail, which are there if one pays attention. Finding those natural steppingstones and foot holds gave me an idea of pacing myself to naturally land in those spots. While the miles were tough, they were meditative. I was tiring out as I reached a gap that opened to a high-elevation cove of tall grass, exposing the vast mountains in the distance. I stopped for water and a rest.

"Hey," a voice came to me from many yards off the trail.

Garlic had dropped her pack out in the meadow and was sitting on a ground quilt that she had spread out. Apparently, she had the same idea at this beautiful stopping point.

"Come over here," she invited from a distance.

"How was your morning?" I sat down on the quilt.

"Okay, I guess. Yours?" I looked at her and smiled with one corner of my mouth.

"You're pretty smooth," she said. "You just ooze everything you do, Music Man. I don't get it. This all seems so easy for you."

"What? This hike is the hardest thing I've ever done!"

Garlic stood up and moved in front me as I sat in a lazy Lotus pose, looking up at her as she spoke:

"Not just the hike but managing everything. It seems natural for you. Don't you ever feel lost or confused like the rest of us?"

"Sure. Not all of us are out here because we're all there, ha!"

Garlic dropped the guardrails back down and made her next move, as I pondered what "managing" anything meant. The thought quickly evaporated when she stepped over my knee, then her other foot crossed my other knee. Her body was right in front of me.

"I don't have anything figured out, except how I'm feeling right now," I said, "There's a lot about me you don't know."

"I'm a quick study when I want," Garlic said with a sultry tease, looking down upon me with the sunlight behind her.

Her thighs turned over in those perfectly vented black leggings. I felt her body heat on my face as she eased down in front of me. Our eyes were locked as she moved onto my lap. Garlic draped her arms around my neck as she lowered herself to me in the meadow. Gripping me in between her knees, her hair fell onto my face as we connected.

"I can't help it."

"It's out of our hands anyway."

"What do we do?"

"Keep taking steps."

Our lips pressed together, and the wind picked up; our bodies gently twisted down into the tall and blustery grass covering the cove, and out of sight.

Love stories are rarely perfect, but that moment was. It was true that there was a lot we didn't know about each other. In fact, we knew practically nothing about each other except for our shared experiences on trail. We sensed that other had suffered somewhere down line in life. That was more than enough, as we gave ourselves to abandon. It was just the way it was supposed to be. Disregarding struggles that drove us out of society, our relationships, our lives, and onto the Appalachian Trail, we easily surrendered to simpler moments. It didn't seem real, and some say that it wasn't. But it was real. We left our homes, our families, former lovers, and society at large, to live out new stories on the magical footpath that stretches nearly the entire length of America's Atlantic region.

"It's not real life," the naysayer's doubt. "It's not responsible," the civilized may scoff.

Nowadays, I respond with a smile and a tip of my hat as I pass on by. We don't know what we don't know, I grant them. I was gaining a new perspective on basic concepts like the difference between making plans or setting goals versus having expectations; adaptability to change. Plans are apt to change, and that is ok. Sometimes goals may not be reached, but it's only a stage of the process. Success comes from turning the cargo shorts of failure upside down and shaking the pockets until change falls out. Each stumbling block that I fumble over presents another opportunity to grow. As my good friend from the rooms Bazooka Joe once suggested while I was faithless in a moment of doubt:

"Don't turn your steppingstones into frisbees."

I want to stay green: Many sojourners find that expectations of what a trail experience should be won't play out that way at all. We found that our expectations were unrealistic or unreasonable. It was harder than we expected. We were lonelier than before, or even more smothered by strangers. Many discover that expectations, in theory, are irrational. I want to stay green.... Travel and trekking experience have taught me that I have no idea what curve balls life will throw at me next. Some days are good, and some days are bad. The trail either goes up or goes down, such as life. A flat and unwinding road will eventually cause me to veer off into a ditch out of boredom and fatigue. The universe and all its life forms and processes are in a constant state of change, from the carbon cycle to my spiritual evolution. I want to stay green.... To remain teachable and adaptable to change, making the best out of situations that could otherwise cause undue suffering. I want to stay green because green things grow.

****

The new partnership with Garlic was coyly evolving into something special, but it had caveats. We discussed the possibility that being lovers could (and would) eventually affect our on-trail trekking arrangement. Our chancing the romancing at many a hiker midnight was *going* to happen. To remain autonomous hikers, however, would be a much tougher task in the early stages of trail romance.

Donatello was far behind by then, geographically speaking, and it was starting to seem like we might not see him again for a while. The thought saddened me. Not everyone deserves a second chance at trust, but everyone deserves any chance to consider something different for their life. That is part of the beauty of the Appalachian Trail. You can leave the past behind and be who you want to be without fear of judgment or persecution. Yes, the trail is getting more crowded every year. With the crowds come the personalities, and I am one of them. As little twos and threes of hikers began coming together, the foundation for a trail family, a "Tramily", was being built.

When it comes to social support, the hiking community is unrivaled. If I had something you needed, it was yours. Even if it was just a shoulder to lean on or an ear to bend. Often it came in the way of places to stay with hot showers, available food or supplies in (legitimate) hiker boxes, random coolers of "trail magic" filled with cold sodas, beers and candy bars left by trail angels, or any other blessing GBITS might place at one's feet. The trail provides, so there was no need to take unfair quantities of rations.

Note to self: "I take me with me wherever I go." If I act like a thieving vagabond, it's difficult to argue with the civilized naysayer who posits that I am only a self-justified Robin Hood. That's not the trail's style. Thru-hiking was never meant to be a permanent change. I never wanted to live on the trail or live off it either. Without doing any sort of serious work on my character flaws, I couldn't expect to out-hike myself for very long. Of all my problems, I am the common denominator. If most human behavior is centered around mitigating stress, how come it isn't working for me? Serious questions lingered and hoped I would find some real answers, but I wasn't projecting a transformation into some impossibly valiant William Wallace either. If the Appalachian Trail truly was the right path, it sometimes seemed hard to see the forest for the trees.

The pandemic was in full swing and trail-town hospitality was a mixed bag. Some folks were happy to see us while others booed us back to the trailhead. Or they honked and pointed away from town limits thru closed car windows as they spun up dust for us and sped away. Garlic and I walked into Hot Springs without a warm greeting from anyone on the streets. We didn't expect a ticker tape parade, but the reaction was still disappointing. I get it now. Nobody knew anything about the causes and conditions of the new and scary ways of the world. But a couple of magical things happened in that little town that day. The first thing, Garlic and I agreed, was a couple of the best cheeseburgers we ever ate from the Smoky Mountain Diner. Citing "new protocols", they kindly told us we could eat at the picnic table behind the restaurant next to the dumpster. We washed the burgers down with a couple of fruity beers and relaxed. As the alcohol rose to my temples, I took a sigh of relief that we were off the trail in the blistering heat of that day. I had a sudden urge to play a guitar again. I had been thinking about it for days. Music Man had no instrument to play! I needed something with strings to strum. The itch was on to make music. What was really going on was as my buzz increased, so did my ego.

We packed up and moved toward the front of the restaurant. Roars from a lively bunch of younger folks rose to a full-on group laugh as we came around the corner. Rowdy rascals: four of them leaned up against a car. A motley crew, they were city-fresh and county-bred. I was compelled to introduce myself.

"Hey, y'all. What's going on?" I chirped.

"Whoa! Hey, you guys are thru hikers!" Beamed the boy.

"That's right," Garlic said with tipsy satisfaction.

"Man, I want to thru-hike the whole thing someday myself," said the youthful ringleader while musing at our equipment. "We just went up to the fire tower on a jettison, out and back overnight. This is my cousin, and that's his cousin, and this is our...girlfriend." She was huge and popped her chewing gum as she winked at me.

"My name is Andrew!" he said, directing the attention back to himself.

"Nice...nice to meet you, Andrew." Fully amused, I jokingly returned the Big Joint's wink. "I'm Music Man, and this is...."

"Garlic." She interrupted me with a glare and punched my side.

"Aye, take it easy lover," I said while rubbing my ribs. "Just joking around, geez."

"Wow! Music Man and Garlic...real thru-hikers," Andrew said in the third person, like we were something he longed to be in another life. He carried on, "My dude, we were just up on the trail two nights ago, partying at the fire tower north of here. You'll reach that after you climb out of town. Whew! That hike up to Rich Mountain Lookout is a son-of-a-bitch, but the fire tower is worth it bros, bras.... Whatever! Hahaha!"

A big climb coming...not what I wanted to hear on this hot day as my insides churned raspberry meade. It was obvious there were some bizarre sexual liberations within this crew, too. I changed the subject.

"So, Andrew. Where can a hiker find an open music store?"

"Music store, music store.... Shit. I don't know, good hiker. All the businesses went down with the disease around here if you know what I mean. You ain't gonna find anything open around this town, except maybe the Dollar General....and this awesome diner! What are you looking for?"

"I need a musical instrument, a backpacker guitar, or something with strings."

He clicked his tongue and shot me with the trigger finger of his empty-handed six-shooter. "Music Man, that makes sense! Your name is *Music Man*, for Christ's sake! But you don't have an instrument to play?"

"I'm ready to kick," said Garlic. She was not as amused by this cast of characters as I was.

"Music Man, check this out..."

Andrew opened the back door of his car and pulled out a little vinyl case. It looked like a shotgun bag or a fancy pool cue. But the treasure he pulled out wasn't a gun and it was a different type of lumber than a pool stick. He ripped the Velcro back and slipped it out of the case. It was the work of an extremely creative luthier.

"WHOA. What is that?" I was transfixed. I had never seen anything like it. It had only three strings attached to a thin V-shaped body, like a backpacker guitar but half the size at a little over a foot long. The fret scale was not equidistant, like a guitar is with semitones.

"That there is a Strumstick."

"Strumstick," I pondered out loud as he handed it to me for further inspection, "I've never seen anything like it!"

"Pretty cool, huh? I got it from Amazon a couple days ago. You know, so I could have something to play while the four of us frolic in the woods. We've been traveling.... ha, we ain't from around here either. I can tell by your accent, Music Man, that you ain't from the North. But you," he motioned in Garlic's direction, "I'm gonna guess, somewhere.... Upstate?"

"Hudson Valley, that's right! I stick out like a sore thumb down here, we all know it." Garlic was proud of her Yankee heritage, and she knew her accent drove all the boys Yonkers in the South. Plus, she was insatiably easy on the eyes. The Big Joint snapped her chewing gum again. Garlic's presence was intoxicating, especially to newcomers. But all I heard was a string band from the deep hollers. Tones of home swirled in my mind's ear as my eyes were glued to the fascinating little hillbilly instrument I turned over in my hands. It looked like a wooden vase with bronze strings and sexy curves.

"How much?" I asked Andrew.

"With shipping and tax, it was around...."

"No, how much do you want for it?"

"Oh, it's not for sa...." *(Twang, twang)*

I interrupted him by delivering a tune from that little slapstick, like banjo music from a bad movie that begged for someone to paddle faster. With their attention on lock, I wrestled with the only dulcimer licks I could remember and held on for dear life. The sparkle of that Strumstick was bound to lure the mountain people down crawling-cliffs into town. I slammed the song shut like a pickup truck's gate, to a burst of applause. Even Garlic raised a sultry eyebrow of approval.

"Ha-ha! Music Man, holy cow! You're a natch! How'd you do that? Bullshit, you've never seen one before! Put your wallet away. That Strumstick is YOURS!"

He didn't want the cash, but I forced three soggy twenty-dollar bills on him. I was so happy to have it and now I just had to figure out how to pack it and how to play it. It weighed about two pounds total in the case. With my luxury item for the trail in hand, we prepared to march on after high fives and new trail memories.

"Dudes! Are you two climbing up to the tower tonight?! We'll meet you up there, but we ain't hiking it again." Andrew hid his pointer finger with his other hand as he motioned in the direction of the Big Joint.

"That big girl didn't say a word," Garlic recalled, as we climbed the beast that is Rich Mountain an hour later. The Andrew Crew ended up meeting us at the fire tower later that night. They drove up as promised, sparing the Big Joint from another hoist of herself up the hill. Andrew brought a case of beer, steaks, and a handle of chilled vodka. We sat around the firepit that night having a good ole time, and I began the "getting to know you" phase of the

Strumstick love affair. Other hikers showed up with other substances. Someone started handing out tabs of acid, but I assumed Garlic didn't see any of that. Andrew was pushy for the party, and I didn't want to say no to him. But I didn't want to go on a trip with Lucy around Garlic's back, either. I wasn't above taking acid though, so I palmed my dose for child's play on another day. Andrew also tried to give me the sixty bucks back that I paid him for the Strumstick, saying he was beholden to the gift. I wouldn't take the money back. But I happily accepted the handful of LSD that he offered me in lieu of the cash. I devised that I would save it for a special occasion.

Later that night, a drunken dozen of us climbed the water tower and spied the town of Hot Springs far below.

"What a day," I whispered into Garlic's ear as I came up behind her and wrapped my arms around her body. She was getting annoyed at the Big Joint, who had turned into a blathering lush and was showing everyone her boobs, which were as big as basketballs. Near hiker-midnight, the Big Joint put all men of the dating scene on blast for us and the valley below. Laughter began to reverberate thru the mountains as she owned the stage....

"If you wanna fuck me, just tell that's what you want!" boomed the Big Joint, "Jesus Christ! Don't give me some bullshit about 'Oh, I'll call ya, babe,' or try and get rid of me with some disrespectful buyout. I don't do that shit! You assholes are killing me!" All the boys howled in laughter. She went on... "I mean, just call a jack of spades a spade, you jokers! If all you want is to fuck me, then be HONEST," the Big joint reached for the heavens.

"*I* want to fuck you!" anonymously rose from a voice in the crowd, inciting a riot of laughter.

"I'm serious! I mean, why can't a guy just be honest? Mean what ya say and say what ya mean! You boys would get a lot farther in life if ya quit throwing all that shade around. Nothing, and I mean *nothing* makes a girl feel worse than to be lied to. It's worse than cheating. If you don't want to fuck me anymore, fine! If that's the case, I probably don't want your ass anymore, either...but it's when you lie. That tells me that you don't even have enough respect for me to tell me the truth as you walk out the door, with nothing more to lose. I tell ya, men have a lot to learn about how to treat a lady." She took a deep breath and sighed. "Now...who spoke up back there? Who said they'd fuck me?"

"Over here, lady," came the voice again. (More howling laughter) "Show's over. You. Let's go."

Hilarious as the pitiful exhibition was, she took a stand for women. Even if she didn't validate her own point, it still meant something. I have no one else to blame for any problem with which I find myself. It was predicated by my own selfish actions. And that selfishness is borne of fear. Fear that I am not going to get something that I want, or the fear that I am going to lose something I already have and want to keep. Selfishness and self-seeking behaviors throw everything off balance. Suspicion of others and doubting ourselves mutates into our DNA when social playbacks are left on repeat. Next, our politics and true spirituality begin to reflect our fears of what we don't know and don't understand. Namely, everything and everyone else. Finally, we pass it on to another generation, placing us that much further away from the natural order. This is just one man's observation. Now let's run it back just one more time.... for old time's sake! Ugh. When will [I] ever learn? I know what you might be thinking, reader, and the answer is *no*. I didn't go anywhere near the Big Joint, who may have been Andrew's sister or cousin or something. But I was making old mistakes, nevertheless. My ego still would have denied it the next day and likely passed a polygraph.

On a certain typical day of mountain hopping, Garlic was leading us along the edge of a steep and sleepy drop-off at the side of the trail. She turned around and was walking backwards to deliver the punchline of a joke she already had us laughing at. With two more steps backwards, she would go over the edge. Suddenly, I lurched forward with my trekking pole, guiding her away from the ledge and back on track.

"Whoa! You gotta watch where you're going, girlfriend! You can't hike backwards near this open cliff!

"Don't tell me how to hike!" Garlic turned 360 degrees on a dime.

"What? I'm not trying to 'tell you how to hike,' it's common sense. Walk facing forwards, not backwards. Especially near a drop-off. One more shake of your tail and it would have fallen off and died."

"I was *fine*. And what's so wrong with walking backwards anyway? Is there a right way to walk, Mr. Thoreau?"

"Garlic, you almost went from Northbound to down, and bound for the coast...one way."

"We all return to the sea eventually. You can't control *that* after you die! Besides, I wasn't going to fall."

"Whatever. Watch where you're going. Now that's about as common as sense gets." "Common sense...common sense? Music Man wants to lecture me about common sense." "You're kidding, right?" "Common sense.... that's rich, Music Man. You know what ain't rich? Me, you asshole. I didn't grow up at a country club in the summertime, or going to the same schools every year, or having real food on the goddamn table. I don't get mail drops from my family! I had to earn this! Do you know what it's like to not know where your next meal is gonna come from? What's *your* path of least resistance' look like? Bet your ass I know mine. I go around."

83

(I wisely dodged some bullets. Speaking up there would have been Russian roulette with a Frenemy's Derringer.)

She had burst forth from all false fronts of failed diplomacy into all-out artillery warfare of hurtful words. Blasting low blows, Garlic had come completely unhinged and she continued the shelling. She wasn't Garlic anymore—she was responding as the traumatized girl of her youth and going by her legal name.

"You can't tell me shit, Music Man. You haven't had it rough. Yeah, you have your problems. White collar problems. I don't have anyone mailing me food and letters on the trail. Growing up, my sister and brother and I had to... They hardly answer the phone when I call. I just barely convinced my sister to watch my cat or even keep my live sourdough yeast in her fridge. They're both probably dead by now!"

I spoke up again.

"Garlic, I went from owning a home and raising a family to copping eight-dollar points of dope under a bridge. I know a little something about struggle, miss 'Upstate'. You have no idea what I have been thru, or what I have put my family thru. I have lost everything! And you're worried about your baking yeast," I snorted, failing to realize that I had justified her point.

"It's special yeast, okay....and I make amazing bread. Everybody wants my bread, like they want your music! I sell it for five bucks, you know! There's a waiting list back at the office."

"Five-dollar bread? At what office? You quit your job to thru-hike anyway, so that'll be the last five bucks you're gonna get out of them. My free bunk in the homeless shelter was the most expensive goddamn thing I ever paid for, Garlic!"

"Yeah? Well, what are you doing about it now? Hiding out in the woods while your kids will grow up calling somebody else "Daddy", because you choose to keep getting high?"

Line crossed.

"Back up! I'm trying to do something different out here, ok?! What is this, rag on Music Man for saving your ass from falling off a precipice? What would you know about my pain anyway?"

"I know that I don't need no man, Music *Man*!"

She knew more about my pain than she let on and she had preyed upon it. I had never seen her so upset, so possessed. Something deep in her soul was driving her to pivot. The verbal expression from her inner child was soaked with pain. Garlic was clutching to a personal purpose that her autonomy as an independent hiker outwardly expressed: complete self-reliance. The pain of her past showed scars of a lost childhood. Now she was angry with me for what I had done to my children's lives; the wrongs I still couldn't right by not being there for my kids. Furthermore, Garlic had to prove to herself that she could do big things despite what she had been thru in life. I was slowly learning

84

what those things were, as we gifted each other trust. She had survived some of the worst of life on life's terms and she was deeply scarred from it. I was quietly paying attention and the flames of my own anger slowed to a simmer back in the moment.

Garlic was alluding to what the future could hold for my children if I didn't get my life together: Resentment and anger. The argument was, however...getting old. I was running out of patience and ammunition. Again, Garlic drew first, gunning for another round of arguments. But I had one last quip in the chamber, and I fired a headshot from the hip.

"You know, Music Man, I grew up poor...."

"Yeah?" I cut in, "then why does it feel like I'm the trailer park, and you're the tornado?"

She fell silent. We looked at each other stoically for a moment. Smiles crept over our faces and we both burst out in laughter. She slapped her knee and put a hand on her belly, her other hand on her hip. We caught our breath chuckling, having broken the feedback loop from hell.

"You're a pretty clever songbird," she said in her sassy-sweet Yankee twang. Just like that, it was over. Killed out with comedy. She kissed me and we started hiking again.

"Sorry, Bae."

"Me too. Now, what were you saying back there before the disaster was averted?" I asked with satisfied relief.

"Nothing. You stole the punchline."

I mumbled under my breath, "Apology accepted."

"Excuse me?"

Moral of the story: Two people can't drive one car.

So, <u>shut up</u>!

She was right about almost everything. The truth felt like a rusty dagger taking another twist. In the back of my mind, I knew that I was trying to uphold a reputation that I didn't deserve. All Garlic wanted for me, was really one wish for my children. The importance of my presence in their lives hiked in front of me on the Appalachian Trail. Garlic was testament to perseverance, but she was deeply scarred from the traumas of her past. She wanted nothing more for me, for my kids, than for us all to be together, and she knew it was critical for their futures. When she knew she had my undivided attention, she told me as much.

"You know, I think I love you, Music," she said at rest with a flushed face and heavy breathing. "But you have good kids waiting for their dad. So, if you think I am going to co-sign any bullshit for you, you've got it wrong, lover."

Garlic and I temporarily split up our partnership at times, hiking certain mountains alone. Or, for various reasons, going at our own natural paces for a day or two at a time. Physical health factors occasionally separated us, and sometimes we would need a break from the company to simply make our own way. But we were loyal to each other, and when the fires of passion were stoked, the moon and the sky became a blur.

Deeper into Virginia, I met a wonderful group of other Nobo hikers who were back on the AT after a brief hiatus around the Smokies. Their moniker was the "Fantastic Food Group," as Garlic affectionately liked to call them. The team was a loyal quartet of friends who had met on the trail. Day after day, they had hiked damn near every mountain together. Fantastic was a rugged red-headed big wall climber who thought he would try his chops at long distance trekking. Each of his calves were as big as the Keffer Oak and he relished any opportunity to strut his "meaty calves" as he liked to call them. We often shared a cherished call and response:

"Hey, Fantastic?" "Yes, Music Man?"

"What do we do every day?

"Why, Music Man, you know that! We climb mountains!"

"Yeah? Every day?"

"That's right...."

(In unison) "WE CLIMB MOUNTAINS EVERY DAY!" It was a positive uplift and made the day job feel as special as it was.

Chilly and Green Bean, a gorgeous young couple from New Jersey, were two of the strongest hikers I ever saw. Green Bean was a power hiker who could climb up a mountain faster than a yo-yo on the rebound, and Chilly (of grace) could carve downhill like a hot knife thru Vermont cheddar. They entertained and challenged themselves, each other, and other hiker in very creative ways.

And Blueberry, the heart and soul of the Nobo bubble, became my closest confidant and friend outside of Garlic. Being an Eagle Scout (though he admitted to failing the navigation component on his first couple tries), Blueberry knew about solid gear and quality food. He hiked with a youthful spirit that was gentle yet focused and regimented, reminding me of NTN (Uncle Ron). As a class, I observed that Eagle Scouts earned greater success on the AT than less experienced outdoors people. Still, navigation was a pesky issue for Blueberry, and we only occasionally had a little laugh about it. This one time at high camp, the rest of the Food Group and I watched from the comfort of a shelter as Blueberry marched past the blue-blazed trail, oblivious of the clear route to the shelter. His eyes were glued to his phone as he tried to let the navigation app bring him home. We saved him.

"Blueberry! Over here! Get that gut-hook out of your cheek and look at the views once in a while!" Everyone laughed as he spiked his way up to the shelter.

"Take me out, coach," he said as he slid onto the picnic bench with a cramp. God, I loved that guy. And he loved all things blueberry flavored. Muffins to gummy sharks to blueberry ales. His passion for what he loved reminded me of playing music with my friends. I missed that part of my former life.

In late April, Music Man was interviewed by a reporter from the New York Times via telephone from Wood's Hole Hostel in Virginia. It was regarding a piece for a series of articles covering the Appalachian Trail experience during COVID. The hostel's spiritual owner, Neville, came out to the bunk house with a phone to her ear and asked us "Does anybody want to talk to the Times?" I was more than happy to. She handed me the phone then whispered, "Family dinner from the wok followed by a gratitude meeting in thirty minutes." Blueberry snapped a picture of Music Man on the front porch of Wood's Hole that he sent to the reporter, and it ended up attached to the Times article. It featured quotes from thru-hikers still on the Appalachian Trail, even after the A.T.C. had demanded our retreat. Blueberry and Music Man took pride in co-contributing to the New York Times article, "How the Pandemic Splintered the Appalachian Trail." The title of the article wasn't great, but there was truth in it. The reporter tried to pin me down on a thru-hiker's opinion of how the A.T.C. handled thru-hiking season by rescinding our registrations as tagged and recognized hikers. When pressed, I didn't feel comfortable voicing opinions on behalf of anyone else so I told the reporter that I believed the A.T.C. must be an incredibly stressful office to work in as of late. I did not envy the tough position they were in at Harpers Ferry. Furthermore, it didn't matter if the AT's governing body recognized my thru-hike or not. (In fairness, the A.T.C. states that it is not a governing body.) I wasn't after a new plaque for a fictitious trophy wall. I just wanted the opportunity to continue the spiritual journey and I hoped a few words might inspire others to hike for healing, too. But hiker beware: You take you with you, wherever you go. Don't take your problems and dump them on the trail when they get too heavy. Someone else must step over it, or worse: pick it up and pack it out for you. "Leave No Trace." (But don't worry about picking up a feather or two for your cap.)

Around this time, another hiker took a keen interest in Garlic. I had felt the pangs of jealousy in my younger days, and I fell back on experience. And so, I thought I handled the new "hanger-on" well. I usually didn't get too rattled by the extra attention my partner received. Meeting new people every day on the trail makes for all kinds of interesting encounters. Garlic carried herself like an ancient soul and a modern goddess. She was invariably tactful at privately diffusing romantic interests from others with empathy. Never at the social expense of the so intrigued. This time was different. I told myself it wasn't her fault, that she had tried to dissuade him even in my presence, yet he was persistent as hell.

Frankly, it seemed disrespectful. The dude didn't give a shit about anything except for what he wanted. Again, I could relate to both sides. I let things go with faith in my woman. But it went too far. Half a day from Damascus, I was flustered with her and took some spacetime to myself. Like clockwork, Donatello appeared.

"What's up, Music Man!"

"Hey, D! How's the hike going? Man, I thought you were at least a few days of hiking behind me?" I queried how he had managed to catch up.

"Yeah, well, I had to make some adjustments," he replied.

It was an unnecessary and rehearsed answer that hid the truth: Donatello had yellow-blazed (hitched a ride) around the recent trail miles for any number of reasons. I suppressed my pink-blazing (tracking the trail's chicks) mentality and welcomed his company. After all, there we were. His presence felt like putting on boots that were well broken in, but I vowed to not be his familiar old fiddle again. We began the descent in Damascus together.

"Are you going to the Broken Fiddle?"

"What is it, fourteen bucks just to pitch a tent in the yard?" he wavered.

"Funds getting low, aye?"

"I just don't think I can swing it if I want to eat. My trip is in trouble, Music Man. No resources coming or going."

He didn't outright lie, at least not that I picked up on. He usually just went about his business in shifty silence. But I sensed that he was being forthright about this very serious issue. What did he have to lose? Donatello was out of money.

"Do you need a bet? A little bit of cash..."

"Naw, man...that's kind of you," he responded. "I can't accept...I won't hike on charity alone."

"It's not a gift, it's a loan." I pulled out a hundred-dollar bill I kept folded behind my driver's license for emergencies and handed it to him. "Go on, take it. We're going to have a good time this weekend. Just try and get a good food resupply out of this too. Drink cheap beer so you can eat for another week."

Donatello let out an embarrassed chuckle, then accepted the legal tender with gratitude. "Thank you, Music. This helps so much. I don't know what to say."

"You just said it, D. And I ain't worried about the payback."

The cash ponied up a fun-rest-stop at the hostel with a great group of hikers and financed a decent resupply. He bought a little flower, and I would smoke some too. I mentioned that Garlic was not far behind and would probably run us down before too long.

"Why ain't you hiking with her today?" Donatello asked.

"Oh, we don't stride mile-for-mile all the time." He suspected it was partially true and didn't press me for more.

It was refreshing to mosey along with his familiar sense of humor again. The skyline was getting gray as the trail dropped down from the mountain and into Towne Park. We ran into Potholder near the caboose. I spotted his guitar hanging off the back of his pack in typical fashion. We always had that in common. Those musical instruments stuck to us like ticks we couldn't reach.

"What's up, Senior!" I hollered.

"Fancy seeing y'all here this fine day." Potholder bellowed with a customary bass that came from the depth of his warm soul. I could hear his whispers from a hundred feet away. Potholder never used digital navigation even for one step: he stuck his thumb in the air and covered the sun to one eye, squinted, then thundered....

"We turn on Laurel Avenue up here, right Siri? You silly girl."

We passed under the wooden sign in Damascus Towne Park welcoming us. During a normal year, "Trail Town, USA," would usually be teeming with hikers in early May. Like so many other pandemic-ravaged communities in the Year of Tears, there would be no welcoming committee.

Damascus seemed like another ghost town. Our feet shuffled down Laurel Avenue, as the squad made its way toward the Broken Fiddle Hostel. We stepped into the only open shop, Mt. Rogers Outfitters, for a can of fuel and a hell of a good time with Lumpy. Eventually breaking down at the Broken Fiddle Hostel, I felt grateful that both places were open for us. The Fiddle wasn't officially open, but they let us in like back door men, so we would all be safe behind the fence. Pandemic protocols had scared nearly every town and hostel out of catering to thru-hikers. But by the time we hit Damascus, the loopholes were slowly opening. Diehard hiking locals were there to support us. We were disappointed to learn that Trail Days (the annual AT hiking festival held in Damascus each May) was effectively canceled. But it didn't surprise us. We almost welcomed the shutdowns and shut-outs. It just added to the adventure of attempting a thru-hike during that Year of our Lord, 2020. Growing more and more attuned to the trail community, our hearts went out to the locals. The vendors and businesses that relied on hikers as a significant source of their annual income, if not the majority or all of it, were getting squeezed. The coronavirus, himself, had come calling from cell door to cell door, raking his empty cup across the bars and demanding: "I'm gonna need better than half of your cookies, Ese." But the trail corridor stayed ever vigilant. "No cookies for you!"

Support for me was echoing from home. Uncle Ron (NTN) and Aunt Janet became strong proponents of the hike, knowing full-well the peace and serenity that can be found in nature. NTN completed a Nobo of the AT in 2005, around age 50. Back then, the age of nifty navigation apps had not yet dawned. NTN hiked the old-fashioned way carrying paper maps and a compass, supported by Janet's mail drops of food. Janet taught my mother how to dehydrate meals and passed along a terrific recipe for trail granola. GORP had come a long way from "good ole raisins and peanuts." Chocolate chips and cardamom...nature's drugs of the finest intents. Mom became an expert at dehydrating food. I told her she should start a small business with those recipes. As a wise retiree of the Postal Service, she was a master at getting a box to the right post office at the right town ahead of schedule. If the timing was off just a little, which only happened a time or two, she would call that post office in the middle of Appalachia and have it forwarded on to the next reasonable post office along the trail corridor. All the while talking shop with the local civil service heroes who tried like hell to carry out their sworn duties during the pandemic. "Hold For Thru-Hiker: Music Man" packages moved like AC/DC current along the trail corridor, especially Virginia into Maryland.

Dad put his expertise with numbers and data crunching to use by making projections on my progress. He tracked changes in my pace, making stunningly accurate guesses as to my whereabouts, like he was handicapping horses. We all hoped and prayed that, with time, the mount would bring home a winning ride. The odds were against me, but there was a team effort behind my hike. I had a huge foundation of support that blossomed into a proper hiking infrastructure chaired by my brother back home, logistics ran the rents, and the walking executed by me on the AT. Bro's contributions were more spiritual than anything. If I needed a positive uplift or motivation to keep going, he always knew just what to say. "Don't Fucking Quit" was his send-off every time. Even if I would crawl on bloody stumps, I must keep going. On a certain phone call with him, I complained of the rugged days ahead.
He wisely exclaimed:

"Twin brother, when you are on that brutal climb in the sweltering heat or sloshing thru the pouring rain; hungry and thirsty; your legs are seizing up and your lungs are burning down; and you ask yourself in doubt, 'What is it all for? Why am I even doing this?' When you waver and entertain thoughts of not— Remember this: Everyone who loves and supports you wishes we were out there, too. We sit at a desk or workstation or at home sequestered from the pandemic world. I am looking out a window to the distant mountaintops on which you dwell, Brah. Know that I would give anything to be schlepping up that mountain with you right now. Don't take this opportunity for granted; a person who doesn't get better only gets bitter. So Don't Fucking Quit."

I tried like the dickens to stay present and connected to myself and keep aware of the needs of others. My trekking poles were constantly clearing twigs off the trail, as my brother had taught me. "Be a good steward of the outdoors," Bro would remind me, and Boomerang would often remind hikers all on the trail.

A few hours after my arrival to the Broken Fiddle, Garlic hobbled in on a terrible limp. "Plantar fasciitis," she finally conceded. I knew she had been struggling with her feet as of late, but she was tough as nails and pain-complaining was never her style. Garlic was the strongest hiker I knew, and I loved to watch her go. I admired her. Walking behind her mile after mile on most days, I got to observe her technique in detail. She taught me how to hike a downhill climb efficiently, instructing me "Don't just slam your feet down. Walk like the Pink Panther when you're descending. Most all movement should happen from the waist down, and you just glide with soft footfalls. It lowers the impact on your joints. Envision a Native bow-hunter crossing a frozen stream." The moccasin-wearing style of hiking we termed "glidding." "Oh, this downhill coming up is gonna be a glid," we'd joke.

Garlic was really hurting when she got to the Broken Fiddle, and it had me worried. "Can I get you some ice, babe?" I wanted to somehow help.

"You're sweet, Music. But no thanks."

"Want me to rub your feet?"

"I said I *don't* fucking need anything!" She snapped, likely feeling smothered. In a mild shock from the foot pain, Garlic had commenced to self-medicate with red wine. Well, so had I. As the night slugged on, she was paying more attention to the other dude, and I got pissed. After he got in my face, I put my opinion of his thru-hiking style on blast for anyone listening, which embarrassed the hell out of both of us. I had a beer in my hand and a half a jar of corn whiskey in my head. Buzzed and surly and having forgotten everything I knew about the terrible feeling of jealousy; I just couldn't act like a gentleman for the life of me. Regret then poured over and I wanted to disappear but there was no place to hide. It was 12:30 am when I donned my pack and burst out the front door heading for the trail. Donatello followed me along the sidewalk of uptown Laurel Avenue and tried to talk me out of leaving town.

"Music, this ain't a good idea. You've had a few drinks, we've all had a few. Don't worry about that other dude. It's her you gotta watch out for." But he backed off that topic quickly. His goal was not to ream her, but to retain me. He was holding firm to genuineness. "Friend, the weather is gonna get bad. It feels like a nasty storm is in the air, eh? You're usually a lock for feeling the weather. You know a storm's brewing." (I could feel it coming in the air that night, too.) Music Man, are you sure you want to hike right now?"

"I'm sure, D. I can't go back now. Everything is screwed up. I'm off track and I need to get myself together. I'm gonna make a push toward Mount Rogers."

"Is this the trail?" We walked me down to the end of Laurel

Avenue. "I'll see you soon, Donatello. I know it's cold and rainy, but I need to walk this off."

I hit the gravel trail and started hiking. The cold air began to close in on my bones and I already regretted leaving the hostel, but it was too late. I was committed. As we parted ways, Donatello watched me from the sidewalk shaking his head as I slipped out of view.

My first stop was the back porch of a vacant rental house along the river. I tried to sleep for an hour but was unable to settle. Around 2 am, I got moving again. What was wrong with Garlic? The plantar fasciitis in her feet was progressing and it was stressful for her. Still, I couldn't decode our seemingly spotty ability to stay on the same page. All the aspects of my trail philoSophy were suffering. Though I couldn't see it, my "self-seeking" dial had been stuck on 11. Set and forget.

"Damn, it's cold out here tonight." The moonshine had begun to wear off and I was in a new struggle to stay warm. My head began spinning in all directions and none of it made any sense. By the time the sun came up, I was having doubts as to my whereabouts. I had not seen a white blaze on the trail all night. I had not even thought to look. Where the hell was I? The trail was wide and rutted as the veiled sunrise began to light up the surroundings. I could see storm clouds bearing down on me. This wasn't right. This is not what the Appalachian Trail feels like. Something was off. I crossed a bridge and approached an information board.

"WELCOME TO THE...VIRGINIA CREEPER TRAIL? YOU CANNOT BE SERIOUS!" as John McEnroe would infamously coin. This was a nightmare. Where was a map on this bloody corkboard? Where am I? I found a red "YOU ARE HERE" arrow in horror, deducing that I had walked ten miles due west on the Virginia Creeper Trail from Damascus, on the wrong trail and in the wrong direction.

10 miles?! "Dang and blast," as Donatello would say. But he would never say he told me so. I wished I had listened to him last night. A huge rain drop hit my cheek as my eyes followed movements up the trail. It was the man in the white suit, and he had a highball in his hand. His other hand signaled me in the direction of the valley further up trail.

"Uncle Jake?"

Another raindrop fell, then another, and another...the sky tore open and unleashed a pressure-purge of rain and noise.

Crack! BOOM Ba-boom-boom! ... Lightning split the air from low hanging storm clouds. VCT board maps indicated it was a ten-mile-get-back to Damascus if I turned around, or four miles and a dime to Abingdon if I kept moving forward. The intervention of my survival instincts forced me onwards as I continued to soak up freezing rain. Sheets of wind and water kept coming harder as the lightning was crashing all around, hitting the ground occasionally. Trail conditions: dark and dangerous. To make matters worse, I found myself crossing a tall bridge with a creaky metal suspension, far above the raging river below. The Old Uncle Jake I had never met, was gone when I passed the spot where I thought he would be.

Boom! The lighting pounced; Again, a white suit flashed on the other side, but how? Uncle Jake had died over a century ago with a drink in his hand.

A rolling black cloud began to envelope the bridge from all sides. The masochistic steel girders glistened with sweaty rain, begging for another whip from a lightning bolt. "No...No...*NO!*" I took the first steps of a sprint, then a flash of atomic white light stuns me with a *"POW!"*

The human body and mind are capable of amazing things, both heroic and tragic. Sometimes the brain says "Stop, we cannot go on" when the body is capable of enduring more. Conversely, the mind will want to go on with every ounce of self-propulsion, but the injured body just won't respond to its pleas.

Unlike the body and the mind, a spiritual bottom out can force so-stricken souls to the edge of a plunge pool. Then looking down, the delusion that a sudden leap is the right solution solidifies. That final way out becomes paramount to those whose grief and despair are so deep, they are seduced by quick and permanent freedom from the bondage of constant and intolerable suffering. Sadly, such states are reached by many every single day, driving some to the doors of treatment centers and asylums the world over. Even less fortunate sufferers hit that point in urban jungles with no chance of rescue.

Consequences may come in the form of court systems, health problems, estrangement, abandonment, or all the above. That's if we don't somehow die from it first. The so-afflicted tell stories of peaceful relief that washes over them when they see the blues and reds of police cruisers light up behind them to pull them over, knowing that the chase is over for now. We can finally get some rest while in jail and find respite from the streets. We don't have to keep spiraling in the deficit cycle of active addiction...for now. Sometimes these institutional interventions can provide just the moment of clarity needed to plant the seeds of change. "I really don't have to do this anymore, if I can make a simple yet difficult choice." Addiction is the only disease that tells the sufferer, "You don't have it." The addict-run mind is so cunning that it uses my own pride and ego to convince me that my condition is caused by anything but the actual state itself. Granted, there are a myriad of emotional conditions that can exacerbate drug abuse. But here, I am specifically referring to "addiction" as a disease of mental illness.

(The Centers for Disease Control define a dis-ease as an illness that is "chronic, progressive and fatal.") After the hopeless admission is made that "Yeah, I got this thing after all," it's usually not enough to effect change. Eventually, I reach a fully savage state of mind where I can't live with it, and I can't live without it. At his point, there is only one impetus for change: consequences. Most effective consequence: the drugs stop working. This requires me to fall thru a trap door hidden in the most recent pit of despair, finding myself in even deeper trouble. Then I try and fail again, and again, but still manage to survive because, well, I don't know.... but "here I am!" Soon enough, I'll hit the "fuck it" button again. I am outmatched and overwhelmed. If overdose or the street life doesn't take me out first, eventually I find myself at the edge of that plunge pool, holding the rail of that sweaty bridge. I am rotating an hourglass with the other hand, but I turn and hold it horizontally to watch the sand settle in the ampules, stopping time. The contorted reflection of my face in the hourglass brought back a memory: I once questioned the dirt under my feet for water under the bridge...my final attempt at self-consolation: "They'll be better off without me."

After dropping and breaking the sandy clock, I hold my nose and my balls; for my fears of physical pain are still there. Addicts fear pain, any pain, even if the coming pain signifies the end of the Great Pain, forever. Alas, I hope for the best and I wish for the worst. Suddenly, I leap. My weight is lifted as I'm falling faster and faster... Then it dawns on me halfway down that help is what I really wanted, that I love my children, I love my family and my friends, I want them to love me, to have me around, I want them to be happy...I want to be happy...like it was before...I want to help others...I want to live! I'M SORRY!!!>>>>>

SMACK!

We hit the water. We black out....

It's quiet and cool with echoes of big reverb; like a dimly lit corn silo with singing dolphins. Fractals of sun rays are pulsing from the surface of the water above. I float in front of you, unfurled. Looking into your eyes, I reach to fix your hair, but you turn toward the flutters of light from above. I leave you and rise toward the light, needing oxygen. Some of us are filled with the breath of life as we resurface and look up at the bridge, then gaze back thru the depths below.... searching. Some of us see doctors and families and cops when we wake up in hospital after lifesaving drips of Narcan during an overdose, finding that we're handcuffed to the hospital bed. Or we taste the cold metal of a .45 that just misfired. We drop the gun and cry with our head in our hands. For better or worse, we weep at another chance to live. What about the other half that didn't resurface on the river with the breath of life? Where was *their* second chance that they prayed for halfway down?

A wise man once asked me a question:
"What's worse than dying of untreated addiction?"
"I can't imagine... What?"
"Living with it."

****

Stunned from the lighting strike on the suspension bridge, I started to refocus on the pieces of my sanity, piled on the far side from where I stood. The bolt had splintered around the girders, but I wasn't hit. I took off running across the bridge and reached the other side safely. I then dropped my pack in an open patch of the muddy forest service road. Rain and tears fell to the ground. I was desperately grateful to have survived the shady alleys and highways of the past few years. Walking the stormy bridge summoned a feeling that resembled the dice game of active addiction, twenty-four hours a day. How I hadn't been struck dead was beyond my comprehension. Something beyond my own efforts had delivered me from the storms and I had no choice but to keep trudging. The microburst storm cloud lifted back to the grayed sky.

Approaching the town of Abingdon that fuzzy day in early May, a motel facade appeared from half a mile across a soupy farm field. I threw my pack over a rusty barbed-wire fence, maneuvered my wrecked body across the razor wires, then schwopped thru the unplanted field of ankle-deep mud. I tossed my ruined hiking boots into the dumpster behind the motel and got myself a room. It was high noon. I stripped my clothes off, crawled into bed and slept until the next morning. Music Man was alone; a creep in Virginia....and far from the Appalachian Trail.

.8

THAT SNOWY DAY BEFORE THE DERBY, when my wife told me to pack my bags, something within my psyche shifted from neutral coasting into a lethal overdrive. A so-called expert later told me that I had experienced a short-term post-traumatic stress disorder. It sounded fair enough at the time. I didn't have the ability to diagnose myself with anything, other than a broken heart. What did I know? Despite the tumult that my inner demons caused me, I had been holding on to the delusion of successfully managing my life, and how I presented it to the outside world. When that false perception of reality started to smell of worn-out brake pads, my broken brain overdrove and jammed cruise control to the speed of sound, with no chance of stopping on my own. I raced off the deep end without a clue or a care. The run was horrendous and there was simply not enough dope around to keep me going or keep me still. Worm-holing from one extreme to the next, I bounced off my city's parklands, stairwells, car bumpers, side doors and floodwalls like a pinball. I experienced frequent states of drug-induced psychosis, whereas I could still carry on the very basic functions of physically existing, whilst tossing any mental or spiritual maintenance tools out the truck window. My last run in the madness went unchecked far beyond what should have been my expiration date. There's no rational explanation for what happened. It took a sober mind for many months before my head started to finally come out of the fog. Then, I was a survivor but not a victim.

When I finally reached that first summit of clarity, the view of the cold and barren wasteland that my life had become slowly emerged from under the cloud cover. Still, my PTSD was working its will in weird ways. My memory banks were opened in little bits at a time. When the door was slightly ajar, new light shone on the destruction I had left in my wake. My engines had in-taken a perfectly good atmosphere and churned it up into toxic chem-trails that streamed for miles. While the fuselage containing my life became a turbulent place to raise children, all I observed from the cockpit were clear skies and clean wind. The consequences of global warming are a tall-tale from forty-thousand feet. (The Lorax sighs)

I am no expert when it comes to physics or cosmology. So, forgive me if I meddle in the affairs of wizards. But here goes my interpretation.... Current scientific evidence suggests that life, at a molecular level, results from organizations of matter and energy in a fine-tuned environment conducive to active chemistry. Mother Nature is faithfully executing her destiny of processes that continually reshape and retool physical reality via that symbiotic relationship between matter and energy. The constant exchange between the two states is nature's way of fighting its own eventual disorder thru an atomic aging process called "entropy". The only thing that separates me from the rest of the Universe is my uniquely human ability to discover and contemplate these scientific facts. Thus, I believe my consciousness is simply the inevitable manifestation of the Universe trying to understand itself. "Who I am" is not simply a decision I make; it's a cosmic reality left for me to embody. "Identity" is nearly a moot point if I'm dying. To survive a self-imposed and wholly unnatural slow-suicide via torching my temple with dope... This calls for swift action— if ready.

In a psycho-social sense, "who I am" is represented by my response to circumstances placed before me. My reputation is based on my responses to life on life's terms. For what it is worth, repetition makes a reputation. Spiritual in principle and simple by design: A way of living modeled after the balance of nature will redirect my collision courses with other people. This includes taking stock of how I treat others. If I take an honest look at it, I am reminded that my ego is the source and center of every problem I have in my life, and every resentment my conscious harbors. For so long, I thought that drugging was just my way to cope with the world around me. It was how I coped with what was going on inside of me. Healthy behaviors will lead to healthy thinking, and not the other way around. Certainly, I will have conflict in my life, just as the Milky Way will inevitably collide with the Andromeda galaxy. But how I take the hit makes all the difference in my recovery. If I don't get up to trudge some more, then it's another moot point.

To "trudge" is to walk with purpose. For me, to simply be present with my being on a nature trail away from Urbania fits the bill. I was inspired by Forrest Gump's response to being questioned about why he crisscrossed the country on foot. "[He] just felt like running." You don't have to be smart, reader, to know how it feels when lost love leaves a hole in your life force. Call it what you want: PTSD, depression, or simply a broken heart. Entropic cosmic conditions are prone to perpetuating psychosomatic changes without my permission. Duh!! So how does this relate to being physically and emotionally present for my children? To get there, I must be the most authentic me I can be, for the betterment of us all. The less conflict I create, the less I'm compelled to escape.

So, who am I? I won't give you another psychiatric textbook answer that I would only be lying about anyway. I'm just another bloke trying to make my way in a dogmatic world that tells me I must play by its rules, or else. Hiking the Appalachian Trail began to infuse new ideas of what it truly meant to be alive and human...to be free. I began to realize that a balance between the spiritual, social, and physical aspects of my life mitigates stress, promotes health, and leads to simple joys. I just want to be happy. How can I lead a life of balance? A new philoSophy for life just might place me in a position to be of service to others. Like helping a stranger with a cup of coffee, teaching my son how to hit a golf ball, or holding my daughter's head on my shoulder when the tough lessons of the first heartbreak will make her want to "Run, Forrest, Run!" If these were things that I truly valued, then it was time to start acting like it. Most of us will reach a moment at some point in our lives when "trudging" seems like a good option. New behaviors turn into new thinking, eh? Why didn't I think of that?

Nowadays, in rare cases like the hiker in Delhi's story, if someone claims that they ended up at the same point where they started all those thousands of miles ago, I suggest they turn around and try it again. So, am I capable of taking my own advice, or is that very idea wise? I digress... Mark Twain famously said, "I'm only human. And I regret it."

****

Music Man woke up in the motel in Abingdon, Virginia, fourteen miles off trail, without any hiking boots, or much in the way of inspiration. He was close to calling it quits when a call to his brother got his attention. Bro told me what he always did, Don't Fucking Quit. Holding the receiver, I looked in the mirror and told myself I would do what he suggested. I reset the dial tone and keyed another Kentucky area code to an old friend and local shop owner:

(*Ring...*) "This is Ryan."

"Hey Ryan, this is Music Man."

"Whoa! Music Man! God, it's great to hear from you! How's the trail going?"

"Well, fits and starts. But I sure am grateful to you and the support crew at Quest. Opening the outfitter for Bro...to get a new backpack for me, Ryan...I just can't thank you enough."

"Say no more, Music Man. I know you are grateful. A thru-hike is forever life-changing, no matter how far you go. Frankly, this whole world could use a touch of the healing that your hike has the potential to provide you. You're not alone. You're not just walking for you, but you are walking for all of us. And we are there with you. March to your drum, Music Man, because it's keeping time for so many more people back home too. If you need anything at all, we're here to help. Whether the store's doors are open or not, we are always available to you and your family. Don't quit, my friend."

"Thank you, Ryan. Today, we ride."

After the dose of homespun medicine for the spirit, I put my big-boy pants on and packed my sack for the trail. Before I left the room, I made one last call out from the motel phone. Garlic didn't answer, but I left a voice message with "I am sorry for how I have been acting." I hung up the phone and donned my pack. As I opened the door to leave, the room's phone rang. I listened to it ring again, watching the phone's red bulb blink like a turn signal. With a sigh, I turned and walked out the door.

In lieu of boots, Crocs would have to get the job done for the foreseeable future. As I walked past the motel lobby, dreading the muddy march back to Damascus, a miracle happened. The all-night hospitality girl working the motel desk was just getting off work and agreed to give me a ride back to Damascus on her way home. It was Sunday morning and Mt. Rogers Outfitters was closed when she dropped me off on Laurel Avenue. No new boots for the Music Man. I waved thank you and headed for the trailhead, trying my luck with finding the right track one more time. In the daylight, I could see where I had gone wrong late Friday night when I missed the white blazes. The experience had humbled me; the humiliation giving way to some much-needed humility over the weekend.

"It's this way, Nincompoop," I cursed myself.

John McEnroe also said, "You can't change your destination overnight, but you can change your direction immediately." I was ready to put my trail philoSophy back in play after a hard stop but no reboot. The trail would dictate so I decided to stop forcing things. Circumstances only got worse when I tried to fix, manage, and control everything around me. It was going to be different now and it was time to get focused on hiking. Maybe traveling alone again would procure new discoveries. I struck out for Mount Rogers, still with rubber Crocs on my feet. It was approaching high noon. Thirty miles in the right direction from town and I would be on the summit before I quit for the day. Sports goal: Check.

Everyone else had left the hostel earlier that morning, so I suspected I would catch somebody I knew by the end of the day. It was a fine time to get the hike on track if the journey had a chance to survive the spring.

The bucolic Jefferson National Forest inspired me to hike in blissful contemplation. Mist and sunshine evoked an early morning feeling well into the afternoon, as the forest's doors of timber often swung open to surprise views of deep gorges and distant ridges. The Crocs were gliding on the cold track. Even though it was veined with exposed tree roots, the surface of the trail was well trammeled and easy to pass. Later that evening, I arrived at Lost Mountain Shelter where it appeared that most of the Tramily had stopped for the night. Hikers were bundled up in their tents trying to stay warm. It was bitter cold out and roughly ten miles separated me from my goal. "It's around 7:30, still some daylight...I can do it." I was gung-ho for the summit of Mount Rogers, and I wanted a "thirty-miler" notch in my belt. Plus, I needed to continue hiking alone for a while. Social goal: Check. After about ten paces toward the next bend, I found two small owls nestled together in the middle of the trail. My headlamp caught their eyes which reflected the beam of light back like a mirror. It was blinding but beautiful. I remembered what Garlic had sweetly said one evening, after hearing the hoots of a distant owl: "I hope she finds what she is looking for." Spiritual goal: Check.

I hiked nearly without stopping, all day and night. It was after three o'clock in the morning when I finally reached Mount Rogers by completing the single longest day of hours and miles on my journey. 29.8 miles of mountainous roam in 15.25 hours, to be exact. Not a record time or a full thirty clicks on the white blazes, but it's a "thirty-miler" in my book. (The purists won't agree, but again, it is my book.) In the loft of Thomas Knob Shelter, I hardly slept because of the cold. Early the next morning, I was heading down the mountain into the Grayson Highlands. The sky had cleared to cool sunshine when I traversed the amazing park where the wild ponies roam. Wildflower meadows and babbling brooks entreat the trail and inspired the imagination. That night found me in high spirits. It was the first and most brilliant of the year's full blood moons. Like a tangerine held at arm's length, the spectacular sphere rose over the ridge and washed the earth with a soft glow. I convinced myself that I could feel the moon's gravity in my core. As I raised my tent, the pole snapped and tore a mortal hole in the ceiling. The Black Diamond tent had been my "old faithful" for many moons since the John Muir Trail with Bro back in 2007. The tent and I had been thru much together over the years. But it was time to let go of the trusted old single-wall Black Diamond.

First shoeless and now homeless again, I laughed out loud. With a sober mind my resolve was stronger with each conquered obstacle. I would not quit, no matter what the trail had in store for me. If I had to hop on bloody stumps and sleep under sap storms, I would keep pushing forward. Not a single blister had dared to form on my feet, thanks to all my homeless schlepping of the streets before the hike. It was "all systems go" and my spirit was rejuvenated. But I would need a major resupply soon. Food and gear items were back on the goods list; services to be determined.

Trekkers often grumble about catching a case of the "Virginia blues" while thru-hiking, due to the sheer number of miles in one state. Roughly a quarter of the Appalachian Trail's entire distance lies in the great Commonwealth of Virginia, which contains around five hundred and eighty AT miles. Without the morale boost that accompanies crossing a state line, it is true that at times you can feel like you are slowly going nowhere. But my hiking experience in the state, named after the Virgin Queen, was far from depressing.

The Appalachian Trail is a masterpiece of wilderness construction, especially in Virginia. The outdoor aisle traverses some of the most beautiful, technical, and historical mountains and valleys along the trail's corridor. Clubsters and maintenance volunteers skillfully carved the trail features in difficult terrain; constructing tight switchbacks and solid bog bridges; clearing dead falls; building stairs with boulders; erecting and updating shelters and trailheads; and keeping a fresh coat of carefully mixed white paint on tree blazes the year round. The volunteers of all the trail clubs along the Appalachian Trail corridor carry out this vital work and Virginia's trail clubs are second to none. Organizations like the A.T.C and ALDHA have contributed much in the way of resources, expertise, and labor towards the existence of well-engineered structures, as well as promoting hiker health and good trail stewardship. Not easy tasks, with as popular and crowded as the trail has become. Hiker access and diversity are growing steadily.

Fixing to shred the Triple Crown, I entered the dragon country feeling healthy and confident. The first of the three features, Dragon's Tooth, is a titanic rock formation in the shape of a giant serpent's tooth. The north side of the mountain is one of the most technical descents on the entire AT for a Nobo. Driving rain and lightning added to the challenge of scaling down the rebar ladders and slick boulder walls. After the recent experience of bad weather that I had endured on the Virginia Creeper Trail, I was enjoying a confident control of my nerves. I strolled into the Four Pines Hostel soaked to the bone but euphoric after the climb. The Fantastic Food group: Blueberry, Fantastic, Chilly and Green Bean, were there along with other friends from the bubble. Garlic hobbled in on her tortured feet a few hours later, but she didn't complain.

Things had been icy between us since Damascus, but she cornered me at the hostel bunks ready to break her silence.

"Hey." She said, as she crossed her arms.

"Hi. How was your climb off the cliff?" I fluffed my pillow.

"Slick."

"Tough conditions up there today. Especially on the ladders in the rain."

"Why didn't you call me back, Music? You know, after you left me that pitiful voicemail back in Damascus, or Abingdon...wherever the hell you were."

"I don't have a phone, Garlic. Besides, I thought you were tired of me. I didn't want you to feel smothered."

"I don't need your help with my feelings. It's hard enough just me to manage, ok? Anyway, I tried to call you back at your motel, Music, like thirty seconds later."

"Oh. I'm sorry I missed it. I just assumed you were..." I was interrupted from across the room.

"Music Man! The New York Times article got published!"

I turned toward Blueberry's voice from the common area, then back to Garlic. The corner of her mouth turned to scorn as she huffed again.

"Your adoring fans request your presence at the piano." She sneered, then walked away.

I was once again oblivious to a teachable moment she was offering. The unwilling student was distracted by the dopey lights and sugary sounds; I was that dude getting wound up like a mini-accordion-monkey-cymbal-circus-music toy; I wasn't in the mood for humble pie. Someone got the attention of the hostel occupants and read the Times article aloud to the hikers gathered around.

"We are on a spiritual journey," he read my quotes "...we're not trying to violate federal law in the National Parks...."

"We sure as hell were!" Donatello added, fueling a few hoots and hollers. I added extra after the read-all-about-it moment:

"This is an epic year to be on the AT! I'm not hiking for a plaque on the wall," I scanned the room, "We make this extraordinary journey together as creatures of the wilderness." I found Garlic's face. She looked away as I raised a glass in toast to the house full of hikers:

"Cheers to Nobo 2020!"

"Cheers!" returned the Tramily of Nobo and section hikers gathered at Four Pines. Then I did my best to strap my ego back down where it belonged. When I stepped out for a smoke, I was startled to catch Donatello with his hand wrist-deep in a tip jar on the windowsill that read "Four Pines Tips." I pretended not to see.

Blueberry and I planned to strike out early in the morning for McAfee Knob, the second leg of the Triple Crown. Then we sat up until midnight chatting in twos and threes in the dark. I played a few songs on the Strumstick, then we listened to a section-hiker sing traditional Russian folk songs with her father. After a night of socializing and restful sleep, Blueberry woke me up before dawn and we hit the trail. I remember feeling embarrassed by my ego.

Our climb together was contemplative and serene. Blueberry talked about his home in Pennsylvania and how the Scouts Camp he managed was struggling in his absence. Boy Scouts had shut down for the year, but there was much to do to keep the grounds going. He felt like he was failing in his duties as a Scout Master, but he was beating himself up too much. He reflected upon his family and his lost love with tenderness and regret. We noticed the musk of a copperhead snake on the trail, like the smell of fresh cut cucumbers, but we never saw it. I told him I had caught Donatello with his hand in the hostel's tip jar the night before. I knew I was opening the casket in the social grave that Donatello had dug for himself. At the time, I believed I was doing the right thing. Still, it haunted me. I wouldn't see Donatello again for a long time and it would be in the most unlikely of places.

Blueberry and I were the first to arrive at McAfee Knob that morning and we enjoyed perfect weather at the iconic outlook, the most photographed location on the Appalachian Trail. The Blue-Ridge mountain cirque guarded the great valley on all sides for dozens of square miles. Fantastic and Boomerang joined us on the ledge. We peered down at the final jewel of the Triple Crown, miles below us to the north, Tinker Cliffs. We would be there in a matter of hours. It was a "Marion Day" as my father would often label afternoons of perfect weather, referring to the Cape Cod town of his summer getaways as a kid. He would relish time spent with Cousin Norman at Horseneck Beach, Buzzards Bay, while Pris would take the ferry from Woods Hole Marine to Martha's Vineyard for her summer nanny job. I was raised in the same way, enjoying the blessings of a family in privileged financial standing. Garlic was right: I was spoiled. Far from my mind was my family's cemetery in the heart of Kentucky, where I would stand over the grave of my great-great-grandfather in disbelief. Beyond the grave marker rose the view of the house on the hill. (By divine intervention, I would muster the courage to walk inside and surrender my freedom for a year.) But amid the AT's Triple Crown of hiking in 2020, I thought about my current versions of Woods Hole. Summer of 2020, it was Neville's special hostel in Pearisburg, Virginia, where the Times finally caught up with the Trail. I pondered the socioeconomic opposites of Cape Cod versus coal mine country, but I didn't consider their commonalities: a high rate of alcoholism and addiction.

The pandemic had not splintered the hiking community. Ironically, it had brought us closer together on the trail, even if a spattering of trail towns chose to reel. I had observed our trekking society to be well-unified. It consisted of people who were doing what they do best: hiking their own hikes and supporting each other all the while. By May, the trailheads were starting to reopen.

"What do we do every day, Fantastic?"

"You know that Music Man. We climb mountains every day."

"That's right, Fantastic, amongst other things."

"Every day," he said while looking on over the valley with a distant, far away sigh.

In the silence that followed, I had revelation, then I voiced it: "I think I have figured out what 'GOD' means to me." Blueberry and Fantastic looked at me sideways, as I offered: "Great Out Doors."

.9

WAKING UP FEELING STRONG AND MOTIVATED became a daily occurrence and the trail offered surprises at nearly every turn. I often walked with Blueberry and the rest of the Fantastic Food Group. It made me feel good when I could keep pace with the twenty-somethings. But I planned my own days and hiked many miles alone, pacing like a metronome but for quiet contemplation.

Strange feelings were starting to wash over me in the woods. Stopping to touch trees also became routine and my connection to the wildlife deepened. Carbon atoms in the trees were the same as those in my own body's structure. I didn't mind the oak tannins that tainted drinking water a ritzy bronze color, even after purification. Ingesting the tree was ok with me. I periodically connected with The Great Spirit who was ever present. I am nature, I discovered. Nature is me. My consciousness simply gives me an opportunity to recognize my nature. Self-awareness, as a human being, is the conduit for the Universe to be aware of itself. Existence trying to make sense of its very own nature: the affairs of nitrogen and carbon... Hydrogen and oxygen...Water. The blood of life.

****

A dear friend from the rooms of recovery once told me a story. We'll call him Freddy. First, we spoke on the reality of death and what it meant to us. Specifically, we shared our ideas on what might happen to our consciousness, or "soul" if you prefer, after we die. Near death experiences (NDE) have been reported for as long as humans have been able to communicate. Explanations abound on both the spiritual and scientific sides of the debate. I was profoundly moved by the story he told me. He recounted his experience in a dream and it was fascinating. But let Freddy tell you in his Guatemalan gangster accent:

"The dream went like 'dis.... Me and Dude were at this housing project, right, and we's about to knock on da door of a street rival called Punk. I was just there to cover his back, ya know, in case some shit went down. Turns out, Dude's woman was in there with Punk. Don't ask me how we knew she was there, it was a dream, you feel me? I waited near the corner of the building while Dude knocked on the door. All of a sudden, we hear Punk yell to us from behind the door:

"You think I'm stupid, G? I know you got pistols out there!"

"Naw, we don't Punk, come on, open da door homie," Dude lied, with his ear on the door listening for stirs inside.

"You got me fucked up, G! Ain't no way!" Punk yelled back thru the door. I could hear him from where I stood a few yards away. I knew he was about to come out that door firing his own pistol.

"Just open the door," came a girl's voice from inside.

"Shut up! I'm about to show these gamberros!" I heard the lock unlatch.

"Dude, Run!" I yelled at him, but it was too late. As soon as we turned to run, Punk swung open the door and started firing shots. "Run, Dude!" We were running in slow motion trying to get back to our car.

"Ah! I'm hit!" I hear him scream out as we're tryin' to run. I turn around and see him hobbling on one leg. He blindly pointed his pistol behind him and fired a shot back as he tried to get away. Punk took another shot at us, and I felt it whiz past my head.

"Move out, Dude! Run!"

"I'm running as fast as I can, Freddy!"

We finally jumped in the car and sped away. I'm driving and Dude be holding his bleeding leg. His artery was hit. He was bleeding out fast, O.G., and turning white. We had to cross the bridge and get back over state lines, ya know. I had warrants and faced deportation if I got hemmed up on any bullshit. That would have been the best I could have hoped for. Probably prison, though, for real. The sirens started as soon as the shooting stopped. I could see the cops gaining on us as we were crossing the bridge.

"Step on it, Freddy!" Punk urgently beat on the dash of the car while looking back at the flashing cruisers. A stream of blood shot out his leg. Man, I was so relieved when we got to the other side. I peeped at the rearview mirror and saw the cops slamming on their brakes and turning up smoke from their tires as they let us go. I was like 'Wha? They're just gonna let us go?' I took the first exit. The sign said "CITY AT LARGE" under the arrow. We were flying down the ramp, homie, and when the turn got too sharp, I started to lose control of the car.

"Slow down, G!"

"Shut up and belt that leg, D.... Oh shit, man...what's that?!"

The ramp just ended, no barricade or nothing. I slammed the brakes then pumped the pedal as the tires cried out in a cloud of burning smoke and rubber, but it was too late. Silence fell, as we dropped off into a black abyss. We flew off that mothafucker like Thelma and Louise! "Whoaaaaa!" As the car tipped forward, all I could think about was my face smashing thru the engine under the hood. Then, I swear to it, we landed in a room. Black walls, no car, just me and Dude. It was quiet, but the room started to fill with a faint glow of yellowish-orange light. We were just standing there, and the room started to light up like oil lamps were fading in. On the walls hung photographs in frames. They were moving pictures of scenes, like out of a Harry Potter movie, or sumptin'. I didn't recognize any of the people or places, though.

"Freddy, these are my people," Dude said as he walked over to the wall in amazement. "There's my brother and sister, and there's my Papa. There's my auntie, too! Look at that one, Yo! That's my daughter!" He pointed at another frame across the glowing room of a beautiful little girl laughing in her father's arms.
I began to get upset. I didn't see any of my people.

"Freddy, these are my memories," Dude went on, "I think we're dead, homie."

I wanted to lose my head, man, but I just kept trying to make sense of it. If we were dead, then where were my people, where were my memories? Why was Dude getting his and I'm not getting mine? I tried to dig up my own memories and put pictures in those frames, but they just wouldn't come. I couldn't get nuthin' to come up on them walls. I started choking up, and Dude's voice started fading. I wanted to see the picture book of my own life, but now I couldn't even dig up the memories. I knew I had them, I knew I had people that loved me. But the memories were fading, and I was losing myself man. I couldn't remember nothing! Then a light at the end of the room started pullin' me in. I tried to fight it and stay with the picture frames where I wanted my memories to appear. Aching for 'em. But the light just kept pullin' me closer and I started crying uncontrollably. Crying harder than I have ever cried, and I am getting too close to the light, and the tears fall harder, and I feel a big squeeze. I emerge on the other side. I am in a bright room; a hospital room and I see doctors and nurses. It's cold and wet. My mother is there with tears of joy as she reaches for me....and I reach for her! I am a newborn baby. I have been reborn."

Freddy shook his head as he quieted himself. He was deeply moved by the telling of his miraculous dream. So was I. His chin curled with controlled emotion as he intimated a final thought:

"Maybe I was alone that night, after all. Getting saved."

****

On the approach to Shenandoah National Park, I was hiking alone one day and looking for a place to lunch. Around a bend in the trail, I came up behind a hiker who was also looking for a place to stop. She heard me coming up behind her and stepped to the side to let me pass.

"Hey there, hiker," I greeted in passing. She turned toward me to reciprocate. I had never seen her before, but she looked pro with her Osprey pack and long Leki trekking poles. Beautiful enough to kill a man. Who was this piece of trail candy?

"I'm Monarch."

"Music Man, a pleasure."

"Yeah, me too. Hey watch out there!"

In the middle of my infatuation, she brought to my attention a snake that was crossing the trail a couple yards in front of me.

"Rattlesnake. See the rattle?" she asked as she pointed.

"Oh, I see it... and I hear it now," I said as it rattled at us for the first time. "He's a bad dude," she said.

"First rattler I have seen on the trail."

"Are you thru-hiking?" Monarch asked as she turned to face me again.

"Yeah, how about you?" I suspected she wasn't a thru-hiker.

"I'm doing a LASH (Long-Ass Section Hike) here in Virginia, three hundred miles."

"That is one serious LASH."

"Yeah, I've been piecing together the AT by states and sections for a couple years. I come out when I can get away from the city for some time."

I thought about Garlic. Where was she and what was she doing? I hadn't seen her in days, and we were very distant. A brand-new inner dialogue started bickering in a knocked-down-and-drag-out brawl between spiritual morals and instincts of the flesh.

"How are we gonna get past that snake?" Monarch asked, now with hesitation in her voice.

"There it goes," I said, as it slithered away to find sleep. "All clear."

A girl's voice came from behind us. "What's up, Music Man?" I turned around curiously.

"Hey, Chilly! How's your day? Haven't seen you and Green Bean for a while."

"Yeah, me and Green Bean and Blueberry got off trail to go with Fantastic to his parents' house in Virginia Beach. Took the opportunity for a sea change and resupply. It was great!"

"Sounds like it! Good for you!" Please don't say anything about Garlic, I thought to myself. Green Bean popped around the corner.

"Yo, Music Man! Good to see you!"

"You too, Greenie. This is Monarch. She's a LASHER. Is that right?"

"Nice to meet you guys. Yeah, I am wrapping up this section at Glasgow in a couple days."

"Coo cool," I said, "well, I'm gonna to push on."

The rest of them stopped for lunch there, but Blueberry kept walking with me. "How was the break, Blue?"

"Oh, it was great. But I'm glad to be back on trail. All we did was drink beer and play corn hole. It was fun, but I'm feeling it now. Verdant Virginia was calling just in time." "Good times," I added.

"Yeah, you know how it is. Once this hiking bug bites you, it leaves a bull's eye."

"I know. They're going to have to pull me off these mountains in restraints. I'm afraid I wouldn't make it back to the trail if I left now. Plus, too much beer slows me down for days anymore. Good for you guys, making it back to the trail and all."

"Hey, I saw Garlic last night," Blueberry said. "She was back at the shelter with the Tramily. She asked if I had seen you."

"Really? I figured that girl was done with me. Probably for the best, Blueberry. She's a strong hiker, but Garlic is always competing with someone." There was a shred of truth there. Still, I was sandbagging him. I was taking her personal inventory when I should have been taking my own.

"I wouldn't know," he said while reaching for his pocket. "Do you want to call her with my phone?"

"Did she say she wanted to hear from me?"

"Not necessarily. But you should call her."

"I'm good, Blue, no thanks. She'll probably catch us by tonight anyway."

"I don't think so, Music Man. Those feet of hers are jacked up bad. She's having another spell with the fascist foot."

Somewhere front and center, I was wondering where Monarch was headed for the night. My instincts were running amuck. Lo and behold, we all ended up at the same shelter. The whole crew from the day, minus Garlic. She must have been hurting, but I wasn't considering it. I flirted with Monarch while Green Bean played the Strumstick around an evening fire.

He loved that thing. He was a small-time home producer when he wasn't hiking. His body's core was built for climbing mountains while his heart was made for music (amongst other noble things). He had a natural talent for playing that mini-Louisville Slugger with a few strings on it. The sad melodies that came from his fingers were rooted in sinister Church modes. I loved listening to him pull dark and romantic lines out of the instrument. Everyone slowly drifted off to sleep and the campsite got quiet. All except for the crickets left to play their bowlegged violins. Monarch and I had rolled our beds out in the shelter earlier and somehow we ended up next to each other. I laid awake tossing and turning and so did she. When at last we faced each other with eyes locked, I whispered to her, and she whispered back...

"Can't sleep?"

"No. I don't sleep well in shelters."

"Why didn't you pitch your tent?"

"Because you were in here," she lusted.

"Want to go sit at the table?"

"Yeah." Monarch made sure I could feel her breath.

We both inch wormed to the edge of the platform and slipped out of our sleeping bags, moving to the picnic table. She looked up at the moon. I swung a leg around and moved close to her back, kissing her neck. She took my hand and led me behind the shelter where we tried to be as quiet as possible. But I knew that if anyone was awake, they might have heard something. With the cheating done, we crept back around the front of the shelter where everyone was peacefully snoring. It appeared we had gotten away with it and laid down giggling, then went to sleep. Early next morning, everyone was moving about with the typical bustle of a summer morning at an AT shelter. Hikers were laughing while tying on bandanas, looking at maps, and the smell of burnt coffee and tired campfire hung in the air. Monarch and I exchanged sultry glances. She didn't know that I was hiding a secret that everyone else knew: There was someone else. I was relieved to observe no one acting awkwardly...*as if* the world revolved around me.

I got out of my sleeping bag and went around the back of the shelter to relieve myself. Glancing past the sinful spot where Monarch and I had sex in the middle of the night, I found to my horror, a tent I recognized. A dozen yards away...it was Garlic's tent. Panic filled me, along with the shame and regret of the convicted. I was busted and there was no way around it. The poor girl had not got out of her tent yet. My mind raced. She couldn't face the humiliation of it. I prepared a confession in my mind so she wouldn't have to cross examine me for the truth.

"Garlic is here," I whispered to Blueberry as I came back around.

"I know," he replied with circumstantial evidence. "She must have got in late. Those feet...that aching...foot."

I rolled my eyes toward Monarch who was chipper and ready to kick off to the trail.

"Are you ready, Music Man? Mind if I tag along?" Monarch spoke with a sparkle. "Hey, who's tent over there?"

"You go ahead," I shooed. "I need to pack up and have a cup of coffee. I'll catch you in a few clicks."

"Okay!" Monarch pecked a kiss on my cheek that burned like

a branding-iron. I felt like the total shard of hambone that I was, but only because I was caught.

"Meet you for lunch?" She was instigating another tryst.

"That could work, let me see how the day shakes out."

(Ugh, I totally suck.)

I felt like the Grinch telling Little Cindy Lou-Who how it was gonna be. With shielded shame I watched everyone clear out of the shelter. No one else alluded to knowing anything, with hikers wishing "Happy Trails," and "Come on, Music Man! It's a day to hike," a reference to the perfect weather.

Blueberry passed me looking askance. I raised one eyebrow back with a grimace. The zipper to Garlic's tent buzzed open just as the last hikers had left. I hadn't seen her in a week. She was a sight for sore eyes and a blackened heart. While standing up to stretch, she instantly stumbled in pain when she put weight on her foot. Garlic was beautiful and resilient, and I was ugly and weak. I shuffled over.

"Hey."

She turned with surprise then opened a perfect smile. "Hey, Music! She hobbled over to me."

"Garlic, I..."

"No wait, Music Man. I'm so glad I found you! Listen, I owe you an apology. I'm sorry for how I have acted."

Wha?

"I have been struggling with my feet...I mean, I've been struggling with a lot of things. My heart, too." She said it with a tenderness that poured gasoline on the fires of my guilt. "I've caught a feeling for you, and I just...I don't know... I'm scared."

"Oh, babe. I am too. We both caught a feeling, it would appear. I don't want to keep making mistakes, Garlic."

That was the best I had. I said I loved her...but I was a royal screw up. "Me either," she cooed, then we kissed.

"Thank you."

The secret sank deep into my heart. Buried at the bottom of the dry well with all the other lies and broken promises. I urged it to join ranks with the grimiest choices I have made in my life. We left the shelter and I immediately stank with sweat in the morning sun.

Shenandoah National Park trailheads were still closed in May when we passed thru, but the waysides (visitor centers) had started to open. I played the Strumstick often and jammed with other hikers whenever anyone was willing. Choogle, a hiker attempting to flip-flop the AT, played a mean harp. We blistered the blues whenever we got the chance. Big Meadows Wayside was a grand time complete with beer and cheese sandwiches on sourdough bread. Garlic watched me play the Strumstick with those laughing blue eyes that spilled love. Monarch had long left the trail.   And so, she had left my mind. Nothing more was said or heard. I hoped what happened in Virginia would stay in Virginia.

While nooning it in the national park, I caught up with one of my dad's oldest and dearest friends from a park phone. "Uncle John" schooled me on the history of the valley and its many battles. A well-versed Civil War historian, Uncle John took the opportunity to tell me about Grant and Sheridan, and a young George A. Custer. As an ambitious brigadier general, Custer cut his teeth at Shenandoah carrying out brutal war tactics for the Union.

"Starve them out or burn them up, that was his style," said Uncle John, "He was a real heathen." Custer would later meet his fate at the infamous Battle of Little Big Horn (aka Custer's Last Stand) against the Cheyenne, leading his cavalry on a suicide mission that not one American soldier would live to recount.

Uncle John told me to keep going and to fight a good fight, and to trust experience in knowing which battles required surrender. He was referring to the struggles within me that were no longer a secret. Keen and sensitive, yet a straight-shooting pragmatist, he told me truths that I didn't want to hear. But I needed to listen. Good friends are like that. He reminded me that people from sea to shining sea loved and supported me; that I needed to cut the bullshit and rebuild some structure for my life.

"Your kids deserve their father. Your parents deserve their son, and you deserve to be happy. Do what you must do as a good man, as a good father. Those things will fall into place together if your foundation is strong. But if you don't do it right the first time, you may not find the time to do it twice. Don't quit and keep making us proud. Make your dad proud." It was stern and wise advice from a man I deeply respected. It had been a long time since anyone was proud of me. I swore to make those changes and I told him I had a good start, for better or worse. He asked about "this Garlic chick" that my parents spoke about. Garlic had begun sending her own postcards to my parents, and even began receiving cards from my dad on occasion. "I have never read or seen anything so beautifully written," Garlic ooh'd, referring to Dad's creative prose and unique penmanship. At first, it made me uneasy. But I let it go. If the correspondence brought some comfort to them both, I had to accept it.

"She sounds like a keeper, young man." cozied Uncle John.

"Yes sir, I will," I affirmed.

Bear activity in the park was exceptional. Garlic and I had a special encounter with a mother and her two cubs. We came between them in a tense moment of triangulation that quickly eased when the cubs bounced across the path and back to momma. The wildflowers were a symphony on land. Bright white blooms of Rhododendron often spread out as far as the eye could see, making the valley appear out like a summertime glacier from any vantage. Spiritual things happen when mountain laurel completely covers the trail corridor in a canopy. It feels like moving thru a tunnel and not knowing what mysterious surprises await at the end.

"I don't think I'm going to drink for a while," Garlic said in northern Virginia as we got closer and closer to Harpers Ferry. "I say things and I do things that I regret. Plus, it just gets in the way of the hike, and it comes between us...." She didn't drink often but she got blistered drunk when she did. Wild nights were loud and animated, usually ending with her wearing my sunglasses in the dark and tangling her words with an exaggerated Hudson Valley twist that sounded like a talking penny whistle. It wasn't hard for her to get the attention she craved, especially when she drank. I didn't argue when she told me the goose was going to hang high for a while. I would still drink but only occasionally, that was my compromise. The last time she said anything to me about my getting wasted on the AT was the day I snuck off to take the acid that Andrew had given me back at Hot Springs.

Donatello and I had decided to take a night hike and trip our way into the Old Schoolhouse near Atkins, Virginia. Trees melted in the sunset like a fire of ice that we could taste as the temperature dropped to below freezing. At some point, we dropped our packs and chased the sun until we almost ran off a cliff. It was dark when we entered the time warp of the schoolhouse built in the late nineteenth century. We were still high as we entered to find Abraham Lincoln sitting at the teacher's desk. Under the soft light of an oil lamp, he looked up from grading rotted parchments and took a bite out of a crisp red apple. Honest Abe never said a word as he chowed down on the apple core while going about his business.

I was trying to hide from Garlic earlier that afternoon. In no condition to talk, I didn't want her to know I was high, but she could tell at first glance. She told me I looked like a ghost, then handed me a fresh clove of garlic she had acquired in town.

"Eat that, you idiot," she said before she hiked on. I thought she was just giving me shit, but she was really trying to help me sober up with the detoxifying clove. She didn't hike with me until I had straightened out a day later. A close relative of hers had struggled with addiction after the military. Her experience of dealing with that meant she understood me slightly more than others when it came to my occasionally bizarre behavior. Festering resentments ebbed and flowed for miles though we would always bounce back quickly from disagreements or moments of disconnection. I was deluding myself and not keeping it real with her. Others thought we were plum nuts. We had said and done some rotten things to each other. But who didn't have skeletons in their closet? Bygones be bygones.

We had a bond that was getting stronger every day. Plus, we often walked alone or with other hikers which gave us both a sense of autonomy and freedom that was refreshing. Walking many miles alone, secrets sometimes surfaced to haunt me. But I would push them back down even deeper and put on a smile when called to attention.

Garlic and I took a double-zero at Harper's Ferry, West Virginia, and we both had friends meet us for visits. On the way into town, we stopped by the closed offices of the Appalachian Trail Conservancy and sat on the dusty porch taking selfies. We met her Godparents for lunch and dinner the first day, then retired to our room at the Comfort Inn.

The next day saw us visiting with family friends Greg and Steve. Respectively, the brother and father of Eddie, one of my dearest childhood friends from Kentucky and my brother's best friend growing up. Eddie, an AT thru-hiker from the pre-Bill Bryson era, had been living in Wyoming for years. Greg and Steve now lived in Washington D.C. They had put together food drops for me at times and helped me resupply fuel for the Jetboil when no stores were open down south. They were champions on my support team, and they had come to visit me as the trail brought us close to their home. We sat in the park near the train yard after lunch and talked at length. Steve, a career lawman now living in D.C., had words of wisdom for me— an old-timer warning yet hope shot:

"Music Man, it's an amazing thing you are doing out there. It's hard work every day to hike that trail, especially when the path that got you there was so tough. But *I know* it has healing qualities. I remember when Eddie walked the trail before joining the Army. He was going thru a lot after his mom died, and he struggled too. But Music Man, you got to get away from all the shit that's going to kill you. In this life, we work hard, then we go home at night, and we keep working. Effort and dedication pay off, as you are learning on the peaceful battlefield. Stay committed to your goals and take steps each day to achieve the small ones that keep you on track. However, if you are looking for something out on the trail, something that is going to change everything back home; a whole lot of nothing is what you're going to find. Everything you need...what God has intended for you...is sitting right here in front of me." He tapped on my chest. Look in the right place and you will find it on the Appalachian Trail, and maybe a few other locales. Get to it, Son."

I was moved by his wisdom and promised Steve that I would work hard. I walked away with the same type of feeling that my talk with Uncle John left me with. I was getting some tough love. Their efforts to connect with me did not fall on deaf ears, though there was still a lot of the trail left to go.

The next leg of business travel was at hand. The pedestrian bridge crossing the Potomac River was closed for renovations. Our safe passage on the trail from Harpers Ferry into Maryland was in question. Logistically, Garlic and I considered a shuttle that would take us miles around town to the next bridge, thereby missing white blazes. The only other option was to hop the barricade to the closed bridge and tie-hop the single-wide rail track across the river. The rails gave track to Amtrak passenger trains flying into town at incredible speeds. It was literally a suicide mission. If a train barreled thru there was nowhere to go except take a plunge to the river below or get horribly smashed by a train cruising like a bullet. The more we talked about it, the more time we lost. We couldn't hear any train whistles or rumbles in the distance. Garlic, ever a purist for passing the white blazes of the official track.... both of us out for adventure; its decision time: "Fuck it, let's go. We did the Smokies! We can cross this bridge. Let's go now."

We hopped the barricade as onlookers yelled at us to stop. "It's too dangerous!" they cried in vain. Another clandestine AT mission was playing out. We started crossing the bridge with no side-rails or anywhere to go except all the way across or over the edge. To make matters worse, the bridge really needed the repairs it was getting. As we hopped the creaky rail timbers, we observed there were ties missing everywhere. I looked down between missing timbers to see the river water rushing far below, and just made another hop. We were moving right along, with a few dozen yards to go, then we heard it from a distance.

"Blewwwwww Bleeewwwwwww!" the overtones of a train whistle pierced the air.

"Oh *shit!* Train's *a-coming!*"

We judged it to be a half-mile away and closing fast. The rails began to vibrate under our feet and the screech of train wheels was approaching from around the bend as we hop-hop-hopped the railroad ties as fast as we could. We were running out of time.

"Oh, my *gawd*, Music, that son-of-a-bitch is right around the corner!

bleewwwWW.......bleeeeEEWWWW!

"Go! Go! Go!"

Hop-hop-hop-hop, Garlic strained with full running weight on her achy foot.

BLEEEEEEWWWWWWWWW!

Crunch! The gravel smashed under our boots as we made it to the other side and safely back to terra firma, just before the passenger train came blistering thru like a silver bullet on its way into the heart of Harpers Ferry. We had made it just in time.

"Yeah!!!!! And another one bites the dust!" Garlic hollered back toward the direction of town. She was a wild and brazen hiker.

Fearless on the AT; the strongest hiker I knew, and I loved her for all that and more. On hiking the Appalachian Trail, we had to assume responsibility for getting the job done ourselves and nothing was going to stop us. When it came to pure adventure, we shared a common penchant for certain reckless behaviors, so we had to have each other's back when the going got rough.

Garlic skipped along the paved trail under the Amtrak rails above us and laughed at the train whizzing by. She thumbed her chin at the last car going by just as the trail delivered us back into the forest. "Adios, A.T.C.!"

Ed Garvey Shelter was sparsely occupied when we arrived mid-afternoon and we decided to stop for the night. We met some hikers there, notably Side-Show Bob and his colleagues. I started singing Rocket Man, accompanied by the Strumstick, when Garlic sat down to a fine duet with me. Side-Show Bob recorded a video from behind us and asked "Would y'all mind if I post that duet to my social media? That was quite a moment." I wondered if cyberspace would agree. But we told him he could do whatever he wanted with his video. Later, I had a wonderful conversation with him. I wasn't interested in his scheme to help "finance" my hike with videos of me "like Hawk, and those other cats that make money off the trail." Nothing against Hawk, I liked his videos enough. But the "Music Man Channel" was out of the question. Regardless of that, Side-Show Bob shared some wonderful thoughts about hiking that I never forgot:

"Relish these days, Music Man. Granted, there are other great trails to explore and a myriad of wonderful outdoor experiences to be had. But you will never recapture the magic of your first thru hike. And there is no greater thru-hiking adventure in the world than the AT, Northbound."

Another fond memory from that evening was playing "the song" for Garlic later that night.

Everyone else was in bed. It was the song that I had first played for her, way back at Standing Bear Farms after the Smokies, as she stood across the fire and opened her heart to the lyrics. On that night, I slowed it down and put all the emotion I could find into the rendition for her. I sang with a whisper to her ear as she sat next to me. It moved her to tears. She turned her head away from me and began to sob. Tears fell from her eyes like clear ribbons. I started to realize why the tune moved Garlic so much. It was like I had written it for her…on her behalf. It was the only time I ever saw that girl cry.

I contemplated the comments of Side-Show Bob, and I had more questions. Did this whole deal have the potential to be better the second time thru? Near the halfway point of the Appalachian Trail, could that answer be a good thing or bad thing, either way?

.10

GARLIC SLAMMED HER SPOON INTO THE EMPTY ICE CREAM carton and rose out of her throne. Rising to the challenge at the Pine Grove Furnace General Store, she dusted her hands in victory and dipped a curtsey before reaching for her backpack.

"And that's how you smash a half gallon of ice cream in one sitting," she beamed with pride.

"Whoo-hoo! Nice going!" cheered the other hikers as we watched her satisfy the requirements for successful consummation of the "Half Gallon Challenge." She curled her lips with satisfaction as she donned her pack. I thought about Grand Master back at Fontana and his Tupperware lunch of melted ice cream with canned tuna and flash-frozen bacon bits. Attempting to eat a half gallon of ice cream in one sitting at Pine Grove Furnace is a right-of-passage for AT thru-hikers. Even on a hot summer day, it's not an easy feat.

Victorious hikers walk away with bragging rights and the coveted wooden spoon; a mini-trophy with a good story behind it. Garlic proudly boasted that flavor selection was key to her success. That and an empty stomach. Don't listen to those who say that a cheeseburger first will help stretch the stomach walls. I nearly barfed up the Coffee Chip runoff in my gut and quit with pints to go. My tail tucked, I snuck away with embarrassment over poor tactical decisions. I knew better than to have a cheeseburger prior to my attempt. It was no mistake; it was a poor choice.

****

During the summer of 2010, a band I was playing in was invited to New York City for a show at the City Winery. It was a great opportunity to open for a local NYC band fronted by Michael Shannon, the Kentucky native turned award winning actor. He was then living in New York and had released an album with his band that included another Louisville native on the drums. We were excited about the opportunity in the Big Apple. With the van packed and spirits high, we hit the road again.

Somewhere outside Cincinnati, I realized to my horror that I forgot to pack my maintenance medicine. The prescription was my lifeline when I couldn't get my drugs of choice. Without anything in my system, I would be dope sick in less than a day and the reality hit like a tour bus. Somewhere around the Pennsylvania state line, sickness came on me like the flu. How could I have been so stupid? This was a total nightmare, a complete disaster. New York City was the last place I wanted to be dope sick and I feared that the others would find out. We arrived in New York, just as the flu-like symptoms worsened. I was desperately trying to conceal my pain and I was becoming antisocial, barely keeping up with everyone who wanted to go out and party the night before the big gig. I couldn't look anyone in the eye.

"The show is tomorrow night. So tonight, we will party!" The rest of the band harmonized. I hid in a corner of the couch.

A hometown friend was putting us up in his Brooklyn flat and he invited us out to the bar he tended. I felt terrible. The last thing I wanted to do was go to a crowded bar and throw shot glasses of neon liquor down my gullet. Just the thought made me run to the apartment bathroom and throw up before we left. I looked at my drooping face in the vanity mirror; it was getting increasingly more difficult to hide my condition. At the bar, I continued to deteriorate and ended up washed out in a corner, as pale as a pillowcase and unable to function.

"Are you ok?" A roadie asked me.

"Man, I don't know. I'm just not feeling it."

"Dude, you look like hell. Why don't you go back to the flat and get some rest. Tomorrow is a big day."

I was relieved to have someone's permission to leave and quickly bounced from the front door of the bar. He was right. Fear was the feeling about tomorrow's big day. I would be worse by then. More dread filled my soul as I awfulize the misery the night would bring, and the further dysfunction tomorrow. I hauled my weak body up Mr. Brownstone's stairs and fell onto the floor of the dark apartment.

After an hour of shivers and cold sweats on the couch, I sat up scared when I heard the door open and close. The footsteps that approached seemed like they came from Death himself, coming around the bend to end my misery. I would have welcomed it. It wasn't Death; it was bandmember Ross.

"Tisk, tisk...." he snickered. Ross stood over me in a showcase of condescension and hypocrisy.

"Fuck you, Ross." I fired back.

"What'd you do, leave your pack at home you asshole?"

He knew what was wrong with me. We shared common secrets, but our drugs of choice were different. He would be no help, so I thought.

"What am I going to do? Tomorrow is going to be a huge day and I'm gonna be ragged. This is bad."

"I can see that. I would offer you a bump, but I know that ain't what you need." Ross was right about that.

"Just make it worse! I'm a screwed man. I'm going to play like a donkey tomorrow night if I can't get well. I'm about to walk these streets and look for something."

"Like hell you are. Look outside! It's Brooklyn out there in case you forgot. You'll get your ass handed to you on the streets, out there looking like that." He reached into his pocket to fumble around for something. I thought he was going for the blow-filled bullet tooter that he never left home without.

"I don't want any powder," I whined.

"Open up your hand, jackass."

To my relief and delight, he dropped two pills into my hand. A wave of relief washed over me as I ravenously chewed them up.

"Oh, my god, man, you're a hero! What the hell, you never have pills? Rainy day fund? Still, I'm hit for tomorrow. These twenty milligrams will only get me to sleep for a few hours. The devil will be back on me as soon as the sun comes up."

He walked back to the door and opened it. Ross turned back and said... "medicine cabinet." He walked out and slammed the door. I sat stunned for a moment, then burst up and ran into the bathroom approaching the huge mirror above the vanity. It just hung on the wall, no medicine cabinet.

"Asshole! How the hell is he gonna play games like that!" Suddenly, an idea.... Maybe the master bedroom has its own bathroom! "Don't go in my bedroom!" I remembered hearing when we arrived. Without hesitation, I ran over to his bedroom door. In a total frenzy, I would pass no chances up and call every bluff. Even if Ross was toying with me, there may still be a medicine cabinet in there. The door was locked. I reached for my wallet and spilled the contents as I fumbled for a credit card. Shaking like a leaf, I slipped and slid the card around at the doorknob frantically. Finally, a pop...the door swung open to the dark bedroom. I flipped the light switch...Another door. Please don't be a closet, please be a bathroom... I opened it... A bathroom. Shit, light switch... where is it? Click, "and let there be light." A sink...a medicine cabinet! I flung it open too fast, spilling deodorants and toothpaste...fumbling, nothing. Top shelf, what's this...I giant Rx bottle with hundreds of pills in it. I read the label... Yep, my mistress.

"There you are, darling. Oh my god." I heaved a quivery sigh of relief. I opened the expired bottle and popped half a handful of pills into my mouth; dozens more into my pockets. "Thank god." A wave of endorphins hit my brain. Just the thought, the fact, that I was going to get well, instantly took the edge off. The brain works like that. The fear alone of not knowing when or where the next fix will come from, compounds a dope sickness fivefold. But with this many pills, I would be fine until we got home. Without regard for anyone else's need for this medication (say, the person who was prescribed it), I quickly popped a half dozen or more down my throat then I sat on the toilet and waited for the fuzzy warmth to fill my temples and run down my spine. Aloha. The medicine massaged the receptors in my gut, sealing the deal. All better. Thirty minutes later, I went back to the bar feeling right as rain; and I got drunk. Ross winked at me from a table as the roadie walked over to the bar corner where my empty longnecks were collecting.

"Glad to see you're feeling better," the roadie noticed.

"Yeah, got it out of my system, I guess."

"I see. Well good, pal."

Really, I had gotten it *into* my system.

The stage was set for the show, at the City Winery. The Manhattan hot spot was packed for a star-studded show. The pearl house lights dropped to a glow of red and blue on the stage floor, then the gate swung open. We were off and running, bringing our contemporary flavor of electrified Newgrass to the Yankees. My head swirled with ego; my guitar smoldered under the shifty weight of my spirited fingers. In real time (black hole gravity time), the illusion that I was slaying that guitar had me fooled. I had been munching and handing out pills like breath mints. The reality was I was so messed up on oxy that I could hardly have played a clean note. Ross came up to me after the set and intimated that I had embarrassed myself. I had played like a donkey, just as I had prophesied. The realization was humiliating. I hardly remember the headliner, but I do recall meeting him and thinking, "This is the nicest guy of all times. For all his rugged handsomeness and ability to portray the most sinister of gangsters during his decorated career on the silver screen, he is literally the nicest human being I have ever met." In the wings, I think I asked him if he liked our set before even giving him a chance to greet us. Not a "Thank you, Mike, for supporting us Kentucky boys...Nope. It was all about me. I look back in horror at the delusion characterized as my thinking. I had gone through so many pills that I was out again and sick by the time the van rolled back into Louisville two days later.

That kind of behavior is far from normal. I was completely powerless over a drug that wouldn't let me quit and it caused me to behave in bizarre and tragic ways. With a little more time, I would reach a point where I couldn't live with it, and I wouldn't live without it. Even now, years since my last opiate, that drug will occasionally make me shift in my seat when I hear a war story about heroin. Then I get grateful to not be dope sick. Being hooked on drugs was like having a jail cell over my bed. When I awoke from the coma, I couldn't so much as sit up without paying the jailer whatever crumpled dollar bills might be left in my pocket so he would let me out. If I didn't have money or the first hit of the day waiting for me on the bedside table, the cell bars kept me down. I remind myself each day of the misery that awaits if I think I can take one more ride with drugs.

Walking away from the Half Gallon Challenge in defeat wasn't that bad, after all. A little lactose induced tummy ache wasn't anything after what I had been thru with drugs. I tried to find gratitude at every opportunity. Having fallen in love with nature again, it didn't matter where the trail led if I was able to find beauty along the way. It was everywhere if I took the time to look.

Garlic and I emerged from the green tunnel of West Virginia (only four miles of trail), sneaking thru the comparably few Maryland miles undisturbed, then across the state line into Pennsylvania.

PUD's (pointless up-and-downs) gave way to great flats of walking that were a welcomed relief from the big climbs in Virginia. We ended up passing thru Boiling Springs a few hours apart. When we reconvened that night, Garlic told an emotional tale of a mother she saw in town, just outside of the boarded-up A.T.C. visitor center in the heart of town:

"He was a special needs kid, Music. Probably fifteen and built like a brick house. His mom tried to calm him down. But that kid was thirsty. She tried to give him water from the hose outside the visitor center, but he spit it out, yelling "Band-Aid! Tastes like Band-Aid! The boy took a swing at his mom and landed one cold on her temple. Knocked her out of her shoes, straight down to the ground. Then he stood over her screaming, as she tried to get to her feet. She wouldn't accept help from anyone standing around, telling us all to back off; that she had it under control. She stood up, sat the boy down, and rocked his head in on her shoulder until he calmed down, repeating "I'm sorry, Mom, I love you," over and over again. Music Man, this woman had to be the best goddamn mom I've ever seen. I just wanted to hug her and wipe the blood off her brow. She had the blackest eye when she turned the other cheek. But she just wanted to comfort her son."

The day before we were set to arrive in Duncannon, I was a few miles ahead when rain clouds began to gather on the horizon past my shoulder. Garlic had urged me to hike on because her feet were hurting, not wanting to slow me up. Reluctantly, I agreed. I never liked leaving her when her pain had reached a certain level. I knew that my presence helped to take her mind off the throbbing. Laughing at silly jokes was great for both of us when morale was wobbly. On this day, however, I was feeling sharp and pushed forward.

The trail was a boardwalk that ran parallel to the river. It was about two feet wide and raised about three feet above the mud at any given location. It went on for miles. I met another hiker who had just arrived for a long weekend on the Appalachian Trail. He was in early twenties and eager to start crushing miles.

"I don't have a trail name. I'm just starting a short section-hike," he informed me when I introduced myself. I passed him on the left as he was cinching down straps of his pack's harness.

"Right on, I'll see you on the trail!" I waved away.

"Alright Music Man!"

A storm was brewing out of the southwest and the sky was graying over the boardwalk. I rounded a bend and stopped dead in my tracks, completely stunned by what crept before me. On the wooden planks just paces away was the biggest damn turtle I had ever seen! It was completely blocking the way forward and there was no way around the monster. It looked like it weighed 100 pounds, but I didn't know for sure. I had never seen a bigger turtle on either side of aquarium glass. And here it was, northbound on the AT, moving as slow as a glacier. As I stood in amazement the young new hiker came up from behind. I pointed at it quietly.

"Whoa! That is a big damn turtle."

"Hell yes, it is."

"Northern Snapper," he correctly identified, "biggest one I've ever seen. She is old, bruh. And just beautiful."

"Spectacular." The antique animal slowly turned herself around to face us, completely blocking our passing on the puncheon.

"What are you doing up here?" I asked the turtle. The new kid answered with knowledge:

"Eminent danger. She probably senses the storm coming up out of the south. It's gonna rain cats and dogs in a little while. Snapping turtles are too slow to get out of the wash in time if the creek rises too fast. She knows she'll drown in a flash flood. That's the kind of smarts that has kept her alive long enough to get that huge."

It sounded good enough to me. This kid knew his nature. Our current problem was how to get around her. She was far too big to safely step over. We would have to drop off the side of the boardwalk into multiple feet of knee-deep mud to avoid the power tool her jaws wielded. Trying our luck with the mud looked more and more likely. The sky was socked in with storm clouds. But the thought of drowning in quicksand or ruining my relatively new Gore-Tex boots was not sitting well with me either. I made a split-decision. "I'm going to try and get around her."

"Be careful man," he warned, "if she gets ahold of your heel, that could spell a season-ender. And she won't let go until she hears lightning. At least you got that going for you." "And what's that?" The new kid was starting to make me nervous.

"The storm coming should be bell-ringer."

His answer for everything didn't bring me any comfort as I inched toward the ancient beast and placed a trekking pole near the left side of her head (trail east) to distract her as I moved in the other direction. Her age and intelligence far surpassed mine and she was not fooled in the least. In a sudden flash I slipped around the side as her head burst forth from the giant shell and snapped for my shin. I swiped my leg out of the way just in time to avoid the clasp of her jaws as she barely missed.

Snap! "Whoa! Whoa!"

"Damn, that was close! Wow!" The new kid commented.

It was too close. I heard the force of her jaws as she went for my money makers. She kept rotating around to keep an eye on me. We had her in a pickle, now. But I was safe, and I backed away.

"How am I gonna get around her?" He fussed as he analyzed the scene playing out. But he didn't need my help deciding what to do.

"I'm just gonna jump over her." "Dude, that's crazy!"

"She ain't looking this way anymore. I think I can make it."

"Uhm...now, if she gets a hold of your heel, your hike will be over before it even starts." I tried to dissuade him. From my vantage point on the other side of Jump Street, I judged his chances at "not good". Even if he did clear the dinosaur, his ankle would be right in front of her nose when the heel landed. To boot, this bog-bridge was very narrow for risking such a calculated jump. Failure to execute could be catastrophic. There was zero room for error. I shook my head as the starting gun fired. The new kid whipped two strides out like Bill Russell flanking into the lane for a shot block, he planted his trekking poles in unison, and let out a rally cry: "Yeet!" With head raised and eyes focused forward, the sprite hiker hoisted himself into the air, in the hopes of flying over the back of the relic reptile. His timing looked good, but it seemed like slow motion. His long hair fell back, as the leading knee came as high as my head. The giant turtle sensed movement in this dangerously exciting game of Man vs. Wild. The point of the new kid's trekking pole grazed her shell as he flew over. Like Pat Day's whip in the final furlong, the tap sparked her head out from the shell aimed straight for his trailing foot...I couldn't see thru the blur of speed with which these two were shockingly matched, his feet crested under her rising head. Toe to toe...pound for pound...trail and tail.... they tangled and I prayed "One Time!" Bigger than my fist, her jaws Snapped!   *THUD* thumped the wooden boards as his feet landed in motion. The new kid trotted off like a cornerback approaching the sideline to sit out 4th Down and Inches.

"A swing and a miss!" I hollered. "Now that was close! She missed you by an inch! What a jump! Eight feet easy, in tough conditions!" I did my best Terry Bradshaw analysis.

"Whew! Ha-ha! I don't want it again," he guffawed, like he had just sunk a thirty-foot sidewinder of a putt to save par and take the Wanamaker Trophy.

"I think you have earned a trail name," I told him as we looked back at her.

"Yeah, what's that?"

"Turtle Hurdle."

"Love it, I accept."

Turtle Hurdle slipped away from his podium-worthy performance and left the valiant yet defeated Northern snapping turtle to affect her own escape. We wished her well and better luck next time, as we all walked away unscathed. The encounter was one of the most memorable wilderness experiences of my trek. The new kid's One Shining Moment: A leap forever etched into my memory as a mid-air black and white still-shot of the hurdle over the turtle. The sky dumped buckets of rain as we finished the climb up to Darlington Shelter. It was packed full of hikers, from the platform to the bunks, but they made room for us. Behind on the trail, Garlic was probably soaking wet in her own battle of "Me vs. My Feet." To fight physical conditions like plantar fasciitis are not only taxing on the body, but they also wear down the spirit. At the same time, true character was built with each step forward. But it's easy to get pressed out. Entering like Special Forces, Garlic didn't make a peep when she sauntered into the shelter well after dark and soaked with water.

Everyone else was asleep or pretending to be, in hopes that they would trick their aches and anxieties away for long enough to rest. I was in my sleeping bag but still waiting up. She sat at the edge of the shelter and found my face with her head lamp.

"Is there room, Bae?" she whispered. "For you? Always."

I sat up in my sleeping bag and inch-wormed to the edge of the shelter. The Deja vu brought a sickening memory back, but I quickly pushed it back down where it belonged.

"What a day, I'm freezing."

"How's your foot?" I reached for her hair.

"It's not good, Music. I don't know what to do. I've tried different shoes and insoles, massage balls, and hyperhydration... Bae, it's only a handful of miles down to Duncannon tomorrow but I feel like it's gonna take me all day to get there. God today was tough. Music, how long have you been here?"

"Not long, just got here a little while ago," but that wasn't true. "Hey, let's zero tomorrow at The Doyle. I'll cruise into town early and make sure I can get us a room before this bubble comes into town."

"Ugh, The Doyle?" Garlic shrugged, "I don't really want to stay there, Music. Is it even open this year? Anyway, I've heard the windows in the rooms are missing panes."

"So, we're glampers, now?" We chuckled at the fresh "glamorous-camping" portmanteau. "Kind Of Outdoorsy Outfitters is gonna be packed with hiker-trash like us," she continued, "some

Sobos said there are a lot of section hikers there for the weekend. Doesn't sound like a restful stop, to me." The trail news about The Doyle was that the following day it would open its doors for first time all season. It was insider knowledge and I wanted to keep it that way until I had the best room staked out for the two of us. My intentions were not to secure a restful stop for her. Squarely focused on my wants, I had a play-date in mind, complete with a party and a bed.

✲✲✲✲✲✲✲✲✲✲✲✲

Someone very close to me once said "You need long-term treatment." Horrified and humiliated, we both knew it was true. My refusal to commit myself to treatment stemmed from reservations about getting sober. I was trapped in the belief that I wasn't that bad; I could quit on my own; I am different from these people; "I'm not like you," I thought when I looked at them. "They," who stand in chow lines at the "homeless shelter turned treatment center." This same line in which I was just another domino. "They" lived at the last house on the block with the other lost and forgotten souls that roamed the streets. Not me. I was just in line for the hot meal. But I was one of them. I had joined the procession and I couldn't even see it. Was it by accident that I ended up at the "safe-place" for the downtown population of downtrodden men? Maybe and maybe not.

✲✲✲✲✲✲✲✲✲✲✲✲

Back to the AT in mid-June... Entering the Doyle seemed like worming one's way into a speakeasy during prohibition. After I said the codeword thru the grill of the door ("Cash"), Vickey opened and rented me a room. Ours was the first room key she rented out that season. Garlic was thrilled when she dropped into town before most of the others to find me on the balcony of the Doyle smoking a cigarette. Rest was eminent. Even injured, she still managed to beat most of the section hikers down off the mountain that day. A seasoned thru-hiker can often still have an edge over fresh-faced new arrivals to the trail. No matter how fit, you gotta have that grit. A large group of us went to The Pub that night and had a hoot. Cheeseburgers and beers covered the table. After a long, rainy hike, it didn't get much better. At the thrift store on the corner, Garlic bought a dress for a dollar. It looked like a universe covered with stars and comets, and she looked perfect in it. Odie took a timeless picture of her wearing the dress while sitting behind the wheel of his Hiker-Yearbook Bus, and it was an instant classic. When we finally retired to our quarters, I realized that she had not had a drink all night. In fact, Garlic hadn't done any serious drinking in some time, save a pint with a pizza here or there. She could stop.

Glassy eyed, I put my arms around her. But when she begged for rest, I got salty and pouted. She just rolled over and turned the light out. "Goodnight."

The weather was brilliant the next morning and I was ready to tee off on the trail. "When do you want to hit the trail, Garlic?"

"I thought we agreed we were gonna take a break today? Music Man, I need a zero day. My feet are killing me."

"Damn. Okay."

"You know...Bae, you should hike today if you want. You're feeling good, you look ready to shred. Go. Besides, you can wake up tomorrow and have a nice morning to yourself. It's Father's Day, tomorrow."

Lost in the selfish waves that endlessly battered the shores of my mind, I had totally forgotten about Father's Day. Did I send my dad a card? My kids...I had not talked to my children in weeks.

"I sent your dad a card, Music. You're covered. I'll give you my phone and you can call your kids tomorrow morning. Then I can call you before I hit the trail and see where you are."

Feelings of inadequacy were surfacing. I was a shitty son, a shitty father, a shitty boyfriend, and a mediocre hiking partner at best. She was right, I needed a day to myself.

"But..." she continued, "I want you to take care of yourself." I knew what she meant. She would never tell me what to do but she hoped I would read between the lines.

"Thanks, but I don't need your phone. Besides, you need it for your own distress calls."

"What'd I tell you about projecting what I need? Worry about yah-self," Garlic belted with the Yankee sass that she used when she meant business, "I just thought you might want to call your kids on Father's Day...or yah dad. Wish I could cawl mine."

We turned from each other on Main Street and started walking in opposite directions. I went to the hotel room, donned my pack, and threw the key on the bed, before continuing down the drag of town headed for the trail. I walked past a liquor store with a neon sign that flickered "OPEN" with an inviting red glow. I stopped, turned around and pulled the glass door open to a cowbell ring. I bought a bottle of gut-rot liquor without so much as an afterthought. The last drops of liquor hit my stomach while crossing the Veterans Memorial Bridge over the Susquehanna River, on the outskirts of town. A train crossing the Rockville Bridge downriver blew its whistle. The piercing cry rang in my ears all the way up the steep cliff side, and into Clark's Ferry Shelter a few miles later. Hammered drunk when I stumbled in, I passed out still wearing my pack, well before sundown; and fell into a strange dream....

****

I am walking thru a beautiful meadow in the mountains, down toward an easy river heading anywhere, and you are there. You cheerfully gesture for me to "come on, slow poke!" The sun shines on the wildflowers and I hurry after you, but I can't catch up. Closer and closer to the river, the sound of the water is soft as it rolls over the smooth boulders. I hear children's voices and I see a young girl standing at an easel. She is painting clouds with a child, who smiles and points at me. He is her little brother. They both laugh and brush the white canvas with white paint, as Old Uncle Jake, in his white suit, approves the work whilst holding his chin. From the top of the easel a butterfly lifts off in flight. Its broad wing-flaps rise above the children, but they don't notice. The gurgle of the stream gets louder. I turn from the children and follow the butterfly, a Viceroy— I think it is beautiful. I come closer to the water's edge and observe the ford to be wider than I thought. The butterfly swoops in and flutters its wings on my cheek with a tease, then darts back up, hovering around, as I watch it shift back and forth, up, and down. I feel your hand slip into mine, we're now side by side. But my eyes are fixed on the flight of the Viceroy and the sun is setting, as it flutters down again and comes closer. Our heads slowly turn toward each other as the Viceroy nears, both of us transfixed on its flight. You grip my hand tighter as the butterfly passes between our faces; our eyes meet and lock as she flutters away to the periphery. You take my other hand and smile. It's getting darker and the river is starting to rumble louder and louder. The water is rising. Your smile turns to a furrowed brow. The long hair covering your face curls up with singe and turns to white dust as you desperately voice "You can run if you want to..." The grains of your dust disappear into the ether. Stuck in slow-motion horror as the river roars, I cry out "no...No...NO!" Then I wake up from the dream in a fright. The rain is pouring into the darkness outside the shelter, and I vomit everything in my system over the edge. Again, all perception fades away with the pitter-patter rain of charcoal-black.

****

"WHIP-POOR-WILL"
I woke up again as rays of sunlight warmed my face.
"WHIP-POOR-WILL...."
"Ah, shut up." I bullied the damn bird. But they don't listen. They never listen.
"WHIP-POOR-WILL!!!"
"Alright, okay, already! I'm getting up, you little bastard."
I vaguely sensed that he'd been cock-a-doodle-doing for an

hour, but I was stuck somewhere between drunk and hungover; unable to respond like a human. That was until the cloaked dagger of bird-cursing had reached the volume needed to pierce the membranes of my throbbing ear drums. I felt horrible. I fried up some coffee. Then I felt horrible some more. I drank the cup and sobered up. I remembered my sweet Aunt Diane reading a book to me as a child.... *Alexander and the Terrible, Horrible, No Good, Very Bad Day*. I felt like I had to hang plain old white shoes over my rebelling feet. Then, it forced its way thru, where I had so longed for it to just...not push thru: "Father's Day. Today is Father's Day."

I thought about the dream and about my children. I thought about my father. I thought about other fathers and sons and daughters. I became very lonely. But I deserved to feel that way. I wondered about Garlic and her father, wherever the hell he was. I thought about what she meant to me and what I meant to her. Moreover, what I represented to her. My mind doubted my heart while my soul doubted my mind. I thought about her offering of the phone yesterday. The offer that I turned down. I remembered things she had told me; I abandoned her again, like her dad, all those years ago. It made me sick, and I hated myself. I drank another cup of joe envisioning my great-grandfather's Guatemalan finca. My own father had never been there to see it. But I had gone? Then I pushed onto the trail feeling no more the father or son that I truly was. What was I doing? What was the point of all this? Why am I hiking this bloody trail? What is wrong with me? Will somebody please help me to under...a family of hikers approached from the north to pass me. The young dad was outpacing the toddler boy and his mother, both dragging in tow but having fun and filled with joy. I stepped off the trail and let them come up.

"It's a good day for it," the daddy jollied as he passed me heading south.

"Every day." I mustered. It felt like a lie.

Mother and son passed next, with the little boy pointing at nature all around. "That's a strong young hiker you've got there," I complimented.

"Oh, we're just trying to keep up with Dad today. It's his father's dream to hike the A.T."

I was deeply moved to record words and I couldn't ignore it. It's a trait I get from my father. I sat down on a blistering hot boulder for ten minutes with a napkin and golf pencil. Three miles later, I wrote the poem in the Rausch Gap Shelter hiker register:

A FATHER'S DAY (UNTITLED)

It was his father's dream to hike the A.T.
But it wasn't his dream to lose him, at 3
Lured by rocky path in the woods
On his knees 'neath the sirens
That sang as they stood
A song up above him
A breeze in the trees
Of picture book moments
That flip thru the leaves
But how is this fair? How is this fine?
And what does Dad wish to glean from the mines?
A harvest of hope from the pastures of plenty
While sonny boy waits,
heart darkened and heavy
To learn an illusion: that once he is free
He'll leave his own son to hike the A.T.

THE 501 SHELTER WAS CLOSED FOR REPAIRS AND WATER contamination issues, but I was prepared with a "camel up" of good water in my pack. There was caution tape blocking the blue blaze to the shelter with a sign posted "No Potable Water. Hazardous." I was relieved at the thought that no one would find me there. I just needed a little more time alone. The 501 had four walls and a closing door, rare for an AT shelter. But the structure appeared closed, locked, and taped off as I approached. I also realized that I was not alone. There was a hiker squatting near the ground with his back turned, as flickers from small flames reflected off gray smoke rising in front of him. The man was lanky with long, white hair pulled back in a tight ponytail and tapered over the ears. He was cooking noodles over an open campfire in the late afternoon when I entered the site. Surprised to see anyone there, I approached with my own caution. Even with the regular checkerboard of closed trailheads and shelters along the entire track due to COVID, the signage for the 501 Shelter closure was still hard to disregard. Anything denoting hazardous water conditions was an immediate red flag. In retrospect, this hiker had reasons to slip behind the makeshift Maginot line as well.

"Hello."

"Well, hello stranger." He responded, squatting with his back turned, un-startled by my presence. "Just you here?"

"Just me," he shrugged, "sorry to disappoint."

The man kept stirring his noodle soup, apparently in no hurry to do anything. His equipment was spread out like a well-organized tag sale with everything in its proper place. It appeared that he had been there a while, but his gear and physical appearance seemed strangely fresh for the location. I came around the fire to inspect a fit, white-haired man that looked just as much "Native-Sage" as he did a hiker. For some reason, I started apologizing:

"No, no...I'm sorry. I didn't mean...."

"Take it easy," he said with a calming smile and continued, "I'm just resting up here. I like solitude. Appears you were looking to hide out, too. No one has been down to this shelter in days. Not with the skull and crossbones on the tape down there. Ha-ha!"

"What's that all about? This shelter isn't under repair....it looks like a temple here. Look at the craftsmanship of this structure! It's like a Hobbit's house, or the inside of a guitar or something. And the water source?"

"All you need to do is boil water to get the little critters out," the man answered. "The real threat are the metal contaminants and the sludge. You know how many toxins we ingest just by walking around that old mining town down there? It's like Chernobyl in that valley."

He had a hell of a point. It made me aware of my lack of awareness. His demeanor was cool and collected and it put me at ease. With a fancy twist of his fork, he brought a noodle up to test it. "Hmm, not quite al dente yet."

"How long have you been here?" I inquired.

"Couple of days. I like these mountains. Peaceful. Medicine Man...." He reached out his hand after wiping it on his shirt.

"Music Man."

"The Music Man. It's a pleasure to finally meet you. How's the thru-hike going?"

"Nice to meet you, Medicine Man. How'd you know I was thru-hiking?"

"That useless A.T.C. tag hanging on your pack there."

"Oh, right." He observed the invalid "thru-hiker" tag with my rescinded number from 1317 to N/A. Until that moment, I felt like it had given me credentials. I vainly wanted people to see it and recognize that I was a thru-hiker. Then when someone finally noticed it, I got embarrassed about my tacky vainglory and felt stupid.

"Music Man, you look like you've had a rough day. Do you always drink alone?"

"If I'm buying, yes. If you're buying, no." I conceded, shunning my own discombobulation.

"Never mind that. You need nourishment. Eat, my friend, EAT. Ha, ha, ha!" The Medicine Man laughed with a gruff grovel that was mined out from the depths of his gut, "Trust me, the water is fine!"

"It has been a hard day, Medicine Man. Father's Day, you know. I miss my kids and my Dad. I'm blowing it, and I'm not treating people right." I was coming correct before Music Man could stop our tongue. It just came out; but Medicine Man wasn't interested in my confession.

"Water," he said. "What?"

"Water, Music Man, water. Your thoughts?"

"Well, it would seem that I crammed my whole life into the bottom of a glass," I replied.

Medicine Man continued "That's right, good hiker. And now, it's about the quality with what you choose to fill your glass, not the quantity. Water is the lifeblood of the land. It's everything living. Nature's perfection can be found in a drop of water. But most of the time, pure and perfect water is not good enough for us humans. "It needs flavor," we say. "It needs added nutrients, and sugar, it needs...alcohol. And we pollute our precious waters with the waste from coal mines, chemical plants and cars, and we wonder why the natural cycle is disrupted. Humans poison each other by what we do to the Earth's water. But in the end, the waters will always cleanse on the rock. The trees will scrub the vapors and tuck away even more carbon dioxide. The water will remain long after we're gone. And it will swallow up the bones of the company towns, and wash everything to the sea; from whence we can try it all again...Look at that spring over there. The water that flows out of that spring is the same water that gave viscosity to the blood of our ancestors. That very water once flowed thru the veins of the ancients that came before us. What happens when we die? Our flesh decomposes and the water returns to the earth. Alas, the cycle of nature continues. The same water in your body right now once gave life to something else. That water gave life to a dinosaur, or an insect, or a tree. Some scientists even suggest the water molecules have their own electromagnetic memory of the DNA structures of living things they were once contained in. Believe this: it's all non-binary. Everything."

"I'm listening."

"Good, Music Man. You need to hear this. You are killing yourself, or your "self" is killing you. What's the difference, you may ask? Well, I just might have an answer." Medicine Man offered they're sage advice:

"When you choose to take a self-destructive path, you disrupt the cycle of a world that you don't even know: Your thinking mind behind your eyes is not the center of the universe. You *are* the universe. And so am I. The center is everywhere." Medicine Man pointed to the setting sun then at his chest and mine too. "The Big Bang literally expanded the space in and around our hearts. Birth to death, the water molecules degrade much slower than the cells of our skin and bones. All molecules are home to the Great Spirit which moves thru water to its own effect. When you find the peace that is possible in your Spirit, you'll know, though you may not understand it. To understand the Great Spirit means to lose it. We can, however, follow the water, coming to simply know the Power. So, how does the water move? According to its Higher Power: Gravity." With eyes closed, the timbre of they're voice changed: "Identify with the fountainhead high up in the mountains. Feel the subtlety of gravity pulling you down, bouncing you off the rocks. You want to find the closest connection with your Higher Power, so you surrender to the flow. Down and down, you tumble, rolling and splashing. But then the grade of the terrain eases, and so, you find grooves and tempos. Surrender yourself; your human ego; which sits right behind your eyes; your "thinking Brain." Give it to the source." Water has no ego. When the water smashes against a rock, it doesn't scratch its head and question or doubt... "I don't know about this whole gravity thing." Without the egocentric self, waters travel freely and seek a natural resting place at the calm, stable flatland of the valleys and plateaus, where it pools with tidal ebb and flow. Sometimes a pond will stagnate, but the water vapor will eventually move back into the cycle. You are water, Music Man. So be water. Behave like water behaves. The quickest way to quit dragging thru mud is to simply let go of the rope. Then stand up, dust off, accept things as they are, and surrender to the Great Spirit." Medicine Man took a deep breath and the timbre of his normal speaking voice returned, as he fixed his eyes upon me with a final question:

"Music Man, what should you do with a glass that is half empty?"

"I don't know, Medicine Man. What?"

"Pour it into a smaller glass."

I felt the doors of a spiritual awakening creak open to let some new light in. He tried his noodles again: "Al dente! Have some."

We fell silent as we ate, then wearily I slept. I woke up with the sun's rays on my face to find Medicine Man gone without a trace. I looked around for signs of his departure but found no tracks or hints of his presence. He had slipped out quieter than a shelter mouse in the night, with direction unknown. I never thanked Medicine Man, but he knew I was grateful.

Carl Sagan once said, when referring to the ancients of the past, that "over the dying embers of a campfire, people watched the stars." What also came with believing that we are the center of the Universe, was the notion of "geo-centric conceit." Wherever we were, so was the Middle Kingdom. Quite vain of us, reader. It took open minds, observation, and imitation before the first scientists weren't burned at the stake for suggesting that all things are connected in material spirit, too. Just as the ancients back then, I fancied that a great Energy was at work. A fresh sense of gratitude filled me on the trail that day, as I was thankful for everything I still had. I loved my children with all my heart, and I knew that they loved me too. There was still a chance to turn things around. After all, every saint has a past, and every sinner has a future. But there can be no salvation without atonement.

After a few miles, I started hearing chuckles and chainsaws and camaraderie. The last switchback of the climb delivered me onto a plateau where trail maintainers from the Susquehanna Trail Club were touching up tree and rock blazes with new coats of the special white paint. I stopped for a look-see and was warmly greeted. Our simple exchange was especially memorable:

"Hey there, friend. Are you thru-hiking?"

"Yep, I sure am. You guys painting blazes?"

"Yep, we sure are. Say... Are you the guy from the paper?"

"The paper?"

"Yeah," chimed another one, "you look familiar. Were you a part of that "pandemic" article the New York Times published about the AT?"

"That was me, amongst others."

"You all did a decent job representing the Trail. Well done."

"Thanks."

"What's your name?"

"Music Man."

"Really? I've heard of you and that instrument you carry. Play us a tune?"

"Sure guys. I'm grateful for the hard work you do out here, keeping this trail fit for fiddling."

"Our pleasure, Music Man. We love it too."

I sang "My Old Kentucky Home" for the good stewards of the Susquehanna Trail Club. They clapped and expressed thanks.

"So, Music Man, would you like to paint a blaze?"

"Would I ever! That would be an honor."

"It's a good trade for the song you gave us."

They handed me a paint brush and pointed out the stepping stone on the trail needing a touchup. I knew it was a high honor and I was truly grateful for the singular experience of dropping a fresh coat of paint on the trail's original mapping. How many hikers before me had used this blaze for direction and comfort?

I was grateful that my new boots, acquired back at Harpers Ferry, were still in good condition. The trail was getting very jagged, more rocks were waiting. Surface conditions were going to get worse before they got better. I sat at a valley overlook and had a snack. Just a few yards away, two rattlesnakes spun around each other like a barber's pole. They didn't pay me no mind, at all. I was glad they had found what they were looking for. Not wanting to interrupt, I walked away.

Later that day, I was sitting next to a stream collecting water when Garlic walked up.

"Hey, lover." she said in sweet Yankee. "How was your Father's Day?" She sat down with me. "It was okay," I mumbled.

"I read the poem you wrote in the register back at Rausch...about your son," she sat down beside me.

I was surprised. At the time, I didn't consider that people I knew were coming up behind and some would read the poem, if they bothered to open the shelter logs.

"Pretty heavy, Music." Garlic affirmed my work.

I didn't respond, but I curled my lips into a half smile.

Garlic shifted the tone, "I was thinking about hiking with this guy, maybe you've seen him? He looks like..."

My half smile widened as she kissed me.

"Let's go." We took each other's hand and stood up.

The rocks in Pennsylvania were especially torturous on Garlic's already shredded feet. As I hiked behind her, the countless steps she took in agony were hard to watch. But not as hard as actually walking in those shoes. She sometimes tripped over her own feet in pain. But she never fell. She just pushed on, building character with every painful rock and root underfoot.

The rocks came in all shapes and sizes. From baseball-sized rocks to beachball-boulders up to the size of small cars. Sometimes the paper-thin shale crumbled with just a little weight on it. We never knew which ones would shift and move underneath our constantly shifting balance. Progress was slow across the miles and miles of rock after rock after rock after rock.... It was exhausting and it was maddening, toiling under what seemed like a Guatemalan sun.   One blazing hot day, we were scrambling thru yet another boulder field when Garlic stopped us dead in our tracks, replete with agony. She was barely able to put any weight on her foot. She was getting emotional because of the searing pain though she tried to hide it.

"It's not far to town. Bae, will you go ahead and get us a room somewhere? I need to get off trail," she conceded. Getting off the trail could mean taking a break and a quick return or taking a break and not returning at all.

"Are you sure you want me to push forward? I don't like the idea of leaving you alone in this condition. If the situation deteriorates, Garlic, there is no one coming up behind us to help."

"I'm sure. Please go secure somewhere for me to rest. Then call from the motel and tell me the room number."

Her voice was shaky, like she needed a good cry and didn't want to do it in front of me. "Ok. You've got enough water, right?"
She nodded as I turned for town. My feet were killing me, too. The trail had been treacherous, and my new boots started to blow out. I needed a break myself. The blistering heat made boulder-hopping a living hell. Transferred radiation from the baked rocks had warmed up our boots to incredible temperatures and fueled the swelling of our feet. Even the wind felt like the opening of a furnace door. The battle was lost, yet I had to keep marching thru enemy lines.

No later than leaving her behind, cloud cover crept in to take the scorching rays of sunlight off my brow. The oasis of shade further reinforced how hot it really was. A breeze crossed my face as the trail turned toward a feature on a ridge that I had been expecting. NTN had marked and mailed his trail maps with granulated details about the terrain. "P.U.D.S. and rocks on the surface of steeply graded scrambles" the map indicated. Mentally, physically, and spiritually fragile, I entered the underwood.   A strange scene of past, present and future spirits was woven into the

134

fabric of my psyche. I think GBITS was trying to tell me something.

The gloomy and spooky walk thru the Rock Maze took on a tale of its own. I kept seeing Old Uncle Jake disappearing and reappearing in, on and around the rocks, like a will-o'-the-wisp. He was wearing his new white suit, as fresh as the day he was buried in it. He was holding the drink he had in his hand just before he died. As he raises the glass, a breeze blows his suit and skin away in a gust of dust, leaving his skeleton to tremble and quake before neatly falling in a pile. His skull lands on top with a clack of the jaw, and shattered glass. Meanwhile, Custer's band of apparitions plays on to the tune of 'Gary Owen' wafting and echoing up the valley, like music up a windy street. But they play it in an atonal raga key that summons the vipers from their off-trail slumbers, without their permission. Old Uncle Jake's smiling skull intimates that "it's for the best." He is almost always hitting the right note, so I'll take him at face value.... what's left of it anyway.

I snapped out of it and climbed down to a trail junction sign: "Shelter 0.2 ↗"

Somewhere, the clouds disappeared again. The rediscovered sun brought blistering summer heat back, which normally didn't bother me. On that day, it gripped my soul as the melting soles of my shoes were starting to lose their grip on the earth. I sat on a demon of a boulder and poured water down my throat and over my head. It seemed like the more I drank, the thirstier I got. Kind of like the ravenous and rabid animal of addiction: Once you fire off the cannon, the shifting target calls for constant reloads but the aim is never as sharp as the first shot. The hissing mark just gets harder and harder to hit. Anyway, I decided to wait there for Garlic. If I was this tired, then her struggle was very real. I waited and waited but there was no sign of her. Nearly half an hour went by with still no sign of her. Then I heard footsteps and the clicking of trekking poles on the track, and thought, "Wow, she's up and moving now." I stood to greet her, but another hiker approached. It was a brown-haired girl cruising down the trail completely covered in sweat. My nerves absorbed a wave of anxiety, and I demanded answers from the blindsided stranger who looked like she'd been bobbing for apples.

"Hey there, hiker."

"Hi!" she returned, not seeming to mind the heat at all.

"Did you see a hiker back there? Blonde girl...."

"Yeah, man, I did. She ain't doing so good."

"Where is she?" I asked impatiently.

She gave me a creepy look before I offered, "that's Garlic, my hiking partner."

"Oh, okay man. I sat with her for a minute. She has water, but that girl is totally overheated with her shoes and socks off. She's just sitting on the side of the trail, man. Hurting!"

"Damn it. Okay, thanks."

"Can you call her or something?"

"No phone. How far back?"

"No more than half a mile. No phone? You or her?"

I took only my water bottle and started hiking the Appalachian Trail south for the first time since Springer Mountain, when I started my hike on that cold and rainy day. A far cry from sweltering Pennsylvania. Without the pack weight I felt as light as a feather on the rescue mission. I feared that a more serious event had happened with her feet.

After ten minutes of foot-pounding the rocks like a jackhammer, I found Garlic right where I was told she would be. She was a hot mess, sitting alone with her swollen feet and nearly out of water. Her face was flushed but she tried to regain some composure as I approached. When I sat down, her head fell on my shoulder in total exhaustion. I wrapped my arms around her.

"Oh, Bae. I can't walk." She was totally defeated. "I can't carry my pack weight. My foot is just killing me. Something popped. I don't know if I can do this anymore."

The words, fraught with self-conviction, were hard to hear. We both knew she was risking permanent injury with every mile. I wanted to take her pain away. But I was powerless.

"Take it easy, babe. I'll carry you if I have to. You're gonna be okay, I promise. (Like I had any control....) We've gotta get you off this boulder pile and out of the heat. I'll take most of your pack weight. You can do it, Garlic."

"I really don't think I can."

"Yes, you can. Garlic, you are the strongest hiker I know. I've watched you walk over hot coals for a thousand miles."

"This is different, Music. It feels like an ice pick is being jammed into my heel. And I'm just sitting here."

"Do you remember the poem I wrote for you? The one I slipped under your motel door in Waynesboro."

"Of course, Music Man."

"This is it—the importance of the moment."

It was the last thing in the bloody world that the woman wanted to do, but she took a deep breath and prepared to stand. I thru her pack over my shoulders and helped her up. Grimaced and grunting in pain, she steadied herself favoring the healthier foot. Downright determined to persevere, Garlic heroically carried herself off that mountain pass in one piece. If her foot was broken, her spirit sure as hell wasn't yet. Jumping off the side would have been easier and less painful. Witnessing my wife go through all-natural birthing experiences at the end of both pregnancies. I recall just like it was yesterday...driving her across the John F. Kennedy Bridge in the middle of that bitter cold night during Christmas week, after she went into labor at home (past full-term) with our first baby. Her hands were planted on the ceiling of the mid-nineties Buick as she bellowed out "I'm gonna drop this baby into the OHIO-fucking-RIVER if you don't STEP ON IT!" Minutes later we pulled up to the Emergency Entrance at Memorial Hospital, and mere moments after that our daughter was born. Women have a capacity for enduring pain that men will never know. "Birthing women" seal the deal for the strongest of the sexes.

I am fully aware, reader, that you find this simile in bad taste. But I lived it. This is my observation as a positive witness. Unaided by any pain reducing agents, Garlic descended the mountain feeling every twist and pang of pain that her nervous system could fire off. At the end of the day, the physical and mental relief of rest was pure and earned.

In the vortex of town, we settled down to complete immobility for many hours. It was taking longer for Garlic to recover each time. Truth be told, I didn't know how many miracles of healing she had left in her. Sometimes it isn't up to us and sometimes it is. In hindsight, it was only partial physical healing that enabled Garlic to get back out time and again. Breaking from the mental anguish of having to manage constant pain was equally as critical to her continuation. When the capacity for endurance was recharged the next morning, she was ready to hike again. We were soon limping around a grocery store in resupply mode getting ready to return to the trail.

"I need Garlic powder."

"I need a King-sized Payday. Dad got me hooked. Oh, and let's not forget Cheez-Its." "Right! The trail-crack."

"I am proud of you, babe," I poured onto her, "but if things get worse again, don't worry about it.

We'll take it one day at a time, one step at a time," I reassured her. "I'm with you all the way."

"At some point, you may need to hike on without me. I know I'm dragging your tempo, Music Man," she lamented.

"No, you're not." Though her "pacing" observation was correct some of the time, it didn't fully apply. Speedy big miles never were in my repertoire, but our pacing and natural strides could vary widely. None of that mattered to me; competition was for horse racing.

"The scope of the journey has evolved, Garlic. Making miles is just the means. I love hiking with you. I love you. And this Tramily is great. The bubble has not burst yet! This crew is going to make it, all of us. I can feel it."

"You think?"

"I believe it."

"You're so positive, Music. I don't know how you manage that outlook all the time. I guess I could do a little more self-reinforcement sometimes."

"Lord, girlfriend, you do enough of that with each footfall. Here's looking at you, kid...ready to kick again. Let's get a loaf of sourdough, what do you say?"

Garlic's face lit up with "Okay!"

At certain points, especially when feet were active and sore, I would ask her to explain the process of baking bread, again. Garlic took great joy in outlining the scale of ingredients around her world-famous yeast; the kneading and rising, and the degassing. It took her mind off the pain when talking about something else she loved to do as much as hiking. She explained the process to me a dozen and one times, but I would still bomb the kitchen if I tried to shake and bake myself.

Garlic meticulously selected a loaf of sweet-smelling bread from the shelf and then looked up at me. In sweet Yankee, she said something to me that I will never forget. I can still hear her voice now...

"Music Man, when we get off this trail, I'm gonna make you so fat. I'm gonna bake you bread and make you pasta...and don't sass me when I'm in the kitchen! And I'm going to keep you grateful for my good loving."

Her glowing face sent a flutter thru my heart. It was the sweetest thing that a lover had ever said to this undeserving man. It was also the first time either of us mentioned a life together after the trail.

"So, you want to be with me after all...this, after all?" I fumbled my words.

"What are we going to do? Run away? I love you, Music. Maybe we could...start to have that conversation...if you want to..." She looked uneasy and a flash of doubt crossed her face again as she judged my reaction. I brushed her hair behind her ears with my fingers and responded:

"I want to be with you and be with my kids. Wherever y'all are is where I call home."

She lit back up:

"Buttah! We need buttah for this bread."

"I'll butter your bread."

She slapped my hand away with playful annoyance.

"You're terrible, control yah-self. What'd I tell you about getting between a girl and her food? When we get off trail, you've got one job to do, Music Man." She reiterated her boundaries with sassy back talk in the kitchen.

"Well, maybe two."

"You know it."

Garlic turned the bread aisle into a catwalk, shaking her hips for a few satisfied paces. Then she turned back around looking serious.

"Wait, there is a third thing, Bae."

"Oh yeah, what's that, hot stuff?"

The serious hiker ran it all the way back:

"If you get high again, just tell me. I know better than to beg you not to get high again, Music Man. If you're gonna do it, you're gonna do it. Or you already did it. Just don't lie to me, *please*. I know recovery is a process. Don't get it twisted, Music Man. I'm not giving you permission to set everything on fire. But tell me if you slip. We all fall short sometimes. If you're honest with me...we have a real chance. Can you do that for me, Bae? You are doing so good."

I took her hand into mine and genuinely made my reply.

"I will. I promise."

Music Man believed it with all his heart. I was getting better, and it felt good. "We" made the oath to Garlic, but I wasn't so sure that I could keep it. If we were post-modern Hansel and Gretel, I certainly wasn't throwing down any breadcrumbs.

.12

THE TOE-TWISTING MINEFIELD OF PENNSYLVANIA ROCKS was in the rear-view. Getting back to simpler trail hiking was a relief. But the challenges had taken their toll. The top of my left foot had begun to hurt. It was dull at first, but the ache worsened as the total days and miles on the AT increased. Progress was inescapable, be it pain or distance, and both brought us closer pivotal moments in our hikes. Garlic had just survived the ultimate physical challenge that would define her moxie as a thru-hiker. Much to her delight, her plantar fasciitis started to improve. My thoughts often drifted to post-hike plans, but we spoke of it rarely. The conversation about our future, that surfaced back at the grocery store, had done well enough to ease some distracting anxieties. And so, we got back to the basics of roaming the highlands of time (for as long as our feet held up). Hike, stop and have a look-see, eat, and retire. We carried on like that for many days, perhaps a week or more. Garlic and I rarely drifted more than a couple miles from each other, locked in unusually tight for us.

The wildlife was terrific. We saw lots of bears and Garlic was tracking what she thought were fox tracks on the trail. She had quite a collection of beautiful feathers too. Every now and then, when she found an especially fitting feather, she would turn around and stick it into my cap with a wink and a kiss. The Fantastic Food Group often leap frogged us and I enjoyed their company whenever I got the chance.

Garlic treated me for my 40th birthday with a surprise restaurant reservation that was just steps off the trail at a highway crossing. She then let me call Bro for half an hour with her phone, while she sat by just looking at me and smiling while I talked. A terrible thunderstorm passed over late that afternoon and we huddled under her pack cover to dodge lightning, squeaking with laughter at each bolt that missed us. The weather cleared for a stunning sunset upon a graffiti-tagged ridge, and she captured my single favorite picture of Music Man on the Appalachian Trail. Garlic spent her day making sure mine would be a jewel in the cove of my memory, and she succeeded. The only thing that could have made the day better, would have been a hug from my twin bro. But Garlic's arms felt damn good enough. She reminded me often of how happy she was to know that the general post-hike location for our settling down would be near my daughter and son. "Those kids deserve their dad," she reflected, "and as they are getting older, so are you. You all need each other."

On our way into Delaware Water Gap, I felt a bite between my pack strap and my back. I shook it off and didn't give it another thought until I took my shirt off many hours later.

"Oh my! Music, you have a bull's eye the size of a basketball on your back!" Garlic cried out in horror.

"Bull's Eye? What are you talking about?" I reached for an itch I couldn't scratch. Garlic came in for a closer inspection and subsequent diagnosis:

"Yep, that's a tick bite, Music Man. No tick hanging on...it's gone. But that bull's eye rash spells one thing: Lyme's Disease," she said with a gloom, "that is, unless you can snub it with antibiotics immediately."

Very fortunately, we were a handful of miles from Delaware Water Gap. Within hours of catching the infection, I made it to a hike-in health clinic and was written a prescription for Doxycycline. I finished the antibiotic as prescribed (there is a first time for everything), and the medicine worked like it was supposed to. I managed to escape the life-long affliction of cyclical Lyme's, thanks to having a solid hiking partner who looked out for me, and luck.

The difficulty of the trail was variable as we moved thru New Jersey. Hikers were generally in good spirits; not terribly beat up by the elements. Garlic and I were well syncopated and squarely focused on the sport tasks at hand. It was hard to keep weight on my body and I was starting to get dangerously thin again, but my body had a strange recollection of the condition and I barely noticed. Garlic constantly urged me to eat more. I tried to take in as much protein as I could with things like lightly salted peanuts and real-meat jerky. I still smoked too many cigarettes, but I was becoming more conscious of my health and trying to make better choices. When I ate right and slept regularly, I felt better. Garlic was pleased with the overall changes in my physical maintenance, and she rewarded me. I registered success. But the ghosts of the past were looming behind the rocks and trees, and they eventually paid us a visit.

The 4th of July found Choogle, Garlic and me cowboy-camped on Catfish Fire Tower in New Jersey, perched sixty feet above the ridge that it crowned. Choogle surprised us with a bottle of bourbon and some firecrackers that he had hiked up from town. As the sun went down, the valley floor lit up with fireworks and mortars popping off from what seemed like hundred different hamlets and towns in a twenty-mile radius, illuminating the Land of the Free with a rolling boil of light.

Choogle's harp and my Strumstick rang high and lonesome from the high tower on the holiday. We decided against lighting the M-80's, we didn't need to. The flickers of a thousand bombs raved the valley like bonnaroo strobe lights. I thought I spied Garlic looking at him with choogly eyes, re-throwing her hair over to one side and recrossing her legs often. I tried not to let it affect me, but eventually I couldn't hide the fact that it had put me on tilt. While damaging, jealousy is so often rooted in the imagination. Unfortunately, for that occasion, my instincts got the better of me. Though I was entirely responsible for the arena of mistrust, I confronted her about my self-imposed and floundering observations the next day. After Choogle bid us farewell to embark on one of his marathon marches, I opened the floodgates:

"So, what was up with you and Choogle back at Catfish Tower?"

"What the hell is that supposed to mean?" she turned and sipped her water bottle.

"I thought I saw you looking at him... I don't know, like...seducing, or something."

"You're out of your goddamn mind." Garlic stared at me, and a put a hand on her hip. "Me and Choogle?"

That put me on further guard. Waves of familiar paranoia battered against my skull-walls.

"I didn't mean 'you and Choogle...'"

"It sure as hell sounded like you did."

"Don't turn this around on me. I asked you a question."

"And I gave you an answer. You're out of your goddamn mind!"

"Cut the bullshit..."

"No, YOU cut the bullshit, Music Man. What about you and...what was her name? Monarch?"

I froze in a panic, feeling like I had stepped into my own hunting noose. A sudden movement would have me hanging upside down. She had never confronted me about Monarch, but I feared that she had heard grumblings about the infidelity back in Virginia. Garlic had asked me if I met the hiker like everyone else, to which I affirmed. But she had never outright asked me...for the truth.

"What about her?"

"You fucked her back in Virginia, didn't you?"

"What? I haven't *fucked* anyone." I lied again.

The retort only made it worse. She stepped closer and lowered her voice.

"I didn't ask you if you fucked *anyone*." As stoic as she could, "I am asking you if you had sex with Monarch."

Crickets.

The hypocrisy of my ways mule-kicked me in the groin.

"Well, did you?" She doubled down.

"NO, Garlic, I did not have sex with Monarch."

It was bullshit in its purest and most harmful form, and it was one of the most wretched lies I have ever told, rivaling the deed itself. Who was I kidding? Only myself. But I stuck to the story and tried not to break character. She looked deep into my eyes. A pause.

142

"Whatever, Music Man. Let's hike. This spot is getting...cumbersome."

Cumbersome? I couldn't understand.

"You take the lead," she added.

I didn't press her, holding on to the deluded hope that my horrible secret was still just that: a secret. I would not allow myself the reality that the jury was already out. The defense would not rest. But no more questions for the cornpump defendant. In a moment like that, all the self-reflection I had done just seemed like writing a letter that I never intended to send, and the carefully crafted cathedral made of aluminum foil crumbles to a sharp and slicing wad of failure.

Her eyes burned holes thru my soul as we silently crossed the hills. We pitched our own tents at the campsite that night, and I even considered going past where we had originally decided to call it for the day. I stayed, however, and we ate dinner silently then went to our own tents. When I woke up the next morning, she was gone.

I didn't see anyone all day and camped alone on a ridge that night. I was thoroughly sick and tired of myself. Garlic had only ever asked three things of me. 1) Treat her right 2) No backtalk in the kitchen 3) Do not lie to her. Still, I was unwilling to face the fear of what I stood to lose if I told the truth, and unable to accept the potential cost of the lies.

It was time to travel alone for a while, I decided, as I hiked thru the desolate Harriman State Park...already alone.

At a trailhead kiosk, a sign read:

"Fingerboard Shelter closed due to bear activity."

We'll see about that. After a water "camel up" with twelve miles left to the shelter I began the trudge, hauling heavy burdens of water and guilt. The landscape was eerie with lots of sparse boulders, thick tree cover and a gloomy sky that just begged to dump a similar load of heavy water. But it never did. Around three miles from the shelter at dusk, I ran out of water. So much for a second thought of passing up the closed shelter. Not a soul stirred in the park for miles and hours. I was completely alone. Making my way down the blue-blazed side trail to the shelter, I passed some steel-fixed bear lines meant for hanging food. Upon closer inspection, I observed the stout metal cables to be thrashed apart over a scrap heap of hiker trash and food wrappers strewn about the ground—definitive signs of aggressive bear activity. Uh...Maybe this wasn't such a good idea, after all. Desperate for water and lacking sufficient light to safely push on, I decided I must stop for the night and risk it. The only bear deterrent I had was that M-80 firecracker that had been buried deep in my pack since New Jersey. I decide to pitch my tent inside the shelter, deducing that no one else was stupid enough to come here. But I took comfort in the notion that I could keep quiet and out of sight. I would not cook dinner here and send smoke signals of scent flying from the roof of the shelter. Late was the hour when I noshed on the last bit of jerky before deciding to walk down to the river for more water. Beams of my headlamp's rays led the way. The water source was two dimes down an open-graded incline. As I crept down, I had to hug myself lest I let go and start trembling at the sound of each faint jingle of slinky little pebbles. Too quiet. The beam of my headlight swathed about as I filled my water bottles and checked all the corners of stillness that never ended. Even the squirrels and birds knew to stay away. Squatting next to the stream, the last drops of water left the filter and dripped into the bottle when I heard a *Rustle... RUSTLE...*

"Who's there?" I turned with a quickness. "Hey, bear, where are you?! Nothing to see here!"

Rustle...Cher, Crack...Sonny, Snap... I threw my light beam back over my other shoulder. Frantically searching for the Ursus-Plus, I put on a laser light show as I hunted. Or was I the game? But there was no bear. I laughed out loud as I rose to meet and talked myself out of the silly pursuit, as I meandered back to the shelter. Better get the firecracker out just in case. I hung my pack at the front of the shelter and brought my food sack into the tent with me. There was nowhere to hang the food. The bear lines were trashed, and I was at the end of my own rope. Time to call it day. I zipped up the tent and laid down for sleep. I kept awake for a while, listening to the sounds of the night. Like a recording studio engineer, I screened the forest noise for thumps and thuds of a hungry Smokey, but he just wasn't there. I drifted off to sleep and fell into a deep slumber. Still, I had placed the firecracker and lighter close by. Many hours went by...

Around 5 am, my eyes opened to the darkness. Why had I awoken? I sat up in my sleeping bag.

Rustle... Rustle...

Oh shit. Close by.

RUSSELL! Garumph...

Very close by. I held my breath attempting to mitigate sounds, scents, or giveaways of the still yet living, and slowly unzipped my tent to the blackness. A tremolo of horror panned against the shelter walls, the sonic source....my hanging pack? I click on the headlamp....

"BEAR!!!!"

Just six feet from my tent, momma bear was on her hind legs, butterfly-floating eight feet in the air, jabbing my backpack around like an Olympic-fit Ali practicing on a speed bag. She turned her head to look down at little ole Music Man at her feet, as I couldn't sing a note. I was stunned. She turned her head further toward the ground. I didn't dare, but I did. I shined the beam down low to the object of interest scampering about at her feet: a cub—

Oh, hellfire. This just got real. I shined the light back up at her face, as she continued to loom over me. We both opened our mouths, but she got the first word....

RAA-ERRRRR!

"Ahhh! BEAR, NO BEAR, BLACK BEAR, GO BEAR...BIG FUCKING BEAR!"

RAAAA-ERRRRRRRR! *Thump-thump...* Her front paws smacked the dirt like Cassius Clay delivering a bee-stinging one-two to the punching mitts of a frightened and grimacing gym scrub. Momma's head dropped within a couple feet of mine—Barely and the Beast...She was huge! I scrambled for the firecracker and the lighter.

"No, No, Bear! You can't have my stuff, BEAR! Go AWAY BEAR! Please don't eat me, *nice* bear!"

Garumph...Snort...Garumph.

I clutched the firecracker. Do I light the fuse and pray she gets away? Damn, the cub. If she didn't have that little heathen, I'd light a blast-off underneath her. But I feared an explosion in the darkness might trigger a deeper primal rage to defend her young. I kept screaming, then I set my headlamp to flash and aimed it at the ceiling of my tent, making it look like a flying saucer or a DeLorean.

"GO! AWAY! BEAR!"

Then the cub caught wind of a chipmunk, or ground animal, or some Holy thing, and took off running. Momma watched her cub run then turned back to me, as she guarded the swinging backpack, still under the roof of my shelter. *My* safe place.

With a final "Garumph" she got the last word as well. Momma gave up and slumped away after her undisciplined and certainly not-as-hungry cub. I never had to fire my only shot, which was a feeble blank of sound that probably would have gotten me killed. Lighter went with M-80 to the back of the pack again. The encounter lasted all of two minutes, and it was the longest two minutes of my hike. The sun rose low and warm over Fingerboard Shelter that morning, but the Music Man was long gone before the first rays of light twinkled against the tattered bear lines that marked the plundered grounds like empty gallows. I survived again, albeit it was a draw. From then on, I stuck to more familiar fingerboards. (Que an out-of-tune Strumstick)

At Bear Mountain, New York, where the trail crosses the Hudson River, I had become increasingly malnourished and dehydrated. After renting a cheap room in town, I barely had the energy or the funds to buy a sports drink and a Clif Bar with the money left over. Furthermore, my foot was killing me. Morale was in the tank with my motivation for life. The shuttle driver dropped me off at the post office where there was a food drop from my parents. That box had saved my ass from famine, and I walked over to my motel room to tear in and chow down, but I didn't really have an appetite. I opened the box to find a full resupply that was packed with Mom's dehydrated meals, high protein grabs (essential) like homemade venison jerky from my uncle, and powdered drink mix for hydration. In this box was a manila envelope. I held it for a moment and closed my eyes. I ran my finger under the flap and opened the end, then I dumped the contents onto the bed: Dozens of letters and handwritten cards from family and friends. Cybil had organized it, and it was the single most heartfelt gesture that a friend had ever done for me...Friends, I should say, who all contributed sentiments of love and encouragement. The letters contained thousands of words filled with well-wishes, we-love-you's, and "Don't Fucking Quit" directives. Moved to a stunning emotional place that day, I detached. Memories of that day are hazy. But I know that I wept while reading your letters. I became, through your words, convinced that I was worth fighting for. How would I ever make things right, with everyone? There is a process for that, in its proper order. So I decided to just keep hiking. Somehow, the trail was mining out the character defects and placing them squarely in my face and unable to avoid them. The trail is long, but it is narrow.

On the approach to the RPH Shelter in Upstate New York, the sides of the trail began to look special, with well-placed stones and strategic aqueducts for diverting water off the trail. Weeds were clipped away, and the voices of jolly trail maintainers rose as I rounded the bend to the shelter grounds.

"Welcome, traveler!" A friendly, red-bearded dude approached to shake my hand and offered to carry my pack the last few paces for me. "This is RPH, the best damn shelter on the AT! I'm Redbeard, and this is Bill." The other guy extended a hand that was as lanky as the rest of him. He leaned in as I reached for it, and quietly introduced himself.

"Bill Bancroft, a pleasure."

"I'm Music Man, nice to meet you gents. What's going on here today, with all these people around?" I noticed Choogle from a distance, with work gloves on, sweating over the removal of a giant tree stump from the center of the greenspace near the shelter.

"Choogle!"

"What's up Music Man! Just doing a little train maintenance!"

"Awesome, my friend! Let me help!" I reached for a pair of gloves.

"Thanks, Music Man," said Bill Bancroft, "giving back to the trail is what it's all about." I see that the AT has had some altruistic effects on you as well. We're all in this thing together. From the moment I found this trail, its spirit found a way into me. You are not alone out here, my friend. RPH Shelter is an example of that, and you can find us here all season, every year. Let us cook you a steak. A little "thank-you" for your willingness to help." A sweet old-soul, Bill was brickish and reminded me of a stoned Yoda.

"Wow, I would love that Bill! Thank you!"

"No, our thanks to you." He gently bowed his head.

"Are you guys with A.T.C., or a trail club?" I asked them, but they looked at each other in a pause then laughed together.

"Get those gloves on, Music Man! Ha-ha-ha!"

I got down to business, helping Choogle dig up the stump. He was so chipper, and genuine, and talked up my musicianship to the others. I thought about how silly my accusations of Garlic had been, and I felt more twinges of regret with how I treated her...what a hypocrite I was. I imagined that the bloody big stump we dug out represented the old trunk of secrets and mischief that were buried deep within my soul. I wanted to dig that stuff out and give it to the Universe. Maybe, I could release that little boy in my ego. Maybe, just maybe, I could let a higher power handle my affairs...eventually. Bill Bancroft noticed my quietly ferocious effort, and mentioned it later:

"Music Man, you seemed very...determined, to get that old tree stump out. That thing was huge, yes, nice job. But once that one is gone, there will be another to remove. That will require your strength as well," he intimated. "Take the obstacles as they come, conserve your efforts, and learn from your methods. Don't chop down a Christmas tree in July."

Bill Bancroft was on to something. He didn't need my context to offer me a sound suggestion; he had his own experiences with the trails of life and life on trails. "Take it easy, Music Man. Good job, and now you can refuel. Here's a steak and a beverage. Thanks for giving back to the path and community."

"No, Bill. Thank you."

"Welcome." He opened a semi-furled smile of the wise. Nobos gave cheers to Bill for the rest of the hike, spoofing the old SNL skit "Tales of Bill Brasky." The toast was warmly changed, "To Bill Bancroft!" Can you imagine the fun we had with that? No example given or needed here.

Amid the more clement climate of Kent, Connecticut, I took the loop trail down to Kent Falls and found Garlic standing on the riverbank still wearing her backpack. She didn't turn to look as I approached and took the spot next to her. We looked at the raging high falls together in silence. As I was about to speak, something moving cast a shadow over us as it flew over the waterfall, and down into the canopy of limbs covering the fleeing river. Its wingspan was huge, as the dinosaur disappeared into the big and tall tunnel that was created by the overhanging trees. The breathtaking creature was likely on a river hunt.

"Bald eagle," Garlic identified.

"Wow, how can you tell?"

"The wings. He looked old and tattered."

"That's a first for me...a bald eagle," my voice cracked.

147

"Music Man, I don't want to hear another word about Choogle, or Monarch, or any bullshit from the last ump-teen hundred miles. Do I make myself clear?"

There was pain in her voice as she was preparing herself for the chest-punch of emotional endurance she was adding to her struggles. She wouldn't accept a confession from me now, even if I was willing. It was too late for that. The slapping tumble of the waterfall sounded like a roar of applause for Garlic, and I felt like hiding in the curtain at the wings. She had taken her own "contemplative stop-and-rest day in Peekskill," she later admitted. She was skilled at the craft of taking abuse and turning the other cheek. One thing is for sure, she wanted no pity and would not accept any. The woman had been thru much in her other life, and I suspected that she was planning to add this latest injustice to her bucketful of "no fucks left to give." In other words, chalk up another resentment then stuff it down and move forward. As the tarnish was darkening, I was reminded that the truth needs no suit of armor. Where was Old Uncle Jake? I needed help.

Another hiker approached us from behind. I greeted him with surprise.

"John the Baptist! Holy.... Man, we haven't seen you since Carolina! I thought you would be long finished by now; with those 30 milers you were pulling every day. Where have you been?" I was optimistic that the mood might shift.

"Music Man and Garlic! I see you two are still fast and furious!"

"Just carving the path," she pleasantly responded. "How are you?"

"Great," replied the religious man. "I'm glad to be back out here! I got off trail in Pennsylvania and went home for a month. But I'm back to finish out the hike. Why not?"

"A month? Damn, son!"

I felt a twinge of competitive loss at this hiker's update. *This* guy was that fast one. Garlic died inside. But she was like her damned cat and shrugged it off.

"John the Baptist! You're a freakin' thoroughbred."

"Breakfast?" He posed, "I hear there's a great Airstream diner in town."

We agreed that is just what we all needed. Eggs and bacon with coffee and juice sounded good.

John the Baptist wanted to hear all about our adventures, and we listened to his tales of occasional forty-mile days, hiking for 18-20 hours without stopping, listening to Jesus, and talking to God. As he spoke about his spirituality, I wished I had what he had. We broke bread, then we parted ways with John the Baptist. Garlic and I walked to the government building together to claim a posted parcel. The general delivery shipping label read:

"HOLD FOR THRU-HIKERS: Music Man & Garlic"

After slicing open the box, I noshed into a Payday candy bar from the supply drop my parents had mailed to the Kent post office. My mom had added a couple homemade and dehydrated vegetarian meals for Garlic. My cousin Gary sent amazingly made-for-me venison jerky, straight from the hills back home. Dad sent some cash too. I was broke. Having run out of divorce money before passing the Nation's capital, I was now completely financially dependent on support from off-trail. I would work-for-stay periodically and take advantage of resupply opportunities when possible.

"Music Man, we'll let you have a free cot in the bunkhouse if you play music by the campfire later?"

"That's a bet...all day and all night."

A former trail club president in Pennsylvania once took me out to Burger King then paid for my resupply. He took me to Burger King again the next morning. Bro and my parents continued to send periodic resupply mail drops and Uncle Ron (NTN) and Aunt Janet sent me boxes of food and supplies too. Cousin Sarah put together a collage of family photos with a handwritten letter of genuine joy and pride. Another note told me that my cousin Patrick's boys were plotting my progress on a map, and Uncle Joe knew that I carried his poem in my wallet, aptly titled "Don't Quit." I read it every night under my headlamp, then tucked the tattered paper away as I tucked myself in. There was real love in those boxes, and I had received at least one in every state. I had picked up several packages from post offices in Old Appalachia that contained letters of love and support, in addition to the consumables. The package was yet another reminder of the journey's team effort. I wouldn't be able to hike without this support, in a spiritual as well as financial sense. Being off the grid without a phone came at a cost, when the time came for "thank-you correspondence." I didn't have that many phone numbers committed to memory outside of my immediate family and friends, but there were return addresses on envelopes. I tried to send a postcard to my parents from every state and call them when it was appropriate. A concerted effort was made to connect our voices after my Father's Day failings. My parents had long since warmed up to the decent idea of my continuing the journey. But I was judicious with using Garlic's phone. I didn't carry that equipment, so using it for calls or texts never sat well with me. But Garlic wanted me to contact my family, and she offered her cell phone for my calls more often than I accepted.

Passing thru the Berkshires of Western Massachusetts, the support back along the trail corridor was incredible too. Our humble bubble of hikers was small in numbers, but big in heart. It consisted of those of us who stubbornly refused to let the pandemic stop us from chasing our dreams.

Thankfully, hikers who had vacated the trail earlier in the season had returned with renewed vigor. Those of us who stayed on to hike protected the precious hope that it was still possible to finish a thru-hike. Roots of real community had tapped into our beings. Bodies and spirits were frequently enriched by altruistic blessings from all kinds of folks, on a scale and scope I had never experienced before from total strangers. (I would experience this again, in similar conditions but a different setting). Trail magic was unusually active, too. There is nothing like coming around a bend to see a strategically placed cooler sitting trailside with a "Trail Magic" sign tacked to the lid. Who knows what mysterious pleasures await on the inside: chilled fruit, cold candy bars, and even colder trail-sodas were commonplace. What a treat!

The 90 miles of trail in Massachusetts gently rise and fall between dense woods and open notches (called "gaps" in the South), across sparkly streams, or under dark cover of the deepest evergreens. Occasionally, however, the trail conditions were horrendous. Scratching past thorn-lined swamps of mosquito-infested mud will drive any seasoned hiker stark-raving mad. But we took the good with the bad. The trail would always open back up to boardwalks and bog bridges over less troubled waters. And a mountain view sunset was available just about any night of the hike if the day was well planned and executed. The summer of 2020 was a special time to be on the Appalachian Trail.

Entering Dalton, Massachusetts, I stopped at Tom Lavardi's house. His yard is a classic rest stop for AT hikers on the march. Tom's warm and transcendental energy was contagious, and he encouraged me to pay attention to the subtle yet powerful energy of nature:

"This amazing trail, Music Man, gives sojourners the time and space to find that which can only be found in the spirit; the decorated theater is Nature. The answers you seek patiently wait in the profound meditative potential that hiking offers. Your community is here to support you in any way we can. Let me know how I can help."

Sometimes while hiking, I said a prayer with every step—A mantra, with each footfall: "Help me serve." If I must act my way into a new way of thinking, I decided that walking with purpose was a start. I called my ex-wife from the picnic table in Tom's yard to see if she would bring the kids over for a visit. I wasn't going to force the issue if she said no. The idea of Daddy blowing into town, with barely time to take off his pack, to hug his kids; just to dash back out again the next day...It might not have sat well. But she agreed. Missing them greatly, I reflected on when I was down South, and I had vowed to "walk to my children." Geographically speaking, that was the case. But the journey had become spiritual in a new kind of way. Wherever I was headed, I had to stay the course.

The idea of simply walking to my children had now broadened in scope; the future was now contingent upon the present. I must finish what I started; the idea that life would fall into place in its own time was driving the fatalistic obsession to finish my thru-hike.

In Dalton, I was grateful for the opportunity to hug and kiss my children and take them out for ice cream and mini golf. I had not seen them in nearly a year. They were so big. The kids were growing up without me. My son wanted to show me his toys with giant smiles. My daughter wanted to hug her daddy and not let go. The dissolution of our family had been especially hard on her. Being the oldest, she vividly remembered what life was like when daddy was around. Even thru periods of emotional unavailability nearing the family breakup, life with her daddy there was still much better than life without dad around. Our family was all she knew. Unexpected tears flowed from the eyes of my children and my ex-wife as they pulled away to leave. It was a bittersweet farewell. They didn't want to leave me, and I didn't want them to go. In a brief afternoon we shared magic. Then it was over. I was back on the trail with my heart full and my soul conflicted. But I knew what I had to do. Though writing about the struggles of the past can be therapeutic and quite natural at times, it is hard to write about those intimate moments I shared with the family that I had destroyed.

The main track of the historic Appalachian Trail had been relatively easy for the past few states. But it was soon replaced by the more rugged and wild walking that was typical of the AT. Mount Greylock loomed in the distance and was feared as "the hardest climb since Virginia." I found it to be one of the most beautiful mountains on the trail to that point. It was a challenge, but the long climb is well graded over a few miles of densely deciduous forests. The AMC Berkshire trail club does a great job managing this section of trail. The stretch between the Saddle Ball and the summit of Mt. Greylock are some of my favorite miles on the entire trail. The hardwoods and underbrush give way to a sample of mossy boreal forest typical of the northern wilderness, with springs and ferns on the earthen floor. It's like a little slice of Canada was placed there by GBITS as a small reward for the big effort it took to reach. A mystical ridge walk near the summit leads to the War Veterans Memorial Tower which presides over the land, topping out at 93 feet above the 3,491-foot summit of the mountain. On that clear day the site offered views of distant peaks across three states. The steep climb down the north slope of the mountain offers dramatic views of the Taconic range to the west and village views of North Adams and Williamstown in the valley. Meditation filled my day as I hiked in step with my spirit, feeling recharged with the love of my kids.

I caught up with Garlic in southern Vermont a couple days later. It was good to be back with my partner and we were getting excited for the Green Mountains, which was the final preparation for New Hampshire. White Mountain National Forest, one of the AT's greatest technical challenges, was just around the corner. My foot was aching with tendonitis, but the pain was manageable as we approached the Long Trail junction near Rutland, Vermont.

We marched toward "The Inn at Long Trail" at a comfortable minimum of conversation. Sport mode led by a length as we entered the far turn of the journey, and the scenery was spectacular. It was a bitter cold evening in the middle of the summer when we made the climb up Mt. Killington. Just as Saddle Ball to Greylock, Mt. Killington had a magic carpet of moss that spread from the forest floor up the trunks of the giant white pines and spruce trees that protect the mountain. Red wax cap mushrooms peeked out from beneath ground ferns that waved to us through an otherwise unnoticed breeze.

"Ladies and gentlemen, welcome to the sunset." Garlic announced, upon our arrival at the summit of Killington.

"Beautiful. I think the cold air is bringing the greens out. What do you think?"

"Music, I can see every color of the rainbow in that sky. Is that periwinkle at the horizon?" She pointed and smiled.

"I see it. Hey, that's Rutland way over there." I stood on the edge and leaned on my walking stick to take in the view. The lights of the town started to dot the valley floor as our plot of earth turned farther away from the sun.

"I miss my cat," cooed Garlic with a sniffle in the cold air.

"I'm sure she misses you, too. I bet your sister has spoiled her rotten."

"Naw, Sis is ready for her to go. I hope Mr. Henshaw is still alive...I miss my sister and my baking yeast." (Yes, the yeast had a name) We let a moment pass in silence. "It's gonna get colder out."

Zipped up to our noses in sleeping bags, we kept close to each other that night in the shelter. Our heads shared my Therm-a-Rest pillow sack. The lessening problems in our relationship took a back seat to the challenging and rewarding trek thru the Vermont wonderland. I kept the worst parts of the dirty truth about myself undercover and did my best not to act up. Deep down I was scared that if she ever found out about my cringe-worthy behavior, she would laugh in horror before trudging away for good. Nowadays, I'm aware that she already knew the turmoil in my heart and suspected my skeletons were many. Garlic was willing to take risks in her life. Furthermore, we were learning how to respect each other's boundaries. After all, it's hard to hike with the same person for miles upon miles, day in and day out. It was a crash course in all things related to building a relationship. There were many failures up to this point. Lord knows I had mine. By that point in the hike, even after brief periods of separation, we always came back together. We were drawn together by a strong force that had intensified past its initial gravity; we stuck together and stayed committed. Just like the Medicine Man might say: You've got to go thru stormy seas to get to calm waters.

Accepting the challenge of the rugged Shelburne Pass, we soon stood in the parking lot of the Inn at Long Trail the next day. While waiting for a room, a familiar looking Escalade with shiny rims and a Yakima rack loaded with kayaks pulled up. The driver door opened, a pair of big feet in Chaco sandals hit the pavement. The other three doors opened, and three smaller pairs of feet with smaller sandals hit the pavement. They had made it.

"Uncle!" The niblings all ran up and gave me a hug. "Hey kiddos! Bro! Y'all made it!"

"Wouldn't have missed you for the world! Great to see you, Brah!" He bear-hugged me off the ground like a twig.

"Whoa, Brah! You got to get some meat on your bones!"

"Dude, I just walked eleventy-seven hundred miles, give me a break!" "Just messing with you, sheesh, it's great to see you!"

"You too, Bro!"

Bro and the kids were on their way to Maine for vacation at Goldfish's family cabin. We had tentatively planned to meet like this, if all the face cards fell into place. They miraculously had. The plan to visit their first cousins in Massachusetts (my kids) had not panned out. But not for a lack of trying. Regardless, the other half of his plan had become real trail magic. Bro met Garlic and many others from the Tramily. The bubble had coordinated a gathering at the Inn at The Long Trail for the weekend to celebrate a hiker's early-August birthday. Tents and Touaregs filled the parking lot across the street; adventurers crossed the pavement like marching ants donning backpacks and mountain bikes; the double-yellow highway lines not too closely followed by bumper-stickered Subarus cruising too fast or too slow with reggae music blasting and smoke pouring from open sunroofs.

"Music Man, come jam one with me after your family dinner!" Choogle demanded with glee, as he rose from a corner barstool in the Pub and slammed an empty pint glass down, nearly shattering it.

"I got you, Choogs! I'll be out there in a little bit."

After a round of drinks, Garlic went outside too. Odie had pulled up in his Hiker-Yearbook Bus and so had Choogle's new lady friend. She and Garlic had become fast friends. I was glad that Garlic had another female that she could confide in; someone else with which she could be honest.

Meanwhile, Bro and I had a chance to catch up over family dinner in the Pub.

"Brah, it's so great to see you man. It's been almost five months since you came by the house to borrow some gear for the hike, looking rough. I didn't know if I would ever see you again."

Shadowy memories of my physical condition five months ago were sobering. I knew how I must have looked when I went to his house for the gear.

"I am so very...Bro, I never want to go back to living that way or put anyone else thru it again. I don't know if I have changed—but the world is changing.

"Brah, something is different about you. You are not the same man that left Louisville in March. This experience is a demonstration of nature's miraculous power to heal."

I was not cured of spiritual sickness, but I was not suffering as I once was. All things considered, it was a miracle that I was alive, given all the shit that I had been thru.

"I love you, Bro."

"I love you too, Brah."

"Uncle, do you want to play chess? There is a giant board over there!"

"Why sure! Sounds like you need a lesson from your elder!"

After Bro crashed the kids and himself out for the night, I rejoined the party outside with a guitar I had borrowed from the Inn. Choogle and I jammed for a small crowd outside and someone hollered out "Can't catch the Covid kids!" I had seen shelter walls irresponsibly tagged with that slogan along the way but had never heard it vocalized. Count me out of that bunch, I thought. No offense to card carrying members, but I was no "Cobo". I think back to what Side-Show Bob had told me at Pine Grove Furnace: "Music Man, there is no greater thru-hiking adventure in the world, than the AT, northbound." I was Nobo, through and thru. The Tramily moved the birthday party to an outdoor Karaoke bar in Rutland. We piled in cars, trucks and buses, and Garlic and I got a ride with Odie in his bus. After a few more rounds of drinks, and listening to the Tramily take stabs at standards, I asked Garlic to duet.

"I dunno...what song do you want to do, lover?"

"Rocket Man."

She let a smile purse her lips. "Okay, Bae."

The deejay queued up the karaoke track, but we didn't need to look at the lyrics. Garlic and Music Man sang the hell out of Elton's flagship hit, complete with a heart-felt call and response in the verses; eyes locked the whole time; and pointing to the sky in unison at just the moment in the song. We exited the stage to a roar of applause. Choogle's new girlfriend came up to me afterwards and intimated "That girl loves you. You could see that up there, Music Man. Don't screw it up dude. Garlic is special."

I didn't plan to screw this one up any more than I already had. But that was the past. I rationalized I was doing her a service by not airing out my dirty hiker laundry. There had been enough toil thus far. So, I continued to walk the tightrope with one foot out in the wind.

At zero-hour-nine a.m., Bro burst thru the bedroom door spilling some of his decaf coffee and beckoned us to breakfast with his classic morning energy:

"Get up, hikers! You've got mountains to climb today...damn y'all stink! Come down for eggs and toast. You smell like a brewery. Geeze! Put some clothes on...No, take a shower first. Brush your teeth...Drink some water, strike a match! Everyone, breathe thru your nose!" He stepped out the door backwards and closed it behind him as he blathered down the hall. We laughed. We brushed the fur off our teeth and went downstairs. Feeling just fine, I didn't care if we smelt like four days' grease, three nights' skin, two days' booze, and a farmed waterfowl. This was the Appalachian Trail, by golly. Day-trippers can bring stink-balm for their upper lips, because long-haulers thankfully get immune to their own "hiker funk."

We joined the breakfast table late and my niece stopped chewing her pancake.

"Oh my god, what's that smell?" Her face scrunched in horror as she dropped her fork. "I don't know, Sweetie. Which notes of the ensemble strike your fancy?" I grinned.

"My fancy? Nothing fancy about that, Uncle! You smell like hot-salted toilet paper. I'll bet your socks are bricks, aren't they?" I put my wretched feet on the table and crossed my ankles.

"I don't know, see if they crack when you pick at 'em."

"Ewe!!!"

"Go on, grab the little piggie and twist!"

We all had a laugh. I leaned over to smack a kiss on Garlic but knocked my exposed foot against the corner of the table and grunted in pain.

"Come, what's this?" My brother eyeballed me, changing his tone.

"He's got tendonitis, but he's pretending like he doesn't." Garlic blurted out the news.

"Hot damn, girlfriend, thanks a lot!" I loosely scolded her for outing me. "Besides, it's not like that. I'm fine."

But Bro quickly called my weak tabloid bluff.

"Looks like it is, Brah. Take care of that foot. Stay fed and hydrated. You know you can't quit this thing. You promised."

"I'm going all the way, Bro. *We* are going all the way."

"He's in good hands, Bro," interrupted Garlic, "I'm seeing to it that he's eating enough and acting right." She turned to me with a squinty smile and brushed the hair off my forehead with her gentle fingers, like I was her kid. "I'll keep your dad up to speed, too," she added, referring to her not-so-secret pen pal. While it secretly embarrassed me, it also secretly comforted me too. Our hikes were autonomous and independent of each other in many respects, but we held each other up constantly. Having that on-trail support is critical and everyone attempting a thru-hike of any long-distance trail needs to have help, just like recovery from addiction.

On the other foot, codependency can be crippling.

"Well, we've got to shove off, Music Man!"

Bro rounded up the kids, with all their sandal-covered feet, and piled them into his giant Escalade. But not before we snapped some great pictures. He rolled down his window and causally put his fist out to bump.

"Brah, I'll come climb Katahdin with you when you get there. That is, if you want me to."

"Bro, yes! That would be amazing! But I won't hold you to that."

"No, I'm holding *you* to that, Music Man!"

He put his sunglasses on, gave a wide toothy smile and pulled away.

"Don't fucking quit!" he hollered. With a couple of quick honks from the SUV's horn, they were gone.

The AT split off east from the Long Trail, out of the Green Mountains and toward New Hampshire. A new relationship with the wilderness was sinking roots deeper into my psyche and I relied on the trail more and more for a sense of connection to self. Spending so much time in nature allowed me to be completely present in the moment and aware of my surroundings. I found myself behaving more and more...like water. But I often bounced back and forth between an external awareness of my ego or being consumed with it. Millions of trees along the trail corridor provide home to countless species of plant and animal life. Realizing the complexity and harmony of nature reminded me of how insignificant I am. Conversely, the concept of natural harmony reinforced my role in its proliferation. The Appalachian Trail was showing me how to live life as a creature of nature, and as a human being with character defects. The Great Out Doors was working a warm spiritual magic upon me, changing how I see myself and others—how I view the world in and around me. John Muir once said, "Of all the paths you take in life, make sure some of them are dirt."

.13

THE GREEN MOUNTAINS OF VERMONT had lived up to their name, as the waning days of summer gifted the trail that singular New England charm. The trees were lush with the deepest greens, and there always seemed to be a breeze. Sitting atop an outcropping just above the treeline, I gazed out over a dirt road that twisted in and out of a grove along a stream. Beyond the hills, there were red-walled and brown-covered bridges, Cape Cod-style houses snuggled up close to the narrow roads that cut thru towns and hidden hamlets in the valleys between the mountains. Around another bend, there was a Vermont Country Store that sold sarsaparillas, sharp cheddars, and maple candy all year long. "I wish my kids were here to see this," I whispered along with the sound of the sun-soaked leaves and branches of plant life twinkling in the wind; the cedars and poplars stayed perched on the muscles of the mountains as they flexed their might. The honeybee that was sniffing around on my knee finally flew away. My imagination heard her wise-crack, "Gee, that guy was heavy!" All seemed right with the world from the vantage of Appalachian Trail in 2020. But looks can be deceiving. The world out there was far from perfect. A raging pandemic, along with other socioeconomic, health and political crises, were ripping people apart across the land. I prayed for those who may be suffering in the jungles of addiction, unable to access resources of rooms of recovery. I rightly assumed that relapse rates were likely on the rise. Sitting atop the Green Mountain outcropping, I breathed in the light and exhaled the darkness, thanking the Great Spirit that I was alive. I then said a prayer for the families of those who have lost loved ones to all manners of battle. Ready to descend out of the Greens and into the lower elevations of eastern Vermont, I stood up, still gazing at the rooftop of the forest and took a step.

"Ouch!"

My left foot usually ached for the first few steps after a brief cooldown, before it realized there was nothing it could do to stop the march, for now. Then the pain would be reluctantly dull, trying like to hell to hurt. But walking it off didn't take too long. I minimized my worsening tendonitis while passing thru Hanover, New Hampshire. After stopping in the quaint yet trendy Dartmouth College town for a resupply with a few other hikers, I tried to affect a delay at a pizza parlor with hiker rates. "A pie and a round of longnecks, on me!" But there were no takers. Garlic's eyes rolled.

Back to the trail.

The fateful day arrived on the doorstep of White Mountains National Forest. While climbing up Mt. Mist in great pain, my foot rolled over a root and audibly popped.

"Ahhh! My foot!" I doubled over in agony then fell to the ground. Garlic was on the next switchback above me and looked down in horror as the temper of the mountain tore me down.

"Shit! This is bad, this is bad!" I panted in pain. My foot felt broken. I feared that a hairline fracture had cracked open; that it was not tendonitis after all. It didn't feel like a muscle or tendon problem, but a bone-break instead. Garlic dropped her pack and was back down to my location in an instant. She gave me some water and tried to calm me down. The pain was searing enough to take those warm breaths of light away leaving a vacuum behind.

"Ok, Bae, calm down. Nothing is broken. You have over-strained the tendonitis." Garlic's voice was even-keeled and sympathetic, but it didn't have the effect she had hoped for.

"I don't know, I heard a pop! It feels like the top of my foot just cracked in half!"

"Easy does it. Calm down and drink some water."

The thought of taking another step put the fear of God in me. I could not put one ounce of weight on my mangled foot. We tried to place a call to Hikers Welcome Hostel just north, but no one was picking up the phone.

"You're going to make a battle march, Music Man."

"Are you crazy?" I struggled to focus on her face. I knew it was calm and beautiful, as it could only ever be. Then a shot of molten pain in my foot made everything dark and jagged again.

"No, I am not crazy. You can and you *will* climb to safety," she ordered, "I'll hustle to the hostel and arrange a shuttle to your location. From here, it's just over two miles to Glencliff going north with a short road walk at the end. Or it's a mile south back to the last road crossing. You can walk the two-point-three miles north, or you can take the mile and a dime back to the last trailhead. We've been thru this before: I'll take your heaviest gear to lighten your shoulder load. And you can take my phone. Decide which direction you want to go."

"North. I'm walking north," was my decision. By that point, I was beginning to fear the worst. The injury was surely going to take me off the AT and I was not sure when I would get back on if I even made it back to the trail. Awfulized was the thought that this could be "all she wrote" if my foot was broken. My thru-hike was hanging in the balance, next to Garlic's goose. My brother's instructions rattled thru my head: "Don't Fucking Quit."

"If these are the last two miles of my thru-hike on the Appalachian Trail, they are going to be northbound miles. I'm not fucking quitting and turning around."

Garlic nodded with approval.

"Okay, Music. Be prepared for your body and mind to start shutting down; hold onto your awareness for dear life if you start hallucinating." She took a few of the heaviest pounds from my pack and handed me her cell phone, along with the rest of her water. "The hostel is half a mile east when you get to the road. Hopefully I'll be at the trailhead when you get down there, with a ride up to the house for us. Now get ready to hike and don't second guess the white blazes. Follow them and don't stop. I love you." She donned her pack then charged up the mountain on a mission. And, to just leave me to it. Garlic, of all people, knew it was going to be a living hell-trek. Better to let me face it alone.

After Garlic walked away, I sat fumbling with my headlamp and cursing at it. But I would need it before the end, if I hiked any less than a mile an hour. Evening was approaching and time was of the essence. "Calm down," I told myself, "You can do this. You don't have a choice, anyway. Might as well embrace the suck." I strapped down the harness of my pack and hoisted myself up on the trekking poles that would be my lifelines. The throb of blood pressure in my foot was nauseating. Light as a feather, I lowered the injured foot to the ground in tremendous pain and immediately lifted it back up. It would be three-legged hiking, like a ball player on crutches after a blowout on the field. Only, I still had to finish the game before my ass would hit the bench. Two miles and three dimes to the road, but then what?

Never mind the morrow: Stay focused; stay present; stay aware. My head was spinning whilst I tried to manage the pain. Each step was torture. I stopped every few paces and couldn't get a groove. Finally, I slumped back down in front of a tree to wallow in misery. Pops and groans rose from my foot and out of my throat. I hobbled on three points for about a half mile, then stopped at a stagnant brook and drank muddy water straight off the dirt. Critically thirsty and operating on instincts, I forgot about the extra water Garlic had stuffed into my pack. Wiping the grit off my lips, I looked up to see a perfectly placed white blaze, elegantly painted on the White pine tree above me. It was the most perfect blaze I had seen. It reminded me of that fresh coat of paint I meticulously brush-stroked for the trail club back in Pennsylvania. What an honor: to touch up a tree blaze for the Appalachian Trail. I took a moment to reflect upon what it represented; where the blazes had led me, and where I was headed.

It was decided that I would not stop until it was done. The time to walk with purpose was at hand...and foot. I got up once and for all and began to hop–double-click... hop–double-click... repeat. Delirium started squeezing my brain, as my body temperature swung wildly. Cold sweats accompanied trembles of pain and itch. How does one persevere under this stress? Experience and instinct.

159

"Dope sick," I said aloud. Not so long ago, I had been so sick and strung out from drugs that I wanted to die. I had experienced a certain physical, mental, and spiritual misery that I would not wish on my worst enemy. I felt like I *was* going to die in many of those drug-induced moments of illness and confusion. But I got thru those struggles knowing that one way or the other, relief was on the other side. "It won't feel like this forever." Even though it doesn't take the pain away, a small self-reassurance, however meager, can go a long way in sweating the shit out.

"I can do this...I must do this; I have no other option; I know what to do; I have watched Garlic persevere; what a soldier of the trail, that Garlic. Strongest hiker I know. Is this what she goes thru on the daily?! She wants this thing with a vengeance. Well, so do I. This is the part of the story where I climb myself off this scrap heap of a mountain...just like I crawled out from under the scrap heap of life to get here in the first place." The pep-talk to "self" had an empowering effect. There were examples to follow and experiences to fall back on. I began to walk for real, into the pain. It was time to turn my pain into purpose. And so, hobbling along, my exhausted consciousness began to close shop. Lizard Brain stepped in as Acting Commander.

Survival Mode: "ENABLED"; Memory Bank: "REBOOT" Awareness Systems: "DETACH" and... "We're away."

The pace seemed much slower than a mile an hour. Each footfall resulted in searing pain. If I rolled over a root the wrong way, nerves screamed like glowing daggers on tender flesh. My heart rate and breathing patterns were elevated. The sun was getting low, and it seemed like a race against the darkness. I began talking to myself out loud, but I don't recall what I was saying or who I was addressing.

I loosely recycled a meditation from Marcus Aurelius as mantra: "Labor not as one who is wretched, nor yet as one who would be pitied or admired; but direct thy will to one thing only, to put thyself in motion and check thyself, as the reason requires." The canopy of the trail corridor started to move faster in my peripheral vision, seemingly faster than I was hobbling. Then, a shift in headspace...

I look to the side and watch the trees go by, The passing miles, the passing time. This magic of the mountains...Rise. To greet our feet in a falling stride. The sun is high. The rain is dry. This magic of the mountains... Rise. A wind away from whence took flight, To strip away the teardrops.

The forest walls were whirling past me a mile a moment, like a wormhole in a celestial highway, as my pain transported me to a yet unknown location in spacetime.

****

The brown sunlight over the last day's madness gave way to night. I drove my Ford Escape down under the bridges and off-ramps of the freeway and into the bowels of the city. Pulling into the homeless camp, on the banks of the Ohio River, the tent city sprawled out before me with zombies shuffling around as usual, in slow motion and leaning at the waist. One nods off in a frayed camp chair while his partner coughs at the push of a needle. I had nothing but the clothes on my back, a driver's license in my pocket, and my guitar in the backseat of the truck. I was out of money, out of gas, and out of ideas. The structure of my life had once again been built up even higher and torn down in awesome fashion. I had really set everything ablaze this time and the firestorm burned hotter than the rest. What was there left to do? Get high again. I had been awake for days and real insanity ebbed with fits and starts. I couldn't tell the difference between reality and illusion. The medical term for it is "drug-induced psychosis". I pulled the truck up next to the biggest tent in the middle of the camp. It belonged to Fitty-Seven. He was a short, bald, tattoo-faced pusherman from New Orleans who said he "came to Louisville after the hurricane in oh-five, looking for change."

"Why do they call you Fitty-Seven?" I asked, when I first met him in his super dome tent, complete with a soiled Persian rug and a loveseat.

He opened a dirty rag to reveal a beautifully polished .357 Magnum. It was the biggest handgun I had ever seen, and it twinkled like a gold tooth when he turned it under the freeway lights.

"Because, Census Man, I'm fifty-seven years old for good reasons." He spun the chamber and belched a sinister laugh. "But if you fuck with me then call me Katrina."

That day, I sat in my truck a few yards from the row of tents, trying to think. Not a penny to my name. I turned to the back seat and looked at the guitar case. My beautiful Taylor acoustic guitar had been a gift from my father. I exited the truck and got the guitar case out, then walked over and scratched on the sidewall of Fitty-Seven's tent.

"Who is it?"

"It's me, Fitty.."

"Census Man, back for a recount! Have a seat on the couch. What's the number today, D?" I sat down and gave him a serious look. "Fitty, I need a bet. I don't have any cash." I eye-balled my guitar case with fear. I didn't want to do it, but the monkey was on me; I was desperate for a fix.

"D, I can't do it right now. I gotta re-up. I need cash money for the last gram I got." Silence again.

"Fitty, how about, I'll give you...my truck."

"What? You'll give me your truck? For a goddamn gram of dope? Are you out of your... Yes, I can see that."

I clutched the handle to my guitar case. I didn't want to get robbed of that too. Take the truck, I thought, just leave the guitar alone. I surmised that I just might go ham for the last time if someone took my Ax. Ignorantly, granted, I trusted Fitty-Seven enough. But I didn't trust the other clientele that constantly came and went around here. Who saw me come in? Paranoia had a grip on me.

"Chill out, Census Man. Smoke this weed." He passed me a smoldering joint that I didn't want, but I puffed it anyway. "I ain't gonna take your truck for a gram," he said, "but I might give you an eight ball and say $300 in cash. That's assuming you got the title. No title, then a gram of dope, it is. How's that sound?"

Fitty had mercy on me. His counteroffer was 20x my original asking price. But still highway robbery.

"I have the title, and it's insured for another two weeks or so before it lapses. You'll be on your own then." It was the truth, I swore. Oh, the irony: I would lie, cheat, and push the closest people in my life away...just to be honest and servile to the dope man. Would I ever reverse the hustle?

"That's a deal, D. Come on, let's go into town. I know a notary public."

It turned out he knew the owner of a funeral home who was able to witness the title transfer, and the deed was done. Elated, he drove us back to his tent in the "new to him" truck and twisted me a huge bag of drugs, then he gave me six fifty-dollar bills. I double checked to make sure they were real.

"D, you crazy as hell, you know that! You've got stones of brass to hang around here like you do. That, or you're a damn fool. Just remember, you ain't got the safety of the getaway truck no more. Camp is a whole different beast now, my man. Take that cash and get a room. People's been watching us. You weren't safe down here before and you really ain't safe now. It would be better to get away from tent city while you've got a chance."

Fitty-Seven gave me a hit of his personal "blue" dope on the house, then shooed me away. I nervously scooped up my guitar case, gripping the handle like brass knuckles, and scurried out. The guitar was all I had left.

The dope hit me hard. I stopped walking and my head spun for a moment. Then everything around me paused. I turned to look back at the homeless camp. No one was around. Everyone had disappeared at the pluck of a rusty string. Only faint glows from inside the quiet tents filled the space as time stood still.

"Hello! Where did everybody go?" I asked the darkness. I walked back toward Fitty's tent. Now the light was off, and it was quiet. He had been there fifty-seven seconds ago...

"Fitty?" No sound, not even a river rat.

Silence and blackness had instantly befell the camp. I felt sober.

"Where the hell is everybody? Are y'all trying to mess with me right now?"

Nobody was messing with me. They were all in hiding. It must have been a bad scene if even the worst of the armed and downtrodden were getting out of my way. I spun around again to check behind my back. More dark tents. I could hear rain beginning to fall. While shifting the guitar case between hands, I looked down to discover that it was no longer my instrument of music. I was holding a large hourglass, and each grain of salt and sand was another heavy burden I harbored from the past.

"What the hell?!" I dropped it to the ground, cracking one of the ampules but not shattering. Was I losing my grip on reality? No, I reassured myself, but still unaware of the only moment of clarity that ever truly mattered.

A crescendo of flashing photons indicated the passing headlights of a car. I turned toward the entrance of the homeless camp thirty yards away. A car had pulled up in the distance, but I couldn't see anything else, except for the rain falling in front of the bright headlights. I shielded my eyes from the direct glare. The car door opened, and a shadowy figure exited the vehicle then slammed the door.

"Hello?" I yelled into the darkness. No answer. Too far...can't hear me in the rain. "Hello?!" I repeated louder. But I dared not move in that direction. The figure walked around and sat against the hood of the car with arms and legs crossed. All I could see was the silhouette of a human being that clearly wanted to remain anonymous. The headlights continued to obscure my vision. I turned around again to escape the glare.

Not far from me, a tent with a faintly lit lamp inside came to focus. I could see the shadow of a woman inside. She was brushing her long hair in front of a mirror. She looked naked. As the lamp light faded, her shadow on the tent wall put down the brush and turned toward someone else on the ground. She swung a leg over to straddle and flipped her hair to one shoulder, then the light faded out. Above the tent, another light came into focus from way down on the other side of the camp. It was further and deeper into the camp than I had ever dared to venture. The light shone up from the ground, illuminating a woman in an ancient dance. I squint, she looks like...A belly dancer? "What the hell is going on?" I ask aloud to the ears of no one. I was the tree that fell in the woods...and nobody could hear me... The khaleegy dances seductively, a hundred yards away in the opposite direction from the headlights of the car. I turn back to look at the car. Still there, headlights and the silhouette...watching me thru the rain—they had me in a pickle. The dancer is trying to lure me deeper into the rows of tents, up under the viaduct where she swirls. Her face is veiled but she is beautiful, with a traditional Arabian bra and belt set, complete with a coined hip scarf. She tries to beckon me hither. I shake my head to signal "No", so she dips and twists, putting more curve in her hips. *No*, I assure myself, it's a trap. I shake my head again, so she swings her hip in a full loop, just begging....

My foot hurts...I lift it up.

"HONK!!!!" blares the horn from the car behind me.

"I'm not going!" I yell back at the silhouette leaning against the hood of the car. "My feet hurt!"

The corner of my eye catches something off to the side: a shadowy playground, and a swing set with seagulls perched on top. More in silhouette, the image of a father and daughter go down the slide and tumble out. They stand up and keep playing. From behind them, the belly dancer is surrounded by others now...they move closer to her. They look like pirates; she reaches for me as if to plead for help. Distressed, she disappears amongst them, devoured by the crowd. The light that once illuminated the belly dancer fades out as a ship leaves the harbor painted on the viaduct wall. Emotions are welling up inside and out. What was happening to me, to my mind? These scenes, all strangely familiar, were playing out clearly and I felt my human emotions come alive again. Like a shell was cracking; it felt like it did before; like when I was younger and not so mangled by toxic living. I turned in another direction, to the other side of the freeway. The building that I had never noticed, it looked like a castle on a bluff, all lit up with stripes of neon colors. On the shore below, there was a hippy girl with dreadlocks down to her knees and a large butterfly on her shoulder that was slowly flapping its wings. She blinked at me thru thick eyeglasses that magnified her big brown eyes as the butterfly left her shoulder, charting a new course for itself, toward a humble house on a hill with coconut candles in the windows. It was a simple looking Appalachian home, with twelve stepping stones carved of magnificent marble. There was a woman out front leaning against the porch post, with cowboy boots crossed at her ankles. I had never seen her before. She looked peaceful and patient as she sat down on the stairs to light a candle on a dish, and she began to play a mountain dulcimer: safety beacons for a wayward traveler. I looked back at the car and the headlights. Still there, the silhouette watches as the windshield wipers blast back and forth, swishing the rain off the windshield in huge waves, then I accidentally kicked the hourglass at my feet, causing it to ring with the timbre of a triangle. The pings kept ticking like a clock stuck at a Grave tempo.

At the banks of the river, an apparition appears in the distance. I turn round and around as fright and wonder dance around me in a black-tie ballroom waltz...My eyes shift to the colorful coliseum of neon...no longer there, now replaced by the distant ridge of a faraway mountain. The valley beyond the ridge ignites with the soft glow of a country town far below. I could see the shadow of a man approaching the precipice, with the city lights below revealing his silhouette. He stops, his back turned to me, and leans on his walking stick admiring the view of the village lights. He tips his hat, as the dots of light go out one by one by one, removing the traces of his outline, and the visions of everything else. Miles in the distance, only the weird and beautiful hometown skyline remains. Then, it too fades away. Finally in the darkness of the abyss, I kept turning, looking for more images to wrap me in some companionship with comfort. What does any of it mean? Wait...these are my memories; a moving picture-book of my life. *These are my songs!*

I close my eyes and sit down in the rain. Enter images of a trail in the woods: I am hiking! Yes, that's more like it. But it is late Autumn, and the day is cold and cloudy. And there is Garlic! She's on point, leading us up a trail and hiking healthy and steady on her feet. She's virtually skipping! We are back in the Deep South, and the trail blazes are unfamiliar. Trail signpost: BMT? Garlic turns to me looking lost, and I drop a baggie.

"What is that?" She asks without a mask.

"I don't know what you mean." I responded furtively.

"That bag of drugs you just dropped!"

"That...it's not mine! It must have been here on the trail."

"But I saw you drop it!"

"No, you didn't!"

"How could you! You promised!"

Garlic's voice trails off and the outline of her body reduces to the emptiness that surrounds.

I am alone on a new trail...It is late winter but sunny; I have a ponytail of healthy new hair and twenty more pounds on my bones. I am farther south, way back down to where it all begins. The trail seems familiar, but there are strange blazes on the trees... a turkey foot? Medicine Man emerges from the wood and speaks to me....

"Pinhoti," he intimates, "means 'turkey home' in Creek. When you are lost, follow the river, Music Man. It will always lead you home."

"Medicine Man, where is home?"

"Ha-Ha-ha-ha!" he laughs with the rasp of a diesel engine. There is a signpost at the trail junction, it reads: "ALL POINTS—>"

Oh...a sigh of relief at the sight of the end. Is that someone waving over there...near the river? The windshield wipers wave and pump on the car in the distance and all I can see are the headlights. But I hear something from the riverbank. With renewed fear, I see the outline of a hooded man. I check back in with the headlights, the silhouette leaning on the hood stands up abruptly and is firmly focused on me, concerned....

"Swath...Swath...Swath." I hear a whirring and crunching sound from the man in waist high grass near the water's edge, as his chopping machete decapitates seedheads of the grass. I approach where the dark of the river meets the dark of the sky, feeling more tired in my feet. He stops chopping at the tall grass with his rusty machete and faces me. The full moon is falling toward the river and its glow brings light to the man's ashen face...It is Black Face. He is white as a ghost. He looks dead. I shudder in fear.

"Black, I haven't seen you for a while." He turns and goes back to uselessly chopping at waist high swamp grass. Confused, I again look back at the headlights and they are dimmer. The rain has stopped and the windshield wipers rest, the silhouette is standing still.

"Black, what is this all about?" He stops chopping and points the rusty blade into the dark aside.

"Over there," Black Face instructs.

I turn yet again with tired feet, accepting his direction. I see a homeless-camp pile of rotting garbage two feet tall. Black Face speaks again: "Looks like as good a spot as any."

Hitting my knees by the trash pile, I bow my head in shame. Black approaches the side of the pile and stands over me clutching the machete in position.

"Look at me," he bellows.

I look up at his ashen face. His teeth clench as he shakes his head with pity and envy. He lowers the sword over my shoulder and turns over stinking trash with the point of the blade, a foot in front of my face. He is right. This is my chance; this might be my last chance. There was nothing left to take but responsibility. I pulled the ball of dope out of my pocket and bit the knot of the baggie with my teeth. The plastic stretched and tore like hot fudge and the taste of bitter metal hit the side of my tongue. I turn the bag upside down and dump the contents onto the scrap heap. Every crystal. Then I drop the baggie on top and stand up, looking over the waste. Moving light reflects off the dope crystals from the distant headlights' shifting positions. I reproach Black Face, who is back to chopping.

"Black, that night in Shorty's tent under the viaduct, with the cops...."

"Yeah, I remember."

"I didn't take your stuff."

This infuriates him. Turning towards me in a flash he places the edge of the blade just above the crown of my head, between my eyes.

"Haven't you seen enough, mothafucker?!"

"Wait, I...."

"NO! No more, 'wait, I'm sorry' bullshit.'" Black Face moves the point of the blade to the tip-o-me nose. I can smell the sour screwdriver on his breath as me moves in to speak, gritting his teeth:

"You get the fuck out of here and don't you *ever* come back. Do I make myself clear? Do you understand what I'm telling you, Mr. Census-Taker? Now.... You can run.....if you *want* to."

We stand face to face, motionless and silent, with our bloodshot eyes deadlocked. After tense moments, he whirls the blade out of my face and starts to chop at the tall grass again.

"Don't forget your guitar," Black instructs with his back turned and blade flying. "That's about all you got left, *Music Man*, or whatever the hell they called you."

There was one more scene to be revealed: Behind the trees over there, what's that? I walk over to the short tree line and pull pine branches back to reveal a billboard that I had never seen before. Advertisements for the freeway. The billboard glows bright white with three simple words in bold black letters:

"CONSIDER SOMETHING DIFFERENT"

At the bottom corner of the billboard, the credits simply read "Family. Life. Bio Work." I let go of the branches and stumble backwards in exhaustion. I had harmed so many people. Everyone who ever cared about me had been hurt in one way or another. I had taken more than money. I had stolen peace and serenity: my children were robbed of their father; the entire family scarred; friends and colleagues mistreated...And most of all, most importantly, I have harmed myself. But I am a survivor. Holy Shit.
I turn to the silhouette between the headlights.

"Help me! I need help!"

The silhouette from the hood moves toward me, so I speed up. "Please, can you help me now?"

✴✴✴✴✴✴✴✴✴✴✴✴

The headlights dim and fade away behind the nearing silhouette and my feet pound the pavement on approach. It is Garlic on the highway at Glencliff coming towards me, as my tunnel vision begins lifts. (My pain-induced hallucinations were similar by description, but dedicated reader—those real events were coming.)

"Music Man, take it easy...calm down Bae." I fell on the side of the road and into her lap.

"Shh, shh, Music...You are in shock. Try to catch your breath. Drink this water.... But you did it! You climbed yourself off that trash pile of a mountain. I can't believe you hiked two miles in less than an hour on that foot. I just got here, Music. And I was crushing it to get down from there."

I was so relieved that that battle march was over. By then, I needed rest and nourishment. My foot was shredded. It felt swollen by at least a full shoe size.

"More bad news, Bae," Garlic said into my ear as she crutched under my armpit. "Fake or real?"

"The hostel is closed. No one is there and no water, not even a garden hose."

"That's gotta be fake news." I was aghast.

"Real talk," she confirmed, "The neighbor came out when I walked up earlier and told me the hostel has been closed all season. Plus, there is a water shortage in town. She wouldn't even let me fill my bottle from her rain barrels. But she was nice."

"Garlic, I need water." I was coming out of shock and still in tremendous pain. We pitched tents in the backyard of the closed Hikers Welcome Hostel. I had just stopped moving when Mr. and Mrs. Foote arrived from across the street.

"We sure are sorry about the water, young hikers, but here you go." Mr. Foote put a six-pack of cold longnecks on the picnic table. "Hope this helps."

The town was an alcoholic's dream come true! Johnny Cash couldn't get a glass of gray prison water there, but the streets flowed with Boston Lager. Eventually, the beer just added to our thirst when there was nothing left to drink. Given the circumstances, temporary relief in fermented form wasn't altogether unwelcomed by either of us.

"I can give you a ride to the hospital tomorrow. That is, if you want to get that foot checked out. Plus, I am the postmaster." Mrs. Foote continued, "the post office is across the street and just next door. We haven't had many hikers this year. The pandemic ran everyone out of town along with the water shortage and all. Small town, you know. Most of our neighbors went to loll in the Florida sunshine."

"Mail? Yes, I should have a package waiting in there."

"What's your name?"

"Music Man."

"Oh yes! It arrived just today. Nice to meet you, Music Man! I've heard a lot about you...from your Mom! She called to verify that it had arrived. Tracking number issue...not my fault! Ha-ha! Plus, this is small-town New Hampshire. Retired post office herself, yep, she's a sweet lady, 'Music Man's Mom!' She knows her U.S.P.S.!"

"She sure does. Mom and Dad are expert trail trackers. It gives them something to do during the sequester."

"Or they just love being a part of their son's life, living vicariously while you're chasing your dreams. Consider that? Covid misery notwithstanding. [So and so] has it, and [the altruistic town physician] died from it. Glencliff will have the voting districts redrawn because of Covid deaths! It has affected this whole country in ways we won't forget any time soon. It's just awful. Anyway, we'll get that food box for you in the morning, Music Man. Then we'll take you to the hospital. That foot doesn't look too good. But we'll need you two to ride in the bed of the truck. Can't take no chances with the dis-ease!"

"Thanks Mr. and Mrs. Foote. I sure am grateful. And we're sorry to hear about how the pandemic has affected your town and your lives."

"Yeah," added Garlic, "I'll share that sentiment. Good luck, Glencliff Feet."

My unlikely rescue by the postmaster and de facto shuttle drivers in town named "Foote" seemed fictional. It was humbling to see the havoc that a ruthless and indiscriminate disease had wreaked on yet another quaint mountain village. Hell, it appeared that the Foote's were the last two people left in Glencliff, and they were truly good people. But they were not coming off that water. Garlic snooped around later in the dark and came back with a liter of water for each of us. She begged me not to ask how.

"Garlic, you should hike tomorrow. I need to get off the trail. But you are healthier than you have been in hundreds of miles. Get into that park and start climbing those big White mountains."

"Music, are you sure?"

"Without a shadow of a doubt. I will catch you when I get back to hiking. If I don't get back on the trail, then I won't. Either way, you're finishing this thing."

The next morning, I gave Garlic most of the food from the maildrop. Mr. and Mrs. Foote (The Feet) were trail angels with wings for a shuttle. They were left to run that little town all by themselves during hiker season, and the best they had for us was as good as it gets for the AT. I'm not sure if we owe them amends for the water, but I suspect so. We hobbled and hopped into the bed of the Foote's pickup truck and pulled out of Glencliff, New Hampshire. After dropping Garlic off at the trailhead, the pickup zoomed away with me still in the back. I waved to Garlic as she disappeared into White Mountains National Forest without me. She never looked back. For miles I rode on the bed of the old pickup truck, watching the changing ridgelines in the sky, as we all rolled down the two-lane state road at incredible speeds. Mr. Foote was living up to his name.

The end of my attempt to thru-hike the Appalachian Trail seemed more and more imminent, so I was determined to savor what could be the final moments in the foothills of New Hampshire's White Mountains. I gave a lazy civilian salute to the distant ridgeline as the pickup dropped into an unknown town.

.14

CURIOUS PEOPLE NORTH OF THE MASON-DIXON LINE sometimes ask me to play a banjo and they are often mesmerized by the factory licks that I can roll out. However, after about three minutes, the Music Man plum runs out of talent and quits playing before they notice my bluegrass chops are on repeat. But down south in Kentucky, I don't go near a banjo in public. True bluegrass pickers can nail a fraud from two counties away.

That's the story of my life, metaphorically. Deep down, I feared that people who got close to me would see thru the smoke and mirrors. They'd see me for who I really was. Who am I, anyway? Should I dodge the question and flip the script one more time? No, not today. My people-pleasing days are over. The Music Man doesn't play by request anymore. Unless another hiker suggests "500 Miles," the classic Journeymen arrangement. That's the one. Bigfoot, himself, changed my perspective on what I saw as unfair criticism, after I was upset with him over nothing. He said, "There's something about me you don't like about yourself." Huh? And then it made sense. Don't get it twisted, I still hope others like me. I am a human being, but I'm too keen on people-pleasing anymore.

An X-ray at Cottage Hospital confirmed a diagnosis of severe tendonitis across the top of my left foot, but I was relieved to learn that there were no fractures. I would likely hike again, but "Not for a week or more, Sir. You must get into bed and not move unless you are going to the bathroom." That was tough to hear. My very being was built for hiking by that point, and even one zero day left me feeling stagnant and twitching to walk the hills. Hiking and exercising are addictive, just like anything else that fires off body chemistry. But I had to hang my pack for a while. So where would I go?

I called Terradactyl, Nobo class of 2016.

"Yes, of course, Music Man. Come and recuperate at my place. You can have your own room and TV. And there is a pool and a hot tub at the other end of the building. But keep your feet away from that ping-pong table. You gotta heal!"

"Terry, I'm grateful."

"No worries! Get well so you can finish this thing."

"I plan to," Music Man agreed.

After a shift at her second job, Mrs. Foote shuttled me from Cottage Hospital to The Notch Hostel where I spent one night before moving on. I snapped at the owner Serena for nothing; she was busy, and I was in pain. She ended up being the kind and patient human between the two of us that day. I owed her a call and an apology, which was made much later. Serena would say, "I don't remember that Music Man, but thanks for the call. Come up this winter and snowshoe with us!"

Terry's Place was no ordinary hostel experience. It was a high-end condominium on the strip in Lincoln, New Hampshire, under the shadow of the towering Franconia Ridge of the White Mountains. All the amenities were right there. Glistening lights and sounds of the ski-resort party scene filled the living room like the Vegas Strip every time someone opened the front door. Garlic hiked into Terry's Place that night and stayed with me, having tackled Mount Moosilauke down into Kinsman Notch. She was now a full day ahead of me in "trail miles". But we were together again for the night at Terry's Place. We were properly prepared to say goodbye for a while.

"You will be back on the trail before you know it. Few days, I bet." She encouraged me.

"I'm not going to push it," I responded. "If I need to stall for a week to heal up, then that's what I'll do. But I'm not going to quit, even if that means I sit down for a bit."

"Ok, Music, but don't just marinate your organs all day. Drink lots of water and milk, Bae. Please limit the beer."

"I probably won't drink any beer." I posed like a poser.

"Don't be an asshole!"

"I don't plan too, geez!" But I missed her point.

Garlic changed the subject. "Look, I'm going to hike slowly, like five to six miles a day. That's about half what we planned to do in the Whites, anyway. If it takes me two weeks to get thru, so be it. That way you can catch me somewhere near the state line.

"I'll catch up with you in the Whites." I insisted.

"That's lofty. Just take it easy. I know you want to finish the hike…and you need to finish," urged Garlic, "But remember this Music Man: thru-hiking the AT isn't for people who need it and it's not for people who want it. It is for those of us willing to *work* for it."

That was my woman—wise in her thirty-three years. She had much to be proud of and she had earned every bit of it for herself. I secretly envied her for that.

Garlic left the next morning for Franconia Notch. As she walked out the door she brushed past an old friend with a warm hello for us both. Potholder cruised in on greased skids.

"Hey Garlic," he greeted with a cheerful boom in his voice. "I see you recovered from kicking that hornet's nest back at Antietam Shelter."

"Ha-ha, yeah, good thing you had that Benadryl. Saved my ass in fourteen places! Geez, has it been that long since we saw you, Potholder? Way back in P.A.?"

"It's been too long, good hiker. Looks like you're hitting the track. Happy trails!"

"Sure am, but it's great to see you, Potholder. Take care of this songbird for me. I want him on my heels by the state line."

Garlic kissed me goodbye and bid us all farewell. Then she headed out the door as was her style: never looking back.

"Bruh! Where have you been?" I painfully smiled and made a wobbly attempt to stand and properly greet Potholder.

"Catching up, Music Man. I heard you're gonna be hemmed up here for a while. Figured you'd want some company. I'm due for a good vortex especially since there is new music to share! I have a new song, what about you?"

"I wouldn't call it a vortex per se, but I would love some company, Potholder!"

"You want a smoke?" He asked politely while sealing up his freshly rolled cigarette.

"No thanks. But I'll have a beer...just one. That's my limit. I might have two if there is an Anchor Steam around here somewhere."

"Yeah, well, Music Man... You gotta hydrate and heal, my friend," he said with a fatherly tone. "Let's just chill tonight and roll cigarettes. Maybe we'll go to the Pub for dinner tomorrow night if you're feeling up to it. I'm meeting some friends in town that you probably know."

"That sounds like a winner, my loyal friend."

The next night, my short hobble down the block to the Pub was exhausting. A bubble of hikers was coming thru town and the social gathering was a positive uplift. We shared stories about the trail and its trials. Hikers recalled tales of glamping with trail angels and visitors, the writhe of the rocks in Pennsylvania, the mystical Green Mountains, helicopters in the Smokies, spiritual hiker-chaplains and restful religious hostels, the angels and demons, arguments about who made the best pancakes on the AT and rendezvouses with free-loving gypsies. I told the tale of the American-Gothic farmers back in Maryland, who abused our labor with promises of drip coffee. We ended up having to break new trails for them while carrying thirty-pound buckets of gravel, IN EACH ARM, halfway up a mountain to their construction site for a new spring. We returned to the porch completely gassed, to find they were only serving us decaf. Score one for the locals.

Terry's Place was essentially a high-end condo. Nearly all my waking time was spent going back and forth from the pool to the hot tub. The temperature shifts felt good on my body, and it seemed to quell the throbbing in my foot. My right hip was now aching because of overcompensation due to the injury. Even the smallest aches and pains can result in other inconveniences. Minute weight shifts had begun to strain everything else in my body. I had to be smart so that I could heal and hike. Sooner or later, I would have to walk thru whatever pain was leftover if wanted to finish the hike. It was advised that I put full weight on the hurting foot to build stamina and mitigate complications due to load-shifting.

As the self-discovery process on my physical healing continued to play out, I began weighing my options. Potholder discussed it with me in depth, committee-style.

"Right now, my hike could go either way, and I'm okay with that. You bet your ass I want to finish, though."

"Fair enough, Music Man. That's a good reminder for me to appreciate the journey as the destination. But let's be pragmatic. There's no appreciating a journey if it's like walking on a bed of coals."

"Maybe and maybe not, Potholder. I have seen things. I've seen people come back to life after terrible ailments out here."

"I know, Music. Garlic is a soldier of the boulders. It's amazing to see, but is it any fun for her?"

"It's not really about the fun at this point, my good man. It's about not quitting on a bad day. And yes, it's still fun for her, I know it. It's one hell of a life, isn't it? Got one more silver dollar."

Potholder and I had a fine couple of days at Terry's Place in mid-August. By the fourth day of my leave from the trail, there wasn't much improvement with my foot. Still, my mind drifted back to the trail and by the morning of the fifth day I wanted to try a day-hike. I decided on a slack-pack over the South and North Twin, then back to Terry's to evaluate. My one and only slack-pack. It was a brutally long day for me, but when he picked me up along I-93 that evening I knew I was ready for Franconia the next day.

"I'll be donning my pack in the morning, Terry."

"Yes! Way to go, Music Man! You can do it, my friend! It may be painful, but nothing worth achieving comes without hardship. I believe in you." That sounded great coming from him, and I was so grateful for his willingness to help me, virtually for free. He shook my hand firmly the next morning, as he dropped me off at the Franconia Notch trail head. "This is great, Music Man. Just great!

You're gonna make it, I just know it!" He had raised me from the dead and back to better health, at the very least. My chances of finishing the hike had improved and it was time to start chopping.

Climbing up to the ridge at Franconia was a blast! I didn't even feel the ascent. I was overjoyed to be back on AT and my foot was doing great. When I emerged onto the ridge, I was stunned by the beauty of the long views. The earth crunches forth in all directions from up there. I imagined the billions of years of tectonic pressures that created it by visualizing explosive moments of granite plates and mountain peaks bursting forth from the Earth's crust, spewing debris with each new jagged explosion.

It was Saturday and the ridge was packed with hundreds of day hikers and weekend warriors. The vantage over the valley and of Lincoln was stunning, and in the opposite direction the first dubious views of the Presidential Range came into focus. Mount Washington ruled them all; dignified and irritable.

But there was trouble already brewing on Franconia— I was out of water. It was a miles-long schlepp down a side trail for water, then a climb back up. It was looking like my only option. Then I got an idea...It was time to Busk-n-Yogi. I dropped my pack and got the Strumstick out at a crowded vista where lots of fit-looking weekend warriors were resting and taking in the White Mountain scenery. There was a group of women that looked like they hiked up together by the laughs they were sharing. No one paid any attention to me as I tuned up the Strumstick like a toy: plink, plink, plink...until I started strumming.

"Weep no more, my lady. Oh, weep no more today. We will sing one song, for My Old Kentucky Home, My Old Kentucky Home, Far Away!" (golf-claps y silbato de niña)

"That's such a great song! Are you from Kentucky?"

"Yep, I sure am. I'm thru-hiking the Appalachian Trail."

"Wow, and you started in Georgia??"

"Yes, ma'am. Everything is going fine, just fine. Except for the fact that, well... I ran out of water climbing that cliff."

"You are out of water? Here, have a Polar can. Hey, that song reminds of the Kentucky Derby! Is Kentucky grass really blue?"

"No, the grass is green. But the music is blue. And thanks!"

"Here's a bottle of Aquafina!" Another one of the pretty faces offered me more hydration. The day hikers all smelled fresh, like laundry detergent. The amazing group of trail angels lined up to fill my bottles and bladders. They encouraged me to keep trudging, and not give up; they asked me questions about weather in the mountains, bears, and if we experienced the pandemic like the rest of the world.

"Hikers experience the pandemic, but not like the rest of the world. I wouldn't trade this day, up here with y'all, for nothing!"

"Wow. I want to hike the "AT" one day," said a young boy.

My time on Franconia Ridge is a beautiful memory: A social moment with strangers unique to the rest of my hike. I walked away from those amazing people feeling spiritually, mentally, and physically refreshed. Waves of goodbyes came from a dozen day-hikers as they called my name in encouragement.

I pushed all the way to Mount Garfield that night and pitched an amazing camp overlooking the valley far below.

Slicing up and down fantastic ridges of the White Mountains, the trail took me across the tree line with each summit before again plunging into the boreal forest canopy. Trekking poles were often stowed away for bouldering because the climbing required scrambling on both hands and feet in certain sections. It was terrifically fun exercise. Crossing the New England mountain scenery was like stepping into a favorite postcard. Nature's elements are brought to life, intensified, and swapped on the senses.

Sometimes I could smell rain on the boulders before the water fell from the sky. At one lucky stop, a Canadian "Gray" Jay, that had been following along landed near my feet. It asked me for a peanut with a turn of its head and a chirp. I was happy to oblige. It grabbed the nut with its feet and flew away to cache it for the winter. Ten minutes later it was back, but I revealed my empty hands, so the clever Gray Jay moved on to beg another.

I bottomed out at a notch, and as I turned for the climb up to Lake of the Clouds Hut, I encountered a Lasher I had met way back in Maryland, at the beginning of his hike. Zoom was a long-ass section hiker, having completed Springer Mountain to Harpers Ferry in 2019. Now back for the second half of the AT in 2020, he picked up his hike from Harpers Ferry and was coming on strong in the Whites. At fifty years old going on thirty, he had youthful grit and a Keto diet that kept him lean and fast. A Navy veteran of significant rank, he was great with logistics and motivation. Thrilled to see him, I asked if I could join him on the summit push to Mt. Washington.

"I wouldn't have it any other way, Music Man! I hiked hard yesterday to catch you. I heard you were up here trying to run down your partner. I know I can't replace the one and only Garlic, but I would love to hike those Presidentials with you. If you'll have me? Of course, until you catch her!"

"It would be an honor and a pleasure, Zoom. And for as long as possible!"

"Great, now let's kick. We have a lot of climbing to do!" He took lead for an epic hike up and over the iconic Mt. Washington. It was a perfect day on the mountain known to have the most temperamental weather in the lower 48 states. The views of the rest of the "Prezzies" were splendid. We stopped in the gift shop and bought sweets. I convinced him to send his wife a postcard and we watched the Cog Rail locomotive climb straight up the face of the mountain. It seemed like we could go to Canada from here.

Zoom knew I was partially injured and hiking the Whites alone. Loyal by profession—and out of the kinship that hikers share—he committed to help guide me safely thru the park. But he was far too humble to let me believe anything other than our temporary partnership was on equal footing. He kept repeating, "Thanks for letting me tag along, Music Man." It was quite the opposite. In faithful service to others, ever the loyal friend and American soldier, Zoom was there to help...and I needed it.

Like a great leader who leads from the rear, Zoom let me believe I achieved it all by myself. He encouraged me when I struggled; he asked for my guidance and experience when he sensed my confidence; and he took charge when things got too flimsy. Damn good man that you want at your six when the shit goes down. The journey thru the most challenging peaks of the Presidential Range was regal and rewarding.

The rainy and windy conditions on Mount Madison made the descent into the pass exhilarating. We skipped into Pinkham Notch soaked and wide eyed and congratulated each other's survival..." Nice job! That was intense." Zoom had plans to rest in Gorham with his wife for a night or two. I didn't know if I would see him again. I didn't know if I would see anyone I knew again. I was now far behind the pack. He offered to call Garlic for me, but I thanked him anyway. I had made it this far; I was going to catch her soon. I bid Zoom farewell with a lazy but respectful civilian salute, as he extended his hand for a good shake instead. He tapped his trekking poles together twice and offered "Happy Trails, and congratulations to both of you! Now go get her!" He turned down the road into town and let out a "HOOYAH!"

The Whites felt like a dream. I missed Garlic, but I was having my own spiritual experience with these mountains and the people covering them, and I suspected she was too. Things were exactly as they were supposed to be. Heading north from Pinkham Notch, the trail got tough again while traversing the knobby peaks of the Wildcats, which offer no relief from steep climbing. I took my time and took care of my feet on those awesome scrambles. With a solid stock of food in my pack, I climbed the Wildcats alone enjoying my own company and meditating. The next afternoon, I crossed the Rattle River and descended into Gorham. Rattle River Hostel was buzzing with hikers I knew.

"Blueberry!"

"Music Man! Great to see you hiking! I've been rooting for you!" Fantastic hopped up with his meaty calves. "Hey, hey...it looks like we're going back to business, Music Man!"

"That's right," I gleefully joined, "to climb mountains every day!"

"You know it!"

Green Bean and Chilly approached, "Yo, Yo! You crazy Nobo! You can't climb mountains on a peg-leg, you pirate!"

"Like hell, I can't! I saw it done on day one in Georgia! Green Bean, it's battle of attrition."

"No, it's a pilgrimage." He answered with check-mate.

"Touché. It's only a miracle of healing. All I had to do was rest a little, but I'm not quitting! The foot didn't stop hurting for real until I got back to hiking."

"Hey Music Man," Chilly pulled me aside, "You just missed Garlic by a half day. Are you going to try and catch her?"

"Not today. It's all good though. I will soon."

In all reality, I had no idea what she was thinking or doing. Chilly added "I think she is getting nervous, you know, about after the trail. Like...what to do."

Garlic and I had plans, complete with potential jobs lined up in the New England town where we planned to go. We had not spoken in nearly a week. Now I was hearing thru trail hush that she was having second thoughts. I guess I should have seen it coming. My heart wrung like a sponge, but I tried not to show it.

"Who knows what any of us are doing when we get off trail." It was a silly and self-centered thing to say, and my ears were burned by the torch of my own words.

"*We* do," said Chilly with sympathy, "but who knows where your journey leads, mate!" She laughed and jumped off a stump like walking the plank.

"My path leads to Pioneer Valley," I claimed.

"Where is that?" Blueberry probed.

"Where the heart is. But first, I'm going up to the Barn Hostel. It's a little too wild here."

"Headed to town, eh...do you want a dab first?" Anonymously offered.

"Thanks, but I'll pass."

****

"Pinwheel" was the name of the first band I ever played in. When we were 12, I rode my bike over to Kyle's house to jam with my guitar and practice amp hanging from the handlebars of my Huffy. Kyle was born one day before me and Bro. Last I heard, he was working on a decade of sobriety. He was one of the early ones to surrender. Kyle was one of the first people in my life that tried to help me in my early thirties, when I showed signs of substance abuse. But I wasn't ready. At 12 years old, we weren't screwed up yet, but were singing a song we wrote called "Five Dollar Wine" when a gentleman from the other side of the neighborhood approached us. (How's that for ridiculous? 12-year-olds, Dude, singing about cheap wine that they haven't even tasted yet.)

The gentleman wore a fedora and a tie, on a retired Saturday morning, like a caricature of Frank Sinatra meets Jerry Lewis, both in their sixties acting like it was still the 60's.

"Have you kids ever even drank wine before? What the hell are you singing about?"

"Um, no…. It just sounds cool."

"Your sound needs work! What are you, thirteen?" asked the original-lounge-singing-looking-older-neighbor-guy.

"We're twelve."

"*Twelve?* Not even a teenager?"

"Boys, you need some help with your sound. You know where I live, right? The last house on the other side of the neighborhood. Do you remember my name, boys? Never mind…it's Mr. Fowler. Just call me Bill. Listen, I have recording equipment in my basement. I have a two-track tape machine and a decent Peavey speaker tower. Best of all, I've got an old German microphone, too. A Neumann. It can hear a house fly fart."

"Okay…" We had no idea what the hell he was talking about, and just gave him blank stares. "Forget about that. Look, if you want to come over on Saturday, we can record your little "Wino Song" and I'll help you work on it. I'm a musician too." He took his fedora off, moved it to his chest, and belted out an old show tune that neither of us recognized…but it was so good, it was funny. It made us laugh out loud. He didn't care, as he sang like the sands of Heaven's beach. We applauded his brilliant tenor performance.

"Okay, Mister…."

"Bill, call me Bill."

"We'll see you next Saturday, Bill."

"Great! Come in the afternoon, after I'm finished cutting my grass."

He popped his fedora back onto his head and walked away whistling the tune he had just performed.

The following Saturday, we showed up as planned. He opened the front door and let us in. The house smelled musky, but not in a bad way. Just old, like someone opened the ancient Bible on the table and walked around with it while they read. And man, that recording gear looked ragged! But again, looks can be deceiving. Kyle asked him if all the gear still worked.

"Does it work?!", Bill repeated the question back, "Are you kidding me, boys? Wait till you hear your song on playback after we lay it down to tracks. He smiled as he pointed to what seemed like a ten-foot-tall speaker cabinet in the corner. He set up two mics for us. That great old German mic was used as an area pattern for the whole room. Then he set up a SM-57 to get a small pattern mic on the vocals. We plugged our equipment in with classic-static buzz; the amps and drums and electric guitars; and Bill queued up the microphone.

"Ok, boys. I'll point to you when we are ready. When you see the red light, HIT IT!

"Three, two, [one]---> "ON" the red light glowed. "One-Two-Three-Four," Pinwheel struck the chords, and it was magic! *"I drink five-dollar wine, chills and bumps all thru my spine."* Um hmm, that was the Gold record we were trying to make at twelve years old. It was terrible, yes. With his eyes closed and shoulders rolling, Bill rolled his hand in a gesture to "Keep going, it's great!" We were transported into that special realm where musicians can go; where nothing can invade the creative space, and everything's safe. (Athletes call it "The Zone.") The purity of the waves moving the sound...music is the true universal language of the world, transcending native tongues. Having a verbal conversation is one thing. I think of something, then I tell you. Now, you have that thought in your head. Knowing the language is prerequisite, though. Not so with music: Sound knows no language barriers; music transcends all limits of emotive communication, barring an airless vacuum. Music is the first language of the Cosmos. Stevie Wonder reminds us that "Music is a world within itself...and you can feel it all over."

It's the magic of the moment when a Russian youth hears a foreign sounding Rhumba for the first time; it's the Persian khaleegy dancer who seduces a young man from Harlem; it's the overhead clap moment in "Radio Ga Ga" from Freddy Mercury at Live Aid; it's Louis Armstrong singing "What A Wonderful World"; it's Kurt Cobain's Unplugged "All Apologies"; it's that feeling I got each time I walked into Blue Moon Records as a teenager and it's Bill Monroe's Blue Moon shining over Kentucky; it's Taps on a lamenting trumpet at the foggy Arlington National Cemetery. If we peek into the mysteries of music, the rewards wrap us like a warm blanket in winter. It brings understanding thru processing emotional experience, instead of trying to reconcile heartbreak with logic. The cosmic and quantum worlds of physics both lust for the Theory of Everything. Humbly, I say the proof is in the music. String Theory checks out, Rumbles to Renaissance to Rock.

Bill invited us back for the following Saturday. He had mixed last week's recording (all two tracks of tape) with equalization and a drip of reverb. Crude, low-fi, and amazing. That German microphone caught all the best and worst of our talents; we loved it.

"This recording is awesome, Bill! Thank you. Hey, will you sing for us again?" Kyle asked. Bill Fowler's face lit up with excitement. "I would love to sing for you fellow music men."

"Cool! Sweet! Go for it!"

Bill took off his fedora and drew a deep breath. Pausing in silence, he locked into the moment to collect himself and properly greet his inspiration. When his mouth opened, the most beautiful thing happened. His seasoned tenor voice gave into opera. Just like

179

the oldest of my father's records, the crescendo of velvety vibrato told a story of classic Italian heartbreak. Bill Fowler sang us an entire aria that Saturday afternoon, shifting and swaying back and forth, painting the heartache with his hands. I didn't need to understand the language. I could feel his pain. He had endured the heartbreak he sang of. But, Oh, the music! This was the first time I had ever witnessed someone truly emote with music, right in front me. For me, and for Pinwheel. Tears fell from his eyes, but he did not wipe them away. He summoned more tears, yet he took his comfort in the melody that he had earned with painful authority. Then the outro gave way to silence. I was moved to the stars and back. After a moment, he sat down to speak words of real significance for us: the importance of which I only had the faintest idea at the time.

"Young men, I want you to pay attention to what I am about to say. And hopefully we make a pact. You boys have talent for this thing. Music is a wonderful way to use your God-given talents and earth-fed energies. But the path artists can take is hard and destructive sometimes. Promise me...that you will never do drugs. Never do drugs, okay?" His eyes fell again. Bill was suffering.

"This is very important. Promise me."

"Okay, Bill. We won't do drugs, we promise."

I went home and told my parents about the amazing day that Pinwheel had at Bill Fowler's basement studio. I told them about the recordings, and the German microphone, and Bill's amazing aria.

"That's wonderful." Mom said. "I told the neighbor that you boys went to Mr. Fowler's house to record some of your music. She said the Fowler boy, Bill's son, moved to Seattle three years ago to join a band. He died last year of a drug overdose. Very sad. Did he mention that?"

I wanted to cry and play music forever...but I would never do drugs, I swore to myself. I wanted to keep that promise to Bill Fowler.

"Yes Mom, he mentioned it. And he taught me music."

The front door to the Barn Hostel in Gorham swung open.

"Welcome, Music Man!"

"How did you know my name?" I asked.

Paul stepped to the side and cheerfully invited me in.

"Music! Oh, Bae!" Garlic came thumping around the corner.

"Oh my God, Garlic!"

She hugged and kissed me, then wagged a finger.

"Why haven't you called me, Music Man?"

"Oh, I'm sorry lover. No phone, you know that! But I was sending you good vibes!"

"You've got a bad habit of leaving a good girl hanging, you know! But it's alright. I'm just glad you're here. I was worried when you didn't call but Zoom told me you were coming for me. I had an awesome hike up in the Presidentials. Oh, my gawd, those mountains were incredible! You kept your promise, you animal! You caught me before Maine! *Way* before Maine! I waited here for you today, thinking you'd come here. I took a couple zero days too. Zoom was here earlier. He said you would be hiking thru town...I hoped that you'd come here. And here you are!" She kissed me again. "Zoom said you guys had an amazing time in the Presidentials. We had bad weather on Mount Madison, too. It was that gnarly side rain. I hiked into Pinkham Notch with Jay and Silent Bob." Garlic had so much to tell me and listening to her recall her adventures was energizing— like the Smokies again.

Jay and Silent Bob were a middle-aged couple from down south. The gal, Jay, did all the talking. Silent Bob said literally two or three words a day. They were more like grumble-gestures. He was basically mute. But he was always smiling, and they were just incredible people. Silent Bob had more quality things to say in his few words than most with their many. He didn't need verbals; his body language and smile poured out like rays of sunshine.

Paul was more than happy to facilitate my reunion with Garlic. It gave him satisfaction, like Terry and the rest of the trail community, to help us hikers make it out there for another day.

Garlic and I shared a cozy bed upstairs and got some rest. I let my feet off the hook for nine hours straight. I was so tired of climbing mountains and all I wanted to do was a whole lot of nothing. I laid awake running my fingers thru her unbraided hair while she slept. Her phone rang and it was my brother.

"Brah."

"Bro."

"You didn't fucking quit?"

"I'm still hiking. I'm in Gorham."

"Good. I booked a flight to Bangor in a few weeks."

I sat up. "You're really coming?"

"Put a step on it, Brah. I'll see you at Katahdin Stream Campground in three weeks."

OUR BUBBLE OF TIGHT-KNIT TRAVELERS was mostly intact heading into Maine. Blueberry's hike had blossomed into something special to witness. His skills as an Eagle Scout were shining and he was so humble about it. Watching his confidence soar was inspiring. Fantastic was crushing climbs with his ever-expanding meaty calves. He was great fun to hike with for his unending sense of humor and his tall tales of taller big-wall rock climbs out west. He made hiking fun and he never got tired, especially if a cold can of beer was approaching. Chilly was finding out what she was truly made of. After a period of self-doubt about her hike many states ago, she had emerged as a true champion of long-distance trekking. She persevered in New York when her mind told her body that it was all over, but she kept going anyway. Green Bean led the charge each day—solid as a rock. With boots to dirt, he was the first hiker out and first into camp every day. That man just knew how to move across the earth. He also learned how to play the Strumstick.

Potholder was making his way up the trail, doing his own unique thing that only Potholder can pull off. We would have laughed them away in disbelief, if someone would have told us that one day we would harmonize our voices into an old German microphone: eerily like one in Bill Fowler's musky basement.

Garlic and I were back to our usual positions and in good strides together as we made our way into the magical state of Maine. I was happy to be hiking with her again and our comfortable partner-pace was damn near unison by that point. Plus, she ate most of the morning spider webs that crisscrossed the path after a calm and quiet night. "Cobb-knocking" was the price she paid for favoring the early morning lead and I never complained about that. We were mostly healthy, though the foot problems continued to pester us both. Our connection was strong as we enjoyed the first couple days in Maine, with sails set in easy wind. Then the smoothness of the track was shattered by Mahoosuc Notch and the Mahoosuc Arm. The Notch was exhilarating for Garlic, Blueberry, and me as we traversed that pitch as a team, for strength in numbers. Trail bosses say it is the "hardest mile" of the entire AT, and it was a very technical section. Rebar ladders and tunnels thru ancient glacier-placed stones trick the hiker underground in spots, then back out and across the sides of boulders that looked like asteroids. Traversing the obstacle course was terrific fun. The slick climb up the Mahoosuc Arm topped off the section like a real-life game of Chutes and Ladders. Maine was already delivering on promises of bold beauty in the isolated forest wilderness.

Even with the excitement surrounding the final phase of our thru-hikes, the trail had worn our bodies down by way of attrition. It had been a long hike, to say the least. In between rounds, Garlic and I laid on the sunny beach of a mountain tarn fully at ease. The water stilled us like a field-sized flag at a halftime show.

"Bro is meeting us at Baxter?" She asked.

"That's what he says. Pretty amazing...if he pulls it off." I explained, "Bro has climbed Katahdin before with NTN, Eddie, and other friends. But he said he has never climbed up the summit sign. Bro said it's "sacred." Only the deserving should hoist themselves up onto it for a picture.

"Does walking here all from Georgia qualify as deserving?" Garlic asked with a chuckle.

"In his mind, it's the *only* qualifier. He wants his own thru-hike someday."

"That's great, Music. I'm happy for you both...I'm happy for all of us...I'm just happy today. So, I think my Godparents are coming to Millinocket for my summit. They don't want to climb the mountain. It's too big. But they can give us a ride to my brother's house in Virginia so we can get my car. We'll get that Acadian lobster dinner we talked about in P.A."

A thousand miles in the rear view, Garlic promised me a Maine lobster prize if we reached the summit. She had asked me what I would do if I finished. "Go to Bar Harbor Lobster Company," (I fantasized about wearing a lobster bib for an hour or more) "From there, will you drive me down to Georgia to get my truck? It's supposed to be in long-term parking at Amicalola. At least, that's where GOAT said Paul has left it."

"Of course, Bae. You know, we could keep...doesn't it feel strange to be talking about post-trail plans?"

"Maybe we should stop, huh?" I pretended to agree.

"Yeah, why don't we go into Rumford now and get a room to ourselves for the night?" We were approaching some significant mountain ranges like the Saddlebacks and Bigelow's. A recharge in town was a solid suggestion. I didn't hesitate.

"That sounds great, lover. We've got the time. Let's do it."

I hid behind a tree while Garlic (hair down) hitched us a ride to town. We checked into a charming little nest at The Rumford Hotel, then sat at the bar and watched with amusement as the young couple that owned the place sizzled steaks and veggies burgers on the grill and poured cheap shots of expensive vodka. The place was empty when we sat down, then filled up with people for the dinner rush, then it emptied out again. We never moved from the barstools, and it seemed like there was no one else in the multiverse. We were that "obnoxious couple" that annoys you with how into each other they are. We reached the bottom of a vodka bottle after plowing thru dinner, then decided to call it a night.

Upon retiring, we locked ourselves in the room until lunchtime the next day. The late morning sun just barely broke thru the pulled vertical blinds, casting shadows like cell bars on the walls. Twisted in bed sheets, she rolled onto me, flipping her hair over one shoulder, and her breathy whispers were music to my ear:

"Can you handle another night?"

"Well, since you put it that way...."

We parlayed the day, but we laid off the booze. Instead, we walked around the town and went to candy shops and antique stores and bought expensive coffees and veggie wraps and tea leaves and took goofy selfies. At one dusty palace of relics, Garlic bought me a beautiful sterling silver ring with a treble clef etched into the band. Then we returned to the room and hummed songs to each other in bed. It was a wonderfully romantic stop.

Getting back to the trail, we stepped into the wake of the dynamic father/son team of Direction and Apollo. Getting a surprise late call, the Nobos were very spiritual and more like best friends than anything else. But Direction's story was most inspiring and instructive for those lucky enough to hear it. Apollo had well-aligned footprints to follow, and I was inspired to pass on the wisdom of my forefathers to my son. In my own words, it goes something like this:

WHEN THE WORKING IS DONE

"When you get home from work, Son,
A man keeps on working 'till the working is done."
Hang your hat, drape your tie, fold your shirt, lean your cane
Why, the corn and tobacco and soy took the rain
Tapped are the roots, the crops reach for the sky
A working man raises his harvest up high
He leaves nothing to chance, for he does lest he try
His hands are for working, he reaps what he sows
Preparing the earth 'round the cold rain and snow
Only then washing up on the land, he can place
His prayers and dances of faith in the space
Finally, he'll rest as the sun paints the west
Feigning of nothing, the man's done his best
With his grandfather's, grandfather's, good father's plans
(this county and country hard won by our clan)
For his children's children, says his father's son:
"A man keeps on working 'till the working is done."

There was clearly more footwork to be done on the trail. The weather was treacherous in the Saddlebacks. Sheets of fierce rain came sideways, and the temperature was near freezing. My feet were throbbing as I pressed forward. The wind damn near blew me off the mountain.

"Stay low!" Garlic screamed. I could barely hear her amid the roar of gales that met here from all directions. The winds gathered speed as they joined forces like Orc battalions before pressing up the mountainsides, making it all seem impassable. Garlic kept us moving and motivated. I wanted to stop a couple times and ride the storm out.

"Bad idea! Best to keep moving!" Her words were lost again to the winds that ripped over the peaks and passes of the Bigelow Reserve just days later, as we encountered the same dangerous conditions again. Wicked weather added to the challenge of hiking over the dagger-like rock masses already rated "extremely difficult" on a clear day. It felt like we were hiking down and around the summits of upside-down mountains in air that would freeze rain from the inside out. There were herds of unknown animals grazing in the valley where waterfalls poured into the sky from rivers. In the calm of the evening, moonflower blooms popped open one bud at a time. The weird earth was under a myriad of spells...it was great fun.

Garlic took a private afternoon to climb Sugarloaf Mountain and she returned with good Caution-news:

"I saw a moose! She was a mangey cow, but she's my mangey cow. I love her."

I hoped to see a moose in these parts, too. I had the fantasy of glimpsing a two-ton bull with a coral reef for a rack, snorting up from the bottom of a mountain lake after kicking a whale's ass. But no moose for the Music Man.

The Tramily had reformed around Pierce Pond, and we planned a gathering for Tim Harrison's classic breakfast at Harrison's Pierce Pond Camp. A good many hikers attended. We ate the famous pancake breakfast family-style after Tim whipped it up and served it all by himself. Cherished is the memory of my private conversation with him in the kitchen. We shared thoughts about the trials and tribulations of trails, love, loss, and tragedy. Tim spoke about the spontaneity of nature and unpredictable hiking conditions. There were musical instruments in every corner of the cabin. Green Bean and I jammed on the miles on the strings setting about, and Tim played us a beautiful composition on his piano too. He said that he had written it for his son, who had gone "Home." I listened and I prayed, and I thanked him for the nourishment. With single-digit miles left to the banks of the Kennebec River, Garlic and I came around a bend in the trail to find Fantastic soaking his feet to his giant calves in a stream. His face was as white as snow.

"Music Man... Garlic..."

"Uh oh, Fanboy. What happened?" I asked.

"It's gotta be sprained, Music. I came over a root and rolled my ankle clear out of the shoe. Who put that root there, anyway?! It really hurts, guys. Yep, I might be closing my tab."

"Ssss, damn that's swollen up double, huh..." said Garlic, as she dropped her pack and placed his foot in her lap for better inspection.

"Good friends, it's bad news. I can't walk. I can't put any weight on it and we're still three miles from the ferry across the Kennebec."

"Fantastic, we've got you." Garlic looked him square in the eyes and reassured him. Both of us had been thru this a time or two. We determined that our experience would pay off for Fantastic; but he would have to do the heavy lifting.

"Listen to me," Garlic continued, "You need to try and control any shock. You're pale as a ghost. Try to breathe slowly and calm your mind. Think of a big wall you love to climb, or something like that. Picture your family, or the beach. Just take your mind away from the pain."

"What about my family on a nude beach?"

I covered my eyes and choked on a chuckle. The image of Fantastic-looking aunts and uncles and cousins with protruding meaty calves running in slow motion along a sandy nude beach...I remembered the Big Joint.

"What about it, Fantastic?" Garlic was as serious as radio.

"Yeah, I was trying to filter drinking water cause I'm out. I'm so thirsty."

"Shit." She grabbed his bottle and dunked it into the crystal-clear stream then handed it back to him. "I don't think river critters should be your concern right now. Besides, your funky-ass feet are the worst pollutant this stream has dealt with in eons," she said while pointing at the hamburger patties under his meaty calves that were soaking in the river. We all laughed, and the timing was right for comedic relief.

"So," Garlic squarely commanded, "Music Man is going to be your crutch down to the river and I am going to carry your pack."

"Roger that, Ma'am," I obeyed the tactful orders.

Garlic donned her pack as normal, then put Fantastic's pack around her shoulders backwards, carrying it out around the front of her body; looking like she had a belly with child. She must have had sixty pounds on her person. I absorbed a good portion of his body weight on my shoulders as his one remaining healthy and meaty calf hopped-hopped-hopped him down to the bank of the river next to me. Fantastic's job performance was a herculean display of endurance as he made the miles in tremendous pain. I flashed back to Mt. Mist. I knew what he was going thru. Of course, so did Garlic. Those were the true lessons of the trail. How much could a person endure when they must? All of it. And knowing when it's time to abandon self and help someone in need...True character is found deep within our soul, in our heart. Sometimes, too, in the pit of our stomach. We didn't want anything in return, for someone else had done this for us. I remembered Steve Edwards back at Harpers Ferry, and how he told me that true change was an inside job. I could travel from sea to shining sea (and I have). And I go to the infinite corners of the earth in search of the grandeur found on mountains; the tranquility of the forests; or sneak up on the great rivers and ocean vistas. I've watched the movements of celestial bodies; inhaled sulfuric gasses pumping out of active volcanic calderas. But just as easily, I had missed the mystery of myself without even noticing. What was it all about? Finding my eternal connection to the heavenly world around me, then helping someone else do the same if they are in need. Sharing a message of hope and love in a world that so often runs on fear: this is my true purpose. I want nothing in return, but to see you smile again.

I wished it had not taken me thirteen states and two thousand miles to figure out that all I needed to be...was water. It was so simple. Not easy, but simple! What could I do with this small realization? Anything I please when I am free from the bondage of "self". What do I do when I'm not dying from active addiction? Everything else.

When we arrived on the south bank of the mighty Kennebec River, Fantastic fell on the beach in exhaustion from royally saving his own ass. He was folded over in pain, but he still put a smile on his face and thanked us. There was a growing number of hikers at the river, and we added to the bottleneck. It was a chance to rest as we waited for the ride across the river. The canoe ferry was skipped by a fine fellow in the employ of the Appalachian Trail Conservancy.

"Filling Steve Longley's shoes is a tall order; may he rest in peace." He lamented, "Steve skipped this ferry for decades. I just try to be me. We of the A.T.C. are proud to be here today, to help you folks get across the Kennebec River safely. By long-standing tradition of the Trail and the Conservancy, I will not abandon this post." Hikers nodded their heads and gave thumbs up in approval. We gently placed the injured Fantastic onto the first ferry across, and he accidentally farted when he leaned into the canoe. Direction queued right in, reaching for his toilet paper:

"You're gonna need some shit tickets for that ferry ride, Fanny."

****

Once upon a time, Bro went to Thanksgiving dinner to meet his then girlfriend's family for the first time. From the head of the table, her father caught him off guard when he asked Bro to give a dinner blessing for the big family he had just met. Surprised and at a loss for words, my brother took one look at the cooked bird on the table and blurted out:

"God, we thank You for...*breasts*."

Knock, knock. Who's there? A real National Lampoon moment. I would have given anything to be a hair on the gizzard for that one. Bro ended up marrying that woman, called Goldfish. They met on the Appalachian Trail at the north bank of the Kennebec River in Maine while waiting for the late trail angel, Steve "The Ferryman" Longley, as he shuttled hikers across the river in the A.T.C.-staffed canoe ferry. They met for ten special minutes between my brother's arrival and my sister-in-law's departure. Bro had to wait for her to finish her Sobo thru-hike of the Appalachian Trail before she found him back home. They just so happened to be from the same hometown. "Eight more miles to Louisville, the hometown of my heart," as the sweet and snappy old Grandpa Jones tune longs for. Years later, Steve Longley would row both our families back across the Kennebec River, to where Bro and Goldfish first crossed paths, so they could marry on the same banks where they had met in a whirlwind. Of that timeless moment, a classic photo taken of them hangs on the memory wall in their home, commemorating the fateful encounter. True story. Goldfish bestowed her thru-hiked Therm-a-Rest pillow sack to me, way back when Bro had set me up with gear and the first "Don't Fucking Quit" instructions— And after Steve "The Ferryman" Longley earned a special place in our family history.

****

After we ferried across the Kennebec River, Garlic and I sat on the stump, at the very spot where my brother met his wife, and we took a picture there too. She sent Bro the picture and expressed our excitement at his intended arrival at Baxter State Park. Everyone rallied around Fantastic, and we all stayed at the Sterling Inn in Caratunk. We grilled steaks and veggie burgers and twisted around on the porch hammocks with plates on our laps. There was a card game at the table, and somebody yelled "Go Fish!". We had a big time on the wrap around porch with Green Bean as our Strumstick maestro. When he finished, he handed it to me and made his request.

"500 Miles, Music Man. Let's hear it." "Alright, this goes out to Mr. Meaty Calves."

Fantastic faked a head-faint and demanded "Don't tease me, but will somebody please throw me a pilsner!" He belched beer that triggered ankle pain then listened to the old song, noticeably uneasy in his spirit. But he smiled with the rest. We gave high fives in groups but privately sobbed in ones and twos at the thought of the dwindling miles left to hike. The end seemed to be approaching too quickly and we didn't want it to end. I wasn't ready for the chapter to close, but the hiking was getting more and more tiring.

Back on trail the next day, the AT crossed miles of mogul-like mounds in the mossy Great North Woods. The land was mirrored with glassy-topped lakes which shone reflections of the pine covered mountains and big blue skies. The sun was warm, and the wind was cool. Fungus caps and flower pipes that lined the trail were covered in a sheen of moisture, and sometimes we thought we could see the mushrooms moving and growing. The water was crystal clear as it giggled over worn down gray and brown stones that covered the riverbeds. We didn't filter the water or even use our bottles. We simply stopped next to a stream and opened our gullets. The sweetest mountain nectars arched like rainbows of humble pride and poured themselves into our mouths. The land was wild and free, as nature's balanced beauty was on full display.

I walked into Shaw's Hiker Hostel in Monson about three hours before Garlic. Several hikers were there resting up before the long haul of the "100 Mile Wilderness": a stretch of trail separated us from the entrance to Baxter State Park at Abol Bridge by the nonstop distance of one hundred miles without a proper resupply. When I joined the campfire at Shaw's, someone pushed a buzz my way and I had taken it. After a long shower, I woke up on my rack still wrapped in a shower towel. Three hours had slipped by. I yawned, then dressed and went outside in the dark.

"What time is it?" I asked the darkness.

"Midnight," came her voice. "That dab knocked you out, huh..."

"Hey, babe. When do you get in?" I scratched my head and yawned again. "After you checked out, apparently," Garlic said under her breath.

"Take it easy...."

"Music, I just don't know about you; everything tells me to run away from you as fast as I can, but I don't... I just can't. Why do I love you? And you think you get away with everything, but I'll let you in on the secret: you are an open book. When you get high, you change. I'm not trying to be a controlling nag, you know... You act differently when you use. You don't talk to me the same way. You don't treat me the same way. You get cocky and you're just...different. You're not the kind of man I want when you are messed up. I just want you without all that baggage. But I guess we don't always get what we want."

"I know that I'm different when I'm high," I conceded. "Believe me, I know. I don't want to keep losing the most important people in my life. I just want to be happy. I'm sorry, but...."

"You can miss me with the hollow apologies, Music Man. By the way, a sincere apology doesn't end with "but". And a good apology isn't really meant for the recipient. What am I gonna do with it, even if I accept it? It's meant to remind the person apologizing that things said and done have consequences. Maybe, you'll realize...Music, you need long-term treatment."

A lump formed in my throat as my heart dropped a level in my chest.

"Listen, Poet is driving us to the trailhead at 8am," she continued, "Let's be ready, ok? Goodnight, Music Man. Get some rest." She kissed my chin and retired to her tent. Back in my rack, my head and heart wrestled with shame, but I turned myself away from the moment, full of fear.

A rooster cackled and the breakfast bell rang bright and early. The place was buzzing with juice, pancakes, and waffles. There were a few Nobos hanging around including Blueberry, who said he was going to wait for Fantastic to arrive accompanied by Chilly and Green Bean. He was such a loyal friend and teammate. Fantastic was trying to hike but was only making single-digit miles each day. In the meantime, Blueberry, ever the loyal colleague, held up to wait for the rest of his expedition.

After a resupply, and some carefully chosen words of inspiration from the trailhead, Poet delivered four of us to the timber gates of the hundred miles that separated us from Abol Bridge Campground.

"Music Man, if we get a weather window let's do the Knife Edge off the mountain after we summit."

"Garlic, what are you talking about?"

"Oh, Bae...I forgot. You don't have the Internet."

"Nope, sure don't. I guess it will be a surprise."

"It sure as hell will be, if we actually find ourselves up there!"

The first day of trail in the 100-Mile Wilderness was total carnage, even for seasoned thru-hikers like us who are ready for the exertion. But it was so rewarding! The mountains and lakes and rivers turned over in an endless reel of picture book scenes and landscapes. Pine trees covered the jagged climbs and mountain tarns fit for swimming decorated the land like Swiss cheese. Each new bend in the trail shared stories of boreal landscapes that only existed in magical wardrobes before my eyes saw them for real. Lucky hikers have moose sightings most commonly at the remote lakes. Moose wade in the shallows to safely cool themselves and relieve pressure that their immense weight puts on their bones, as well as evade other trouble.

At an early morning river crossing on the third day in, we hopped up on the bridge to an amazing surprise (for me). Crossing the bridge in our direction, was Donatello! Last seen at Harpers Ferry, we heard that he had left the trail. But there he was, pack loaded and heading south and nearing the end of the hundred miles.

"Donatello!"

"Wha-ho! Music Man! Good to see you!" He tipped his cap as Garlic passed, "My lady...." He tipped his coolie with his staff.

Garlic passed him like a ship in the night as he approached me for a hug. Donatello had never hugged me before. Garlic disappeared up the trail in silence.

"I thought you were off trail, D, it's great to see you!"

"I was, Music, but...well, I'm back. I'm gonna try a flip-flop back to Harper's Ferry if I can out-hike the seasons. You know...I walk slow. Ha-ha! Anyway, some resources came available, so this time I can eat!"

"I'm glad to hear that, D. My man, you are about to finish the 100-Mile Wilderness! How's it been, coming south?"

"Hard in either direction. But it's epic, just beautiful. Hey, Music Man, I have something for you." He opened his wallet and pulled out a $100 bill. He handed it to me with a couple trail patches from my old backpack that I gave him in Carolina.

"I figured you wanted those John Muir Trail and Yosemite patches back, too."

"You've been carrying these patches just to give them back to me? Wow, I'm thrilled to have them. But the money, Donatello, you don't have to...."

"I owe you that, from Damascus. I'm thankful for the loan. Wish I could have talked you out of taking that wrong turn that night, but I reckon you needed it. Bro, I have missed you man...I wish I could have kept up. But don't think twice, Music! I'm in a better position out here now; I'm trying to be a better human being. I will always owe the trail."

My old friend and hiking partner who, once upon a time, faced his own haunts and challenges, had overcome something within his spirit, thanks to the AT. His actions were of a new kind of change, unlike all my sanctimonious hot air—Donatello was no longer traveling by wants upon a dime.

"Donatello, I am so happy to see you...and excited for you to give this hike another run. Sobo to Harper's Ferry, aye?! Who'd have guessed it? Shoot, you're more than halfway home with plenty of season left. You can make it...if you want to! Friend, I love you and I appreciate you."

"Congratulations to you and Garlic on your thru-hikes. What a year to be on the AT." "Thank you, Donatello. But we still have one big mountain left to climb."

191

"Music Man, you have reached the summit already. Happy Trails, old friend!"

Donatello pulled a Class-A cigarette out and placed it into the corner of his mouth as he turned to walk away....

****

Back on that lonely and rainy night at tent city, I was a broken mess. I had traded my truck for the last bag of dope, while the silhouette between the headlights watched me pour it out for Black Face. Who had I poured it out for, really? Confusion and misery weighed down every step like I had anvils anchored to my ankles. Heavy, too, was the burden of the last earthly possession that I carried: my guitar. More than anything, I had not the heart to play it. I was physically, mentally, and spiritually bankrupt. No destination, but my feet just kept moving. All I wanted to do was stop dead in my tracks, but the glistening streets showed my fledgling spirit a path. My body was operating on unknown Power. Episodes and scenes from my life's past flashed thru my mind like an endless series of mass extinctions and resurrections; each rise and fall more tragic than the last. This time, I had truly set everything on fire and stepped right into the flames. Still, I didn't have the strength to surrender on my own. Then something like a miracle happened.

As I rounded a dark and drizzly corner of the huge new sports arena downtown, a back door swung open into the sidewalk and almost hit me. The night watchman stepped out to light a smoke. He wore a yellow shirt that read "SECURITY" across the shoulders and on the breast pocket. The door startled us both as it slammed shut in between us, revealing our presence to each other.

"Shit! You scared the hell out of me, man," he exclaimed as he lowered the lighter away from the unlit cigarette in the corner of his mouth. The Latino Watchman spoke in a thick Spanish accent. My soaked and shocked appearance was enough to send a shudder thru any soul or spirit.

"Sorry," I responded, "I'm lost, and....do you think there is a God?" It just came out.

"Come again?" he asked.

"If there is...a 'God', I can't find him anywhere. I don't know what has happened to my life. I am lonely and afraid, and I can't live like this anymore."

The Latino Watchman studied me as I spoke, with the unlit cigarette hanging out of the corner of his mouth, and a look of anguish and love in his eyes. I asked him again:

"Sir, do you believe in God?"

"Yes, my friend. I believe in Him."

"Do you think you could pray with me...I mean, pray for me?"

A lump was forming in my throat. The Latino Watchman took the cigarette from the corner of his mouth and shoved it into his pocket. With empathy and care and genuine love, he responded: "I would be happy to pray with you." He extended his hands in an offering. They were steady and calm; dry and protected from the rain. He invited me: "Take my hands, do not be afraid. Allow Him into your heart."

I peered into his comforting eyes, then I looked down into his open hands. Again, I read the word written across his shirt: "SECURITY". I lowered my guitar to the sidewalk and raised my trembling hands toward his. He immediately grabbed them and bowed his head. I lowered my head as he began praying.

"Father, we come to you in need...."

The Latino Watchman prayed with an accent that reminded me of Guatemalan dialects, like those I had heard a lifetime ago in the travels of my youth. His words and his kindness opened a channel to the Source. I felt spiritual power flow through him. The Latino Watchman was filled with light, and it began to flow into me. Tears fell from his eyes as Grace poured out of his heart. He prayed for my safety and my health. He prayed for my loved ones to find peace. He prayed for this desperate man in his hands: that I might find my way out of this terrible darkness; he prayed for my peace and serenity; that I find healing through the Father; and that I find my own strength. I began to weep too. The Latino Watchman continued to pray as we both sobbed, then he squeezed my hands and closed out his requests:

"Dios, esté música hombre ha caminado bastante. En el nombre del Padre, del Hijo y del Espíritu Santo. Amén."

I don't speak Spanish, but I understood the prayer, thanks to buried shrapnel from the Latin class I nearly failed in college. He covered my heart with his right hand, and his own heart with his left. My voice cracked as I spoke:

"Thank You."

"You are most welcome, my friend. Good luck. Godspeed."

He wiped his eyes and put the unlit cigarette back into the corner of his mouth. But I didn't wipe my tears. I had earned those tears and I would wear them until they dried. I reached down and picked up my guitar case. It felt a little lighter. We passed shoulders and walked away in opposite directions. I took only a few paces before I turned around to say something else to the Latino Watchman, but he was gone. I never heard the arena door close behind him. Even if I didn't have the strength to ask God for help, I asked someone for help, and He showed up anyway. A couple hours later, a pink sunrise broke over the eastern sky. But a new light had already illuminated my path to the front door of The Healing Place. I have not had a drink or a drug since that night.

****

The encounter with Donatello in the 100-Mile Wilderness that late-summer morning in Maine was a spiritual experience for me. He had made amends in his own way, and I did not deserve it. But that didn't matter. The amends were for him. He knew he would eventually have the opportunity and he was ready to act when he got the chance. I was reminded again that the trail is long, but it is narrow. And sometimes the convoluted ink of a hundred paragraphs can be better summed up by a single word: Gratitude.

Crossing the 100-Mile Wilderness, the Appalachian Trail sliced thru old-growth pine forests, up and over strenuous pitches of mogul-like mounds and hills, and tons of fish-stocked water. The rugged climbing didn't stop until we reached the pond and lake region just south of Baxter.

While hiking alone on a particular afternoon in mid-September, I rounded a bend as the trail skirted the shore of a lake, and it hit me....as the first views of Mount Katahdin only could. Towering and treacherous; dignified and dangerous; she loomed over the flat horizon like the Great Sphinx at the Giza Plateau. It was the middle of September, and the northern terminus of the Appalachian Trail was less than ten miles away. I let out a sigh of relief, within striking distance of completing the contract I had made with myself six months, fourteen states, and nearly twenty-two hundred miles back.

Garlic caught up with me and we exited the trail at Abol Bridge Campground with a host of other hikers. Many of whom were ready to complete the last technical challenge of their journeys. Direction and Apollo appeared with a beautifully brilliant Russian-American thru-hiker, who I had just met on the approach to Abol Bridge. She had hiked the AT from end to end in four months, overcoming much toil on her trek. I do not recall her name, so I affectionately refer to her as "Russianonymous"; the one who surrendered her heart to spiritual offerings toward the end of her journey.

The Tramily celebrated in fine form. We ate well and sat around the fire ring telling tales of adventure and war stories of woe on the Appalachian Trail, as the fire illuminated the smiles on everyone's faces. The crackle of the flames fumed off the sweet pine trees that canopy the camp. Many of us were happier people and most of us were healthier for the long haul. Whether we were on-trail or off-trail, we were blessed by GBITS just to be there with a chance to finish the damn thing. It is a joy to watch other people turn themselves on to the wonders of nature and help others to find that place too. A deeply fulfilling spiritual experience is available to anyone who dares to trek. One cannot help but be moved by the rare sighting of a Scarlet Tanager at dusk, with its bright red coat and black wings. The beautiful bird will sit like royalty at dusk, seemingly with the knowledge that its glowing coat holds the best of the late sun's offerings.

After breakfast the next morning, Garlic and I moved in the direction of Katahdin Stream Campground. Garlic wanted to take it very slow. It was an emotional time, and we walked the sacred ground with a soft reverence. After a quiet and steady morning, I agreed to hike ahead then wait for her at lunch, excited to relish in my own spiritual experiences with Baxter State Park and canvas-like views of the mountain.

For the first time since North Georgia, I registered for a permit to hike an Appalachian mountain. It was apropos. We did not have to wait long for the rented minivan that pulled into the parking lot squealing its tires with rapid fire horn honking.

"Bro!" "BrahhHHH!"

"Yes! You made it!" Bro jumped out of the van and hurried over to a big embrace, one like we shared back at the Long Trail Inn. He lifted me high then slammed me down on my swollen feet before slapping my ass cheek.

"Good game, Music Man!"

"Aye, thank you. But there's one last mountain to climb."

Bro turned to my partner.

Smack! "Good game to you, too, Garlic!" She hopped and chirped at the friendly slap-ass of comradery.

"Thanks, Bro. It's great to see you! Yah just like yah brotha."

The mystical campground was buzzing with people for hours. Many of us sat around the field well after dark enjoying the good company in the backcountry vibes of Katahdin Stream Campground. I let Bro crash in my tent for the night and told Garlic I would join her soon in her tent. We had a big day ahead, but my mind was astir. Late into the evening, only Green Bean and I sat around the fire ring as he plucked the Strumstick. The Fantastic Food Group still had another day of hiking before their summit day. "Big day for you guys tomorrow, Music Man," he harmonized with dark Locrian scales under his fingertips. "How do you feel?"

"I am tired, Greenie. I am ready to be done hiking. But I'm just so excited to share the day with...everyone. I'm so happy that my brother here...and Garlic and I made it to this mountain together. It's been quite a ride."

"Yeah, man. It has been a ride. I'm still trying to figure out what it has all been for. We hike all this way and then it's over, and we just...go home."

"Well, New Jersey ain't bad."

"Jersey's a zoo, Music Man! Why do you think Chilly and I are out here?"

"I hear you, Green Bean, but there was more to this than just a geographical change. I am starting to have faith." It just came out.

"Really? In what?"

"That the true lessons of the trail are enduring; this experience could be a microcosm of regular old civilian life; and that more will be revealed."

"That's pretty optimistic, Music Man." He strummed another sullen melody.

"Hopefully more optimistic than the Devil's funeral service you're playing over there," I joked.

He huffed in approval:

"The Strumstick sounds so happy. I want to make it sound angry."

"Are you angry, Green Bean?"

He stopped playing.

"Music Man, I'm the happiest I have ever been. I don't want the hike to end."

"What are you thinking right now?" I wanted him to dig deep, and it gave him pause.

"What if hiking the Appalachian Trail just means we made a decision to do something....and then we did it."

"Ah. A simple task...but not easy."

"Music, this is the hardest thing I have ever done. But you're right. It is simple. All we had to do was follow some paint stripes on the trees and they brought us all the way from Georgia to Maine. Simple directions, huh? Just follow the hundred-thousand blazes while running from them. The blazes run southbound too, you know."

"Already thinking about a southbound bid, are we Greenie?"

"Not until I figure this Nobo thing out."

"Agreed." I said, "My friend, the hardest part of this whole Chautauqua was getting to the trailhead to begin with. From Springer Mountain onwards, GBITS had her own plans for us. On that note...I'm so impressed with all of you waiting for Fantastic to catch up, so y'all'd finish as a team. That's loyalty and humility, Green Bean. Truly."

"You would do the same, Music Man. You already did. You and Garlic showed us how. Thru everything, you stuck together. We had to ask ourselves and each other what was truly important. Breaking up and leaving each other to chance so we could summit on "personal goal" dates? Or finishing what we started: Ending as a team was the obvious choice. We were the fortunate ones this year. We all made it this far with a little help from our friends, a lot of luck, and a wagon-load of determination. Fantastic, Blueberry, Chilly and Green Bean will summit together."

"That's right, good hiker. Way to show up and show out for your partners, all yuns. You helped us too, ya know. I wouldn't be here without you guys either." I realized how little of my story others really knew. Garlic was closed-mouthed and loyal. "I need good people in my life. I've been lonely for so long. I want to be a father again." I voiced with regret, but the hope was there. "That's how I learn what kind of man I want to be, the presence of a Higher Power working thru people and nature. I think that anyone who steps foot on this trail is eligible for a spiritual experience." I stood up to go to bed as he played the sweetest, happiest melody that ever was. "Greenie, I know you produce music back home...but what pays the bills? A day-job?" The shadows of the fire jumped to lick the brim of his hat as he looked up to answer:

"I work at a treatment center for addiction."

I gave him an extended empathetic blink in return, followed with an offering: "The Strumstick...keep it. It's yours after I take it up the mountain tomorrow."

His smile widened as he went back to his draconian Church modes from medieval times. "Thank you, Music."

"You're welcome. Keep it safe...."

"Brah!" Bro called out from across the cold, "your tent smells like wet dogs and stale bronsky!" "Are you kidding me, Bro? What'd you expect after 2,188 miles?"

"I'm just saying...a little toothbrush and bleach one time?" We shared the evening's last laugh, then I crawled into Garlic's tent and exhaled deeply.

"Big spoon." She called with a quickness, beating me to it. I took one last look at the nearly new moon above the pine top shadows, then zipped up the front door to home and laid down with her.

"Best two out of three?"

"Only five more miles to go," she whispered back. "Your data is acceptable, but no. All me." Threading her arm around my chest, the good girl tucked her face into my neck and shoulder. "I can't believe that tomorrow, we will climb Mt. Katahdin, then it's finished."

"The journey isn't over yet, my love."

Garlic removed her oversized coral-rimmed glasses and placed them into the tent pocket, then drifted off to sleep, the sleep of the weary and worthy. I laid awake most of the night holding her tight while playing back my conversation with Green Bean. The wind whispered sweet nothings, but I couldn't understand the words. Inside the tent walls, I could smell the sweet aroma of pine that was strong enough to trigger my taste buds. As I ran my fingers thru Garlic's sleeping hair, I reminisced about the Nantahala cove of tall grass where we first agreed to take things one step at a time before rolling into love. My mind continued to mull over the mighty purpose of the hike. Slowly revealing from the start, simple kindness was the lesson. Much of my life, I failed to see it. The realization hit me that there is not too much worry about things, or at least there shouldn't be, when I am a good man. Sometimes I trudge the paths with purpose, but sometimes I may just drift about. There was much wisdom in the old saying "All who wander are not lost." True, I will occasionally find myself surrounded by thorns and ivy; those times will call for course corrections. But I will get by...I will survive. Thoughts flowed about my mind like a carousel. In all, the night before the final summit found me filled with gratitude. But there were outstanding warrants, a lot of them...Eventually, I must face the music and make proper amends.

Bro was snoring his sweet dreams a few yards away. Kentucky to northern Maine in only one wake-up was a huge travel day for him. The cold was no match for his fatigue. I was so happy he had made the journey and was there with me; for me. His was love and support at its finest and typical of my twin. Mom and Dad were right there in our hearts too. They had come along on every step of the journey as they were never far from my mind and heart, along with all my friends and family. My children, my wonderful kids.....everyone was peacefully sleeping. At dawn, the sunrise came to illuminate the pine-covered floor of the Great North Woods.

.16

MID-MORNING LIGHT BROKE THRU the tree cover and illuminated the trail register kiosk at the junction of the Hunt Trail system. Underfoot, the brown dirt was covered with orange pine needles like chilly and cheese. Bro insisted on bringing up the rear of the group. Garlic took the point as she so often led in good form. There was no other place I would have rather been that morning. It was a clear day, and no rain was forecasted with highs in the upper 60's. There was not a cloud on the horizon.

"What do you think, Music? Knife's Edge? "Knife's Edge, Garlic. Let's do it. Bro?"

"Haw-right! I was hoping y'all say that!" Bro exclaimed, "Third time's the charm! The weather was too bad for the east ridge when I came in 2000 with Eddie...same thing with NTN. This is fitting, Brah!"

The "Knife Edge" is the hair-raising northeastern route off the mountain beyond the summit. It would be a tremendous technical challenge with thousands of feet of vertical drop off both sides of the trail that followed the great spine of the mountain. And the track consisted of boulder after boulder of serious hops, skips, scrambles, and jumps. Never was there a more dangerous section of the trail, but it wasn't technically the AT. We would be officially finished by that point if we reached the summit. But we still had to get to the top of Mount Katahdin.

Ascending the Hunt Route was numbingly difficult, yet a visceral thrill. Still, I didn't physically feel the pains of big-mountain climbing. This was really it: our destination after a six-month journey along the highest ridges of the Appalachian Mountains. The banter between the three of us was worthy of meeting minutes. We laughed and laughed ourselves farther up the mountain. At one point, Bro said "You two have your own damn language!"

As we rounded the corner of a switchback to face a ladder scramble, someone was coming down the trail toward us. I recognized him, it was...Shorty? I stopped as he whizzed past us on the trail headed south.

"Look at that white boy go!" He chuckled away and out of sight.

What the hell was he doing up here? And where did he get those shiny new shoes? Well, good for him!

"Take care of your shoes, Shorty!"

We kept going and there was someone else coming down, slicing back and forth...Monarch? Garlic was cutting it up with Bro to distract herself. I was focused on who was coming at me. Monarch zigzagged around Garlic, fluttered in front of me and winked, pleasantly announcing that she was "just passing thru". Nobody but me noticed. "Hey!" A voice from the lichen patch bellowed, "Ya need to be home with your families!" The postmaster from Fontana was wagging a finger at us. "I'm headed there now, Sir!" I began yelling over the rotor wash of a helicopter hovering overhead. The chopper from the Smokies? Piloted by Zoom wearing dark aviator sunglasses and having big laughs. He gave me a lazy civilian salute and turned the chopper away, chewing his gum.

"Whatever you do, don't take the Knife Edge!" Is that Krystal? Coming down the trail with her hands up, Kalik was riding a unicycle behind her holding a short rope that was tied around her waist. They blitzed past us in a cloud of single-track dust. But I would go to the Knife Edge. For that is where I would face my fear. One deviation from the path to salvation and the consequences could be disastrous. I must take the Knife Edge. Everything worth having is worth taking a risk for. Just like thru-hiking, recovery is not for people who want it or even need it; it is for those willing to work for it.

Climbing higher and higher toward the summit, we passed Steve Edwards and Uncle John, moving like Special Forces, carrying resupplies and a bugle: "Remember, Music Man, stay prepared. All you need is already within you. Fight fair and work hard!" Uncle John blew the Call to the Post with his bugle.

"Yes sir, Steve! Uncle John!"

In the distance, the sharp Knife Edge twisted down for miles to the dark blue water of the mountain tarns far below, as White Cap gated the horizon a lifetime away, toward the direction of Springer Mountain. There was John the Baptist and Grand Master, parkour running across the face of the mountain and speaking in Dutch tongues about chess while carrying the train of the Lord's robe. They looked satisfied and serene. Medicine Man appeared near the switchback and kneeling at the feet of Bill Fowler, who was fanning himself with his fedora. He turned to me and sang in an operatic voice,

"Music Man, it's not too late to keep a promise to an old friend!"

We kept climbing the boulders whilst more friends emerged. A hundred feet in the air, Turtle Hurdle was taking the summit with a single bound, under the admiring eyes of Mr. and Mrs. Foote! Delhi pointed to him and laughed in approval. Side-Show Bob gave me thumbs up from the edge of a trail-side shelter, then swiped at his cell phone screen. Jimmy Banks was there with his arm around his wife and guitar slung across his back. "She says you can keep the Jetboil," says Jimmy, as his wife's arms wrap around his waist.

Future friends, K-Bar and Coco, passed like bursting Roman Candles and advised me to "Use that sunblock, Music Man!" Andrew and his crazy crew of cousins came bounding down the mountain. Andrew headed straight for me extending a closed-hand offering. But the Big Joint pushed his arm away and urged him forward. She tried to say thanks, but Garlic didn't flinch, focused on the last pitch. She already had her sight set on the Knife Edge, but just a little further...just a little further. We could see the sign at the top of the mountain...the end was in sight... "Bro, is that Mom and Dad?" Bro smiles and nods, "Just a couple more turns!" Garlic sings a familiar melody in overtones, like fairies from a dream:

"Music, Sweet Music, let's hike the Benton Mackaye!"

"Now?"

"After the Knife Edge, silly!"

Sitting perfectly straight next to the "Bob Ross" moss was Tom Lavardi leading Neville and Tim Harrison in a guided meditation. Tom Lavardi opened one eye and folded his hands in a spiritual gesture. With the half-smile of the Buddha, he slightly bowed in approval before going back to breathing suggestions. Who is that? White-haired and silver-bearded.... It's Nimblewill Nomad! Passing on my left, he repeated his parting words to me from Flagg Mountain when I thru-hiked the Pinhoti Trail, completing the "1000-Mile Challenge". Nimblewill said: "Music Man, you're on the right path." Here via the Pinhoti Trail is Raven, tugging her dog leash taut as Swiss Cheese keeps up with her. They bounce by—Swiss Cheese prophesied "Write that book, Music Man! Now say Cheese!" He points to Freddy, who snaps a Polaroid for his wall of memories. He winks at me as he begins to fan the picture after pulling it from the old camera. Holding my hourglass, I look inside to glimpse Nimblewill Nomad now slipping thru the grains, taking the form of Dr. Ron Whitehead when bottlenecked between the ampules; then the sand and dust reform into Old Uncle Jake wearing his new white suit. But Uncle Jake looks young again and he is smiling! He no longer has a drink in his hand. He has a baton, and he is conducting a symphony in the sky! Potholder and Choogle strike happy-blues chords on que.

As we neared the summit, Uncle Jake pointed his baton to the edge of the mountain. My eyes follow and I freeze—I hear...chop...chop...chop....

"Black Face, what are you doing here?"

"Shh...." he hushes while raising the machete. "Remember what I told you, Music Man...." He turned the blade up to show me the delicate balance that would be needed to safely stay the course on the edge of the knife...life on life's terms.

"If shaped in a good foundry, the blade of a knife can't cut itself." It was Black Face's final gesture.

He tucked away the machete with a quick flip and stuffed the sheath away into his hooded trench coat, then lowered the hood over his eyes. As Black turned his back, he revealed the Latino Watchman who took an unlit cigarette from the corner of his mouth and shoved it into his pocket, then placed his hand over his heart and lowered his head in prayer.

I saw the swaying Uncle Jake, in his perfect white suit and waving baton, laughing heartily as he conducted his masterpiece atop the mighty Mount Katahdin. There was Leadbelly magic in his music. Uncle Jake's waving baton traced the Knife Edge in the sky, as the wind on the hill blew like the Breath of God. Father Time and Mother Nature are fairly ruling the Great Out Doors, as it has always been and will continue to be. Ironically, as a sojourner of the wilderness, I had found the spirit of community, and a reawakening of my own humanness. I had been a part of life again. The hiking community helps each other get there. The beauty of the whole adventure is that where we are going and where we have been don't matter anymore. Our awareness in the present moment... that's what counts—at that place can be found peace.

I have kept and guarded those moments, fancied or real. And now I share them because each step is vital on the spiritual path of life. I am so grateful for the ability to tap deeply into the well of love that resides within me. Loving myself and treating myself accordingly is the basis for gifts of genuinely shared love. I can't give away something I do not have and finding that interconnected love is an inside job that never ceases, and never ceases to amaze. The voices of my children are telling me that they are proud of me, and they love me. The silhouette from between the headlights of the downtown car reveals itself to me, and I cry out:

"It was *you*, all this time? Of course!"

Reaching the Table with only a mile to go, the capstone of the peak appeared like the Great Jaguar Temple at Tikal for a fleeting moment, before the outline of the sawhorse sign returned. Thomas Merton once said, "We are always traveling," and Thoreau wrote that he could not trust a man who didn't know how to properly walk. I will split the difference with the rest. The mountains will always call me away from the summits of the city and I shall answer whenever I can. Ne'er can I forget that I owe the Appalachian Trail and not the other way around. It is a familiar refrain: the trail provides.

With the KATAHDIN sign in sight on Baxter Peak, and...It's "Hard Way! What are you doing here?!" I laugh with him.

"I'm here to take your picture!" He wails, "It's the whole reason I climbed up this rock today. And to return the Therm-a-Rest pillow sack! You've earned it, Music Man!"

"Thank you! Pay it forward, Hard Way!" He laughed and stepped back with an open hand to point the way. Bro reached for camera and let out a laugh and dropped a single tear that landed near his lip. This accomplishment was just as much his as mine. Bro taught me how to pay it forward. But his tear of joy was for me.

As we approached the peak of the mountain, a crowd of great spirits were gathered in glee. They quieted and cleared the way to the summit as we trudged toward the sawhorse sign marking the northern terminus of the Appalachian Trail.

"Thru-hikers," they whispered, as we took the final steps...click-click-click.... top.

When it was his turn, Music Man climbed onto the summit sign of Mount Katahdin and looked south. He could see all the distant mountains and valleys and he appreciated where they had led him. He turned to face northeast, with its Knife Edge, and to the horizon beyond...toward new challenges to come. Filled with gratitude, he would continue the journey ahead one step at a time.

At the end of the Appalachian Trail on the 15th of September, Music Man surrendered:

"I am finished now. You can call me Dave."

.17

BACK FROM THE CLOUDS, THE KATAHDIN EXPERIENCE
hadn't been surreal—it was ethereal. The climb and summit were
filled with peace and serenity, fond reflection, and quiet regrets. We
climbed the mountain on its own terms, just as life should be lived.
The zenith of my journey was shared with Bro and Garlic, in
intimate moments of joy and grief and laughter and tears. Such
singular experiences of depth and human intimacy cannot be
conveyed with anymore paragraphs of ink or sounds of the tongue,
but simply expressed as cadences of pure love; a kinship between
the darkness and the light; the great reality of Ralph Waldo
Emerson's most famous quote:
    "It's not the Destination, It's the Journey." We had lived it.
    Trekking from Georgia to Maine was over. I spent three days
on the Acadian Coast eating lobstah with buttah with Garlic,
courtesy of her Godparents. After which we made the drive to
Virginia to get her car, then to Georgia to pick up my algae filled
and covered truck, which was right where Paul and GOAT said it
would be: in Amicalola State Park's long-term lot...parking
validated. Angels. Three day's motor travel cast the six-month
journey by foot into a shocking perspective. That part was
downright depressing: 183 grueling days to walk it, and 3 lazy days
to drive back. We took our time, both ways.
    Garlic came to Louisville and stayed with me. I introduced
her to my parents, who longed to meet her. We stayed in the house I
grew up in for a couple of weeks. Mom and Dad were thoroughly
proud of everyone. There was a sense about the house that I had
saved my own skin by sticking to the woods for six months. They
loved having us there, and we were happy to be there too. That's
when it became surreal, much like the not-yet-lost sensation of
touching the sign atop Mount Katahdin, allowing the reality of the
journey's end to continue its cool drizzle over us.
While hiking, I could not imagine how I would feel after the hike. It
turned out that it felt damn good. We never gave ourselves the
chance for the very-real "Post-Trail Depression" to sink in.
    Many thru-hikers experience serious blues after returning to
the "real world." We skipped that phase by skipping down another
trail instead. With everything happening on the ground in Louisville
and elsewhere in the world, during the Year of the Rat, Garlic and I
decided we had better keep hiking. We packed our bags and boxes
full of food and headed south again. This time we set our sights on
the Benton Mackaye Trail from Georgia back up into the Smokies.

Our fledgling bond was shattered and scattered there, in the backwoods of North Georgia. I finally lost Garlic once and for all, after I had royally screwed up again...In typical fashion. The cunning and pale-blazing demons of the past caught me when guards were down. But you have already read about that. At the end of the BMT, Garlic and I waved goodbye. Each of us traveled in different cardinal directions, in the gas-guzzling maze of the million American highways that branched out like blood vessels. Alas, we left the long yet narrow footpath in the trees; that seemed like it could stretch for a lifetime; only wide enough for two feet, a backpack, and a dream; that long yet narrow footpath that all but ensures that we find each other, if only we keep walking, allowing our unique strides and tempos to bring us back together; that long yet narrow footpath that guarantees we will have to take a good look at ourselves mirrored in the eyes of the others we share the adventure with. Garlic was finally able to flee without the premise that we'd eventually see each other again. The open road freed her of the bondage of our partnership. At the time, that's what it felt like to me. I realize now that we were not running from each other. We were running from ourselves. My harbored hopes held onto her with that old familiar grip around not letting go. Slowly but surely realizing that I'd never see Garlic again, I let go of the rope. Over the course of time, the sense of loss lessened as I picked up the precious gems of wisdom that she left behind for me.

As for dreams kept for the end of a journey, they can inadvertently be left in the tent and stuffed into a backpack to be tossed down the basement stairs until the next wilderness escape. Then some sunny spring day, when the tent is unfurled on that first night out, back in black, the sleepy-eyed but excited dreams burst forth to exclaim "Here I am! Remember me? Let's take another adventure!" The memories of old places and worn faces cloud the walls of musty thought-bubbles as they pop one by one. But the ever-vibrant spirit of adventure, determined to "glid" once again, emerges hungry for new context, new places and fresh faces animated to the backdrop of an idyllic countryside. But if we're lucky, once or twice in a lifetime, a "Garlic" shows up to brand our memories and hearts with a magic that can linger long after the person is gone. The most profound gift of love she gave, was giving me back to my children. My heart secretly thanked her, while taking a stroll on the flat trails outside of town with my kids. As they ran ahead to explore the mysteries of the Great Out Doors, I thought back to that cold night in the Smokies. Her headlamp beam that shone in my eyes; blooming to illuminate a long-lost world of real emotion that returned me to my children. Garlic wouldn't have it any other way. And neither would I.

Ironically, she handed me over to new brothers first....

The final piece of hope, committed reader, came in the form of miracles that I never expected or asked for. They were not my prayers being answered, that ultimately brought me out of self-imposed isolation and misery. Those prayers sounded like "God, if you get me out of this one, I swear I'll never do it again." No, not those same foxhole prayers again. Answered were the prayers of all those who cared so deeply for me and wanted a new me back and wanted to see me reunited with my kids. After your desperate pleas were heard and answered, GBITS got around to letting me know that I was not alone either. Hope arrived in the form of a house on a hill, in rural Kentucky, where I finally sat still for long enough to analyze the past with some clarity of mind. Real help and reasonable hope came in the form of genuine human connections with others who were just like me. I was desperately groomed and ready for help. With faith and assurance, they said:

"You ain't so special, Dave. That terminal uniqueness is gonna kill you—unless you're willing to sit and listen for a change, instead of doing all that walking and talking. You're not fooling us, brother. We have it too. So, why don't you let us love you back to life? Welcome to Power greater than yourself."

Hope arrived with the acceptance of there being nothing left to take, but responsibility. Hope possessed the Latino Watchman, who prayed over me that special night, after I had sold everything off except my guitar, then dumped the contents of my last baggie on the trash pile. Hope came from within the walls of the Healing Place, that house on the hill that stands above the monuments of my ancestors, where Uncle Jake, who a century ago, died with a drink in his hand. But Jacob reached from the annals of family history to pay something forward. He provided a guiding light in times of darkness. Along with Garlic, and Dad's letters and Mom's nourishment and Bro's wisdom—ALL rays of light shining on a path; leading to a chance for a certain kind of freedom that an ancestor didn't get to experience. The spirit of Uncle Jake walked the entire way with me and ended up embodied in the Latino Watchman. They led me to Healing Place where I realized that I could once again walk amongst the living, free from the bondage of the very thing that had stood in my way for all those years: Me.

I'm not a specifically religious man, but I have found a new sense of spirituality that connects me with who and what I am: One with a cosmos that created me; a small part of a Power far greater than myself that saved me: You, and the Great Out Doors.

It may appear that "The Story" was presented as one of Mr. Vice and Mr. Virtue, but the truth is that responsibility rests squarely on the shoulders of one. Was I rendered white as snow the moment I put the bottles down? No way. But each day that I wake up, I am grateful for another opportunity to try and get it right. The little things in life don't pile up as easily, either. I can walk home in the pouring rain without an umbrella or even a rain jacket, getting soaked to my skivvies, and it doesn't bother me.

Eventually, after the baptism, I will find myself warm and dry again— likely refreshed. I thank the trail for those simple enduring lessons which occasionally whisper to me, as intuition. I would have never had the courage to sit still for nearly a year, and work on myself, if I hadn't found the strength to keep trudging the trail. thru both the mountains of Appalachia and the rooms of recovery. I desperately wanted and needed both. However, fresh perspective can be deceptively easy to find, when clear and lonely mountaintops offer unencumbered views of moral high grounds. What truly counts are the actions that follow a return to the trailhead where the rubber meets the road again. Garlic's prophetic words played out as I believe she hoped and prayed they would: Thru-hikes and recoveries alike are not for people who need them or even want them—they are for those of us willing to *work* for them. I hike one step at time, and I stay sober one day at a time. My sanity requires both. And just like NTN, I can no longer drive past a trailhead anywhere and not be a rubberneck...looking for a white blaze on a mighty oak trunk just beyond the treeline.

I live in New England now, one town over from my children. I am an active co-parent in their lives, and they are thrilled to have their father back. My son's car seat is buckled into the backseat of my car, and my daughter braids a new bracelet for my wrist every time I see her. I have a lot of beautiful bracelets now. The colors look like Killington sunsets. Her hands twist and tie those bracelets just for me. We sing, then I clap and hug them after they blow out birthday candles. When I pick up my son and daughter from school, we experience the smiles, the disagreements, joys, laughter, and tears that accompany my son's skinned knees. I can tell him "Everything will be ok," and he sniffles "okay." He believes me and smiles when I tell him "I will never leave you," then we go back to raking leaf piles he can bounce into. They know they can count on me to be there, and we are all better off for it. Garlic would be happy for my daughter. She never leaves go of a hug first. I have a good job and a place to call home. I have friends and family that want the best for me. They tell me so and show me. Sometimes, they show me how. Sometimes, I show them how. And that's how it works, one day at a time...one step at a time.

All these gifts bestow upon me as I continue to do the work necessary to set and keep matters straight. Life is simple and good, in a wonderful world that I never could have imagined as I sat under the freeway in the rain that night, looking up at the billboard that read "CONSIDER SOMETHING DIFFERENT." When it comes to fighting for my life, being there for my kids, or taking a long walk...
—DON'T FUCKING QUIT.

As for the last material possession I carried thru it all...I strum those strings every day. When inspiration strikes, I write the song that awaits.

Recently, I attended some festival gatherings for hikers. I was invited to Alabama to play music and talk about my hiking experiences with the Pinhoti Trail community. On a stage for the first time in years, I was honest and vulnerable, sharing some of my story between songs. People approached me afterwards to tell me it resonated with them in some way. Everybody knows someone who struggles.

Back in New England a couple weeks later, I traveled to Williamstown. I had recently been elected to the board of directors of a non-profit organization "of hikers, for hikers." Excited to see old friends and meet friends anew, I had butterflies in my stomach for the first time in years. I walked around the artist and vendor booths finding friends. After thanking the Appalachian Long Distance Hikers Association (ALDHA) folks for the "AT Thru-Hiker" certificate they had mailed me in 2020, I found myself catching up with Bill Bancroft from the RPH Shelter, where I had worked on that tree stump with Choogle. Bill had just finished saying "It's hard to lose family," when I froze with surprise as a man I recognized was approaching me. It was my former father-in-law, Bamboo Bob, who is a three-time AT thru-hiker himself. He had come to the festival to participate in a panel discussion with other long-distance hikers. His wife, Just Visiting, was there too. They are my children's loving grandparents and will always be like family to me. It is hard to lose family...and be expected to quickly accept such a circumstance. I had not seen or spoken to them since the divorce a few years ago. A tear wells up in the corner of Just Visiting's eye as she spies Bamboo Bob ferociously shaking my hand.

"Bob, I wasn't expecting to see you here."

"I know, Dave." Bob responds as he continues to squeeze and shake, "but we knew that you would be here. We've seen your name all over the place, with the buzz of the Board's elections. Congratulations on everything, as of lately. You look terrific. Dave, your kids are thrilled you are here in New England now."

"Thank you. It's great to see you both." I send a warm smile in Just Visiting's direction. "It's great to see you too, Dave. You have made your children very happy," Bob says.

In his own way, Bamboo Bob is telling me that he approves of my recent actions as well. Just Visiting fights tears and says, "This is just wonderful," as she watches Bamboo Bob and Music Man continue to shake hands. We're all excited about the weekend's festivities.

"Now, let's talk about hiking."

AFTERWORD

By: Music Man's Father

It is not a selfish act to wish for one's own happiness. As he scaled the mountains and forged the valleys from Georgia to Maine, Music Man learned that a simplicity of life, as it is on the trail, leads to peace of mind and tranquility. He had hoped that such could be maintained when he returned to the "real world". Though the "thru-hiking" part of his story concluded at the Appalachian Trail's end, this was surely not the end of his travels. Truth be told, he traveled miles and miles more; scaling personal mountains and descending numerous valleys in the days that followed. All to embark on the most monumental trek of his life: staying sober one day at a time. It took more than just the six months and 2,193 miles he hiked between Georgia and Maine. He endured loss and pain in ways never experienced on the AT. At times, it was a lonely walk despite being in the company of fellow sojourners. Mere months after the thru-hike, The Healing Place enabled him to become humbler than before. Like the AT, it brought him deep gratitude, and he accepted the circumstances with a sense of relief.

Finally, he discovered a profound new joy in life; remaining grateful for the ever-present friends, colleagues, relatives, and spirits from the past that support him on his continuing quest. It dawned on him, like the sun rising upon Katahdin, that the greatest gift to himself was finding new ways to live in the present, being grateful for each moment of every day. Beyond himself, Dave found a sincere desire to give back to others, just as those that came before had helped him. As his feet keep trudging the path, he beckons You, as you consider something different for your own life; whatever that may be.

And so, Music Man gifted his goods, knowledge, and encouragement to Hard Way as he too set off unto his trail of a lifetime.

AT Journal: final entries by Music Man's Mother:

9/15/20 - Summit Day at Katahdin. First communication came about 8:30a from [Bro]. "In the climb" was the text. We stayed by the phone all day waiting for word. Weather looks to be good there. About 7:00p I texted Ron. "Should we be worried?" Ron quickly responded "No, they are either enjoying good weather on the summit or they decided to do the Knife Edge." Finally the phone rang at 7:45. It was Dave! They'd done it - and did the Knife Edge as well. Eureka! I posted the one picture we got (Dave and [Garlic]) on WhatsApp. First posted NTN's pic at Katahdin, July 2005, Goldfish's pic at Springer, December 2005, and finally [Music Man's] pic September 2020. Dave said they were exhausted but exhilarated. We gushed out congratulations. Food was ordered and we hung up. A very very good day. I thanked God for his safe journey. Also talked with Mom and thanked her for interceding on Dave's behalf all those times I asked. Janet sent me the Memorare to the Blessed Virgin. I appealed to her many times. She answered.

9/16/20 - [Bro] called about 11:30a on way to Portland airport. Said Summit Day was perfect. "It was the best day I have ever spent with Dave, hands down." Said everyone got up at 5:00a after the coldest night on the hike. Perfect weather. Left about 8 and summited around noon. A group of 4 Nobos were just ahead. Hugs all around. Section hikers parted to make way for them to summit. Pictures, videos...Said it was the happiest he had ever seen Dave. They did the treacherous Knife Edge which was a little squeamish. [Bro] said Dave said the three of us were with him every step. After coming down, they tried to find a restaurant. Only a McDonald's. [Bro] asked, is there any other place? Only a place down a dirt road and would close at 8:00p. It was 7:40p (ugh). Turned out to be wonderful. Dave got a T-bone, baked potato, and asparagus. Free desert for summit thru-hikers. [Bro] shared anecdotes from the day. Dave and Garlic telling stories, He said they laughed and smiled all day, said his face hurt from laughing. Chris said it was his "honor" to be with Dave. Chris told the story of DEL-461 who was a 72 yr old doctor who walked the trail in honor of the 461 men lost in his unit in Vietnam. "I did this hike in honor of the 461 men we lost in Vietnam." He said it was absolutely silent. Dave and Garlic will stay an extra day or so in Maine. Not sure I blame him. Must be hard to say goodbye to the trail. Dave had to dig deep to walk 2,193 miles. I can only imagine. Never more proud.

~~The End~~

The Beginning

AUTHOR'S GRATITUDE

All,

Without the guidance, support, and encouragement of so many kind and loving people, The Story and it's telling would not have been possible. Without the journey of the many paths and their peoples, there would be no story from the author's perspective. Without some healing, the feather would have remained in the inkwell. To my family and friends, the "green-suitors," the Trail Angels, and the souls in the rooms—I love you all.

To my parents, for the unwavering dedication to their children and grandchildren, thank you for giving me the courage to follow my dreams. Mom, your grace gave me the heart to write. Dad, your heart gave me the guts to write my truth. Pris, your priceless pieces of original art are family jewels; they come from that spiritual place of wisdom and love. To Betty Jane, for documenting the centuries full of family jewels, for your encouragement, syntax and content scrubs, and for revealing our storied clan-kinship that was over six-hundred years in the making—I could never repay you. My friend, Wesley Holshouser, from the small confines of that second-story room in the "house on the hill," to the design for this book— "hear, hear" to another chance at helping someone.

Bro, you already know: Without you, the story would have a much different ending. Because of you, the story has just begun. I love you and I thank you. People sometimes ask, "What's it like to have a twin brother?" I simply reply, "I don't know what it's like *not* to be a twin."

Garlic, All things said and unsaid. Mostly, thank you.

From the summits down to the waters, let my Gratitude call across the mountains to fill the valleys. By the Light of the Love in my children's hearts, I'll *glid* the path...for us.

Humbly Yours,
Dave

Made in the USA
Monee, IL
11 February 2023

27559162R00118